CURRENT DEBATES IN GLOBAL JUSTICE

STUDIES IN GLOBAL JUSTICE

VOLUME 2

Aims and Scope
In today's world, national borders seem irrelevant when it comes to international crime and terrorism. Likewise, human rights, poverty, inequality, democracy, development, trade, bioethics, hunger, war and peace are all issues of global rather than national justice. The fact that mass demonstrations are organized whenever the world's governments and politicians gather to discuss such major international issues is testimony to a widespread appeal for justice around the world.

Discussions of global justice are not limited to the fields of political philosophy and political theory. In fact, research concerning global justice quite often requires an interdisciplinary approach. It involves aspects of ethics, law, human rights, international relations, sociology, economics, public health, and ecology. Springer's new series *Studies in Global Justice* takes up that interdisciplinary perspective. The series brings together outstanding monographs and anthologies that deal with both basic normative theorizing and its institutional applications. The volumes in the series discuss such aspects of global justice as the scope of social justice, the moral significance of borders, global inequality and poverty, the justification and content of human rights, the aims and methods of development, global environmental justice, global bioethics, the global institutional order and the justice of intervention and war.

Volumes in this series will prove of great relevance to researchers, educators and students, as well as politicians, policy-makers and government officials.

Current Debates in Global Justice

Edited by

GILLIAN BROCK
University of Auckland, New Zealand

and

DARREL MOELLENDORF
San Diego State University, U.S.A.

Springer

A C.I.P. catalogue record for this book is available from the Library of Congress.

ISBN 1-4020-3347-8 (HB)
ISBN 1-4020-3494-6 (PB)

Published by Springer,
P.O. Box 17, 3300 AA Dordrecht, The Netherlands.

Sold and distributed in North, Central and South America
by Springer,
101 Philip Drive, Norwell, MA 02061, U.S.A.

In all other countries, sold and distributed
by Springer,
P.O. Box 322, 3300 AH Dordrecht, The Netherlands.

Printed on acid-free paper

Printed in the Netherlands.

TABLE OF CONTENTS

INTRODUCTION

Issues of global justice dominate our contemporary world. Increasingly, philosophers are turning their attention to thinking about particular issues of global justice and the accounts that would best facilitate theorizing about these. This volume of papers on global justice derives from a mini-conference held in conjunction with the Pacific Division meeting of the American Philosophical Association in Pasadena, California, in 2004. The idea of holding a mini-conference on global justice was inspired by the growth of interest in such questions, and it was hoped that organizing the mini-conference would stimulate further good writing in this area.[1] We believe that our mission has been accomplished! We received a number of thoughtful papers on both theoretical and more applied issues, showing excellent coverage of a range of topics in the domain of global justice. A selection of some of the very best papers is published in this special issue of *The Journal of Ethics*. In particular, we tried to include papers that would reflect some of the range of topics that were covered at the conference, to give readers a sense of both the scope of the field as it is currently emerging and the direction that the debates seem to be taking.

As a result of increased attention to theorizing about global justice, cosmopolitanism has enjoyed a resurgence of interest as well. As Charles Beitz (citing Thomas Pogge) notes, the crux of the idea of moral cosmopolitanism is that every person possesses a global stature

[1]Seminal works on global justice include, among others, Charles Beitz, *Political Theory and International Relations* (Princeton: Princeton University Press, 1979); Henry Shue, *Basic Rights* (Princeton: Princeton University Press, 1980); and Thomas Pogge's several articles and his *Realizing Rawls* (Ithaca: Cornell University Press, 1989). Recently interest in the area has grown considerably, with a number of philosophical works being published taking up a variety of themes in the area of global justice. Prominent among these are Joshua Cohen (ed.), *For Love of Country: Debating the Limits of Patriotism* (Boston: Beacon Press, 1996); Thomas Pogge, *World Poverty and Human Rights* (Cambridge: Polity Press, 2002); John Rawls, *The Law of Peoples* (Cambridge: Harvard University Press, 1999); Ian Shapiro and Lea Brilmayer (eds.), *Global Justice* (New York: New York University Press, 1999); Samuel Scheffler, *Boundaries and Allegiances* (Oxford: Oxford University Press, 2001); and Peter Singer, *One World: The Ethics of Globalization* (New Haven: Yale University Press, 2002).

The Journal of Ethics (2005) 9: 1–9

as the ultimate unit of moral concern. Cosmopolitanism's force can be well appreciated by considering what it rules out. For instance, it rules out the assigning of ultimate rather than derivative value to collective entities like nations or states, and it also rules out positions that attach no moral value to some people, or weights the value people have differentially according to characteristics such as ethnicity, race, or nationality. However, when we turn to examine what cosmopolitanism *requires*, the view is less determinate. Cosmopolitans can embrace almost any theoretical perspective and a wide range of normative theories may legitimately claim to be cosmopolitan, since there are a number of ways of understanding a person's good, or what it is to be an ultimate unit of moral concern.

How should we go forward in developing cosmopolitanism? Beitz suggests that the cosmopolitan project might well be advanced by considering the diverse array of apparent reasons for action which seem to confront us (for instance, some grounded in local attachments, others arising from legal or economic global structures and their consequences for human well-being) and formulating better models of the manner in which various reasons might be integrated when it is necessary to make practical judgments about how to act.

Beitz also discusses global political justice, that is to say, the global provisions for making political decisions. Global processes of public decision-making, or global regimes, are fairly well developed in certain areas, for instance, in the areas of intellectual property agreements and trade rules. Reflection on reforming our global institutions (and global governance more generally) is fairly advanced in political science, but Beitz notes, the discussion lacks moral clarity and this is something that moral and political philosophers might well be able to provide.

A widely held precept of justice, indeed of morality in general, is that we should refrain from foreseeably and avoidably harming others. But if the massive and desperate poverty of the world, which causes some 18 million deaths annually, is the foreseeable and avoidable consequence of social conditions shaped and enforced by us, the advantaged citizens of the affluent countries, then, according to Pogge, citizens of the rich countries are participating in the largest, although not the gravest, crime against humanity in the history of the world. Pogge seeks to defend the thesis that advantaged citizens of the affluent world harm the world's poor through a variety of arguments intended to appeal to adherents of the various widely accepted schools of contemporary political philosophy.

To those who hold the actual history of a distribution is relevant to its justice, Pogge replies that the era of colonial conquest and administration gravely disadvantaged Africans *vis-à-vis* Europeans. To those who hold that a distribution is just if it could have been the product of voluntary transactions by rationally self-interested agents, he replies, following John Locke, that such a view would require that the worst-off in an institutional order be at least as well off as they would be holding a proportional share of the world's resources, and that this condition is manifestly not fulfilled today. To those who hold that the consequences of an institutional arrangement matter, Pogge argues that the radical inequality extant globally will be ruled out by even the most minimal broadly consequentialist standard of justice. Moreover, Pogge argues that various changes in global institutional order, including the elimination of protectionism in the developed world and the implementation of a global resource dividend that places a small tax on the consumption of certain natural resources, taken severally or jointly, would avoid the most egregious harms of the present global order.

David Miller argues against the view that global justice requires commitment to a global principle of equality, in particular a principle of global equality of opportunity. Though he argues against global egalitarianism he is not unconcerned about global inequality. On the contrary, if we are no longer in the grip of an ideal of global egalitarianism we can better focus more directly on how to tackle global injustice in its many forms.

A principle of global equality of opportunity would seem to require that people of similar talents and motivation should have equivalent life chances or opportunity sets irrespective of the society to which they happen to belong. When we try to apply this principle to the global level, Miller argues that we face several problems since, first, there is no common cultural understanding of what metric is to be used when trying to make cross-national comparisons of opportunity sets. Moreover, different cultures value and rank opportunities differently. We can only make confident judgments in extreme cases, but in those cases we notice that it is actually concerns about absolute poverty or deprivation that are in play, rather than equality *per se*.

Another aspect of global equality of opportunity that Miller finds objectionable is that it undermines national self-determination, and this would seriously interfere with one of the key features of his preferred model of Global Justice. The conception of global justice Miller favors has three main requirements: obligations to (1) respect basic human rights globally; (2) to refrain from exploiting the vulnerable; and (3) to provide all political communities with the opportunity to achieve self-determination and social justice. Global inequality is objectionable, but not in the first instance for reasons of distributive justice. Rather, material inequalities transfer too easily into inequalities of power, which can be a source of injustice since the powerful can simply dictate terms of trade and exchange, for instance. Inequalities of power also interfere with nations' interests in self-determination and provide an obstacle to achieving fair terms of co-operation internationally.

Mathias Risse investigates what we know about what makes some countries rich and stable, and others not. Three major positions dominate the discussion in development economics: one focuses on geography, another integration into world markets, and a third maintains that prosperity derives from the quality of institutions (such as, stable property rights, the rule of law, and appropriate regulatory structures). Risse argues that the institutional view is the most promising given the current stage of the debate, and that this has an important bearing on what duties we have to poor countries. Risse's position thus also attempts to provide further support for Rawls' views on duties of assistance as articulated in *The Law of Peoples,* namely, that the focus of assistance should be on setting up just institutions rather than more demanding principles of redistribution (such as implementation of a Global Difference Principle).

Sanjay Reddy cautions against unwarranted empirical and normative assumptions in applied normative reasoning. Reddy argues that in many cases applied normative reasoning mistakenly assumes that apparent constraints are more rigid than they in reality are. So in debates about whether resources should be redistributed either in the direction of compatriots or non-compatriots, we should not lightly assume that there are insufficient resources for both tasks. Additionally, we ought not be too quick in our judgments of the causes of economic growth, especially when developmental economists have not achieved a clear consensus on the matter. Hence, moral judgments that require empirical premises about the causes of growth must factor in the empirical uncertainty. Finally, when assessing moral responsibility for poverty and inequality, we should assume neither that inequality is simply a product of domestic factors, nor that moral responsibility is solely a function of causal responsibility.

In considering our duties of global justice, several theorists advance a thesis of "compatriot favoritism" or a "patriotic priority thesis,"[2] which holds that we must give priority to helping less needy compatriots over more needy non-compatriots. Some of the most well known arguments for this view focus on considerations of fair play, coercion, and autonomy. Richard Arneson examines all of these positions and argues that they fail. To take just one of these arguments, compatriot favoritists maintain that since co-nationals are involved in mutual state coercion – they coercively impose a system of laws on one another – co-nationals are entitled to special treatment when it comes to assistance, because they are entitled to compensation for the imposition of the coercive legal scheme. In response to this position, Arneson argues that the laws prohibiting criminal activities do not actually coerce fully reasonable and moral persons – indeed, co-nationals actually receive benefits from such "schemes of coercion" rather than having to bear burdens which warrant compensation.

The extent and degree of suffering, due to extreme poverty, for nearly half of the world's population in the developing world stands in sharp contrast to consumption patterns and lifestyles of most of the people in the world's richest countries. Dale Jamieson considers the proper application of the moral principle advocated by Peter Singer.[3] The moral principle that Singer advocates is that "if it is in our power to prevent something bad from happening, without thereby sacrificing anything of comparable moral importance, we ought morally to do it."[4] Singer believes that even the substantially weaker principle that we ought to prevent bad things if doing so does not require sacrificing "anything morally significant" would, if taken seriously, dramatically change our patterns of consumption and lifestyle, by requiring us to give substantial amounts of time or money to famine and poverty relief.

Jamieson does not dispute either of Singer's moral principles. Instead he contends that a commitment to them is not incompatible

---

[2] For some good examples of this view see Richard Miller, "Cosmopolitan Respect and Patriotic Concern," *Philosophy and Public Affairs* 27 (1998), pp. 202–224; and Michael Blake, "Distributive Justice, State Coercion, and Autonomy," *Philosophy and Public Affairs* 30 (2001), pp. 257–296.

[3] Peter Singer, "Famine, Affluence, and Morality," *Philosophy and Public Affairs* 1 (1972), pp. 229–243.

[4] Singer, "Famine, Affluence, and Morality," p. 231.

with a great deal of skepticism about efforts of humanitarian aid, development assistance, and humanitarian intervention. Aid, while sometimes achieving good results, can decontextualize, depoliticize, and dehistoricize humanitarian emergencies that are typically the products of civil wars. Development assistance is quite often not terribly effective at promoting development because one of its chief aims is to help donors, or interests in donor countries, not the recipients of aid. Humanitarian interventions, although not ruled out in principle, are often ineffective for several reasons. Armies are not trained to be humanitarian organizations; interventions often compromise the impartiality of humanitarian organizations; and such interventions usually serve various imperial projects of the United States. In short, Jamieson's argument is a plea for humility when advising what we should be doing to help the impoverished of the world even if we accept Singer's principles.

Though cosmopolitan theorists maintain that obligations to distribute resources are global in scope, they frequently do not argue for a restructuring of the global system to realize their distributive goals better. Luis Cabrera argues that this is a mistake and that democratically accountable economic and political integration between states is the most effective way to facilitate these trans-state distributions. He argues, in other words, that moral cosmopolitans should also be strong institutional cosmopolitans.[5] Cabrera examines the European Union as a model for the kind of integration he believes can, in the long run, best realize the key cosmopolitan goal that persons should have access to adequate opportunities and resources, irrespective of their birth-country. As Europe has become more integrated, it has resulted in some significant transfers of resources and opportunities to poorer member states. Also, as integration has occurred, there has been an expansion in the set of persons whose interests are thought to be appropriately consulted in decision-making. There is nothing automatic about achieving the integrated alternative with its more egalitarian consequences. Rather, economic integration, and the process of constitutionalization, can give rise to important opportunities to press for egalitarian versions of integration.

In contrast to Cabrera's position, which recommends more integration between states, Omar Dahbour believes this path to be

[5] For this distinction see, for instance, Thomas Pogge, "Cosmopolitanism and Sovereignty," *Ethics* 103 (1992), pp. 48–75.

misguided – in fact, something like the opposite will be most conducive to global justice, in his view. Dahbour identifies three different models of global community. The first two models discussed are communities of law and trade. Both of these models focus on creating a borderless world by establishing laws, rules, and institutions that govern all people, eventually superceding the sovereignty of particular states, so that global standards of justice apply universally. In contrast, a third model is presented, namely, that of a world of autonomous, self-sustaining communities, which takes as a primary component the norm of self-determination and some conception of sovereignty. Only self-sustaining communities that embody some robust notion of sovereignty can adequately protect communities facing the threats posed by the globalizing tendencies of capital. Dahbour argues we would do better in a world where we coexist in a state of mutual indifference, rather than increased involvement and interdependence, or even "common concern." Indeed, inevitably it is the interference by hegemonic states and global financial institutions in affairs of poor or less powerful states that causes the problems they currently face. Dahbour claims that it is this sort of interference that is in actual fact the cause of most of the oppression that besets the developing world today.

Because customary international law does not contain an amendment procedure, it gives rise to a puzzle, which Robert Goodin observes as follows: How can we distinguish actors that break the law out of genuine respect for its rule and the motive to amend it, from those who merely seek not to be held to the standard of the law? This question takes on special urgency in a world that contains a single superpower that is able to break the law in many cases without significant costs. Goodin argues that an analogy to civil disobedience in domestic cases yields useful criteria. These are that the law must be broken publicly and that the law breaker must accept the legal consequences of the breach. International law is often thought of as soft law without clearly defined legal consequences associated with breaking it. Goodin argues that one rule of thumb with regard to accepting the legal consequences of breaking international law is that the law breaker must be prepared to be held to the same rules – the amended law created by breaking the law – that it proposes applying to others. Although there are cases of superpowers meeting this standard, according to Goodin, the US's preventive war against Iraq was not one.

Should the UN engage in preventive military actions? John Lango takes up this general question, but also pursues the more particular question of whether the UN should engage in preventive military actions to secure the goal of nonproliferation or the abolition of weapons of mass destruction. Lango investigates whether UN preventive military actions could satisfy just war principles, especially the traditional just war principles of legitimate authority, just cause, last resort, and proportionality. He argues that not only the possession of weapons of mass destruction but also the attempt to possess such weapons constitutes a threat to the peace. If a state that possesses such weapons acts in a sufficiently threatening way, a preventive war against it could satisfy the just cause criterion. We should also be concerned in cases where grave harm could be brought about through reckless or negligent activity as well, and it is possible that just cause for UN preventive military action could be satisfied in such cases too. After considerable discussion of the criteria of legitimate authority, last resort, and proportionality, he offers a qualified defense of the UN preventive military actions to stop the spread of, or abolish, weapons of mass destruction.

The World Trade Organization's (WTO) role in international trade looms large. Ninety-seven percent of all international trade is governed by the three main treaties that the WTO administers.[6] The General Agreement on Trade and Tariffs (GATT) and the Agreement on Trade-Related Intellectual Property Rights (TRIPS) are better known than the General Agreement of Trade in Services (GATS). However, a multi-lateral agreement on trade in services is a new and distinctive feature of the WTO regime, and certainly the coverage of the GATS is no less far reaching than that of the GATT and the TRIPS. For example, Gopal Sreenivasan observes that states that schedule health care insurance under the GATS are not permitted to extend any previously existing, if any, public monopolies in health insurance to previously uncovered services without compensating other GATS members affected by the extension. Sreenivasan argues that because the GATS is binding on future generations, and because it is extremely costly to opt out once a state has agreed to the GATS, signatories to the GATS have, in effect, acquired a constitutional obligation and the democratic legitimacy of such obligations requires more than a standard majoritarian decision procedure.

As the summary of the previous papers suggests, discussions of global justice typically focus on which humans, compatriots or noncompatriots, are owed what according to the demands of justice.

---

[6] http://www.wto.org/english/thewto_e/whatis_e/inbrief_e/inbr02_e.htm.

James Sterba argues that all attempts to limit the demands of justice to humans are ultimately question begging. Rather, justice covers not only what we owe all other human beings, but what we owe all individual living beings and ecosystems as well. Hence, Sterba urges, the scope of discussions of global justice must be enlarged considerably. Sterba defends a number of principles that purport to offer guidelines in determining when to give preference to humans and when to prefer other animals in matters of practical deliberation.

As we believe is evident in the volume, there is some exciting work being done in the field of global justice. We hope this collection of new articles will stimulate further reflection in this important area. We are indebted to all of the participants of the mini-conference for doing the intellectual work that will continue to stimulate many of us to think further and more deeply about these issues. For help in carrying out the conference from which the volume derives, we owe thanks to the American Philosophical Association, Pacific Division, for being so supportive of the idea of the mini-conference on global justice and for generously subsidizing the event. In particular, Anita Silvers deserves special thanks for all her hard work and help in making this conference possible. We are also grateful to Mathias Risse for organizing a panel discussion at the mini-conference that provided three of the papers published in this issue. Finally, we would like to thank the other two members of the mini-conference organizational committee for their assistance: Harry Brighouse and Rodney Peffer.

GILLIAN BROCK
Department of Philosophy
University of Auckland
Private Bag 92019
Auckland
New Zealand
E-mail: g.brock@auckland.ac.nz

DARREL MOELLENDORF
Department of Philosophy
San Diego State University
5500 Campanile Dr.
San Diego, CA 92182-8142
USA
E-mail: dmoellen@mail.sdsu.edu

CHARLES R. BEITZ

COSMOPOLITANISM AND GLOBAL JUSTICE*

(Received 14 May 2004; accepted in revised form 2 June 2004)

ABSTRACT. Philosophical attention to problems about global justice is flourishing in a way it has not in any time in memory. This paper considers some reasons for the rise of interest in the subject and reflects on some dilemmas about the meaning of the idea of the cosmopolitan in reasoning about social institutions, concentrating on the two principal dimensions of global justice, the economic and the political.

KEY WORDS: cosmopolitanism, democracy, global distributive justice, global political justice, morality of states, poverty

Philosophical attention to problems about global justice is flourishing in a way it has not at any time in memory. I do not need to say very much to explain why this is a good thing. We face an assortment of urgent practical problems that are not likely to be solved, if they can be solved at all, without concerted international action. Some of these involve controlling the pathologies of the states system – for example, aggressive war and oppressive government. Some are collective action problems – for example, global warming and depletion of fisheries. Some arise from the fact that the world contains such vast amounts of human suffering, much of it chronic and in varying degrees avoidable.

There is at the same time the emergence of a nascent global capacity to act. This capacity is fragmentary and heterogeneous. It expresses itself in the foreign policies of states, in an eclectic variety of intergovernmental organizations, in the institutions and regimes that organize global economic relations, and in humanitarian and human

*Opening address of the Mini-Conference on Global Justice, American Philosophical Association Pacific Division, 2004 Annual Meeting, Pasadena, California, March 27, 2004. I am grateful for comments to Darrel Moellendorf and to my copanelists Michael Blake, Kristen Hessler, Jon Mandle, Mathias Risse and Leif Wenar.

rights law and a series of largely improvised legal and political mechanisms of enforcement. Alongside and occasionally intertwined with all of this is an evolving transnational civil society comprised of a diverse assortment of non-governmental organizations. The urgency of the problems and the prospect that they might eventually be alleviated by political action explain why the rise of philosophical interest in global justice is to be welcomed.

With the exception of the morality of war, philosophical understanding of problems of global justice is still at an early stage. It behooves anyone who thinks and writes about these matters to appreciate that as our understanding develops, we may learn from revisiting ideas that once seemed clear and persuasive. As a step in this direction, I would like to reflect on some dilemmas about the meaning of the idea of the cosmopolitan as it applies to the two principal dimensions of global justice, the economic and the political. These remarks are supposed to be brief, aimed more to characterize disagreement than to advance an argument. Inevitably they will be both incomplete and telegraphic, and for that I apologize in advance.

Global Justice in Political Theory

By way of background, let me begin with an observation about the increase of philosophical attention to problems of global justice in the last 30 or so years. In 1960, Martin Wight, a leading English student of international relations, wrote an essay with the provocative title, "Why Is There No International Theory?" He meant to deny that there is a tradition of international political theory comparable to the political theory of the state. Such international thought as there was, he wrote, was "largely repellent and intractable in form" and "marked, not only by paucity but also by intellectual and moral poverty."[1] As a judgment about the history of international thought, this is too severe – the product of an oddly constricted view of the tradition. But it would have been a fair description of the treatment of international relations in what was then the contemporary literature of political philosophy. With the

[1] Martin Wight, "Why Is There No International Theory?" in Herbert Butterfield and Martin Wight (eds.), *Diplomatic Investigations: Essays in the Theory of International Politics* (London: George Allen and Unwin, 1966), p. 20. The essay was first published in *International Relations* 2 (1960).

exception of a very few works from the mid-1950s about natural and human rights, a few more about the morality of war, the appendix on international relations in Stanley Benn and Richard Peters' important textbook in political philosophy, and H.L.A. Hart's chapter on international law, political philosophers had given virtually no thought to any subject that could be brought under the heading of global justice since the 1930s.[2]

The program of this conference shows how dramatically things have changed. Today, global justice is a legitimate subject of philosophical inquiry. There is a lively and growing literature. People teach whole courses about it. Conferences are devoted to it. Thirty years is not a long time in political philosophy – barely an academic generation – and one has to say the extent of the intellectual transformation is remarkable.

Why the change? Certainly one factor is the broader revival of interest in normative political philosophy since the 1960s. More important is a pervasive shift in understanding of the empirical content of global political life. Brian Barry wrote in 1965 that "in relations between states the problem of establishing a peaceful order overshadows all others." He continued (interestingly, in retrospect):

> No doubt it is possible for substantive general principles to be put forward and widely accepted, e.g., that rich nations have some kind of obligation to help poor nations develop their economies. But any attempt to develop a detailed casuistry of political principles in the absence of a working international order seems a doubtfully rewarding enterprise.[3]

Barry was ahead of his time in recognizing the subject of international distributive justice, but when he described the problem of establishing peaceful order as eclipsing all else he precisely recapitulated the prevailing view.

Today, political philosophy has absorbed a richer and more variegated conception of the content and structure of world politics. This is partly a reflection of changes in the academic study of international relations, where economic interdependence, transnational politics, and the political economy of international regimes have attracted

---

[2] Stanley Benn and Richard Peters, *Social Principles and the Democratic State* (London: George Allen and Unwin, 1959), published in the United States as *The Principles of Political Thought* (New York: Free Press, 1965); H.L.A. Hart, *The Concept of Law* (Oxford: Clarendon Press, 1961), Chapter 10. In fact, Hart's book was published a year after Wight's essay first appeared.

[3] Brian Barry, *Political Argument: A Reissue with a New Introduction* (New York and London: Wheatsheaf Harvester, 1990), p. lxxiv (1st ed. 1965). These passages occur in the 1965 Introduction, near the end.

attention since the 1970s.[4] It also reflects the impact of changes in world politics itself – in particular, the assortment of economic and social phenomena conventionally known as "globalization."[5] These phenomena have become more prominent since the end of the Cold War, which had the dual effect of encouraging a sense of political possibility and removing the principal remaining barrier to a truly cosmopolitan global market. One could not take these developments seriously without being forced to reconsider the sharp distinction between the domestic and the international realms implicit in the perception of international relations as primarily a zone of war and peace.

All of this is familiar enough. Let me add two related cautions. First, one should not think of globalization as a development peculiar to the late-20th century.[6] However it is measured – whether by the volume of trade, capital flows and labor migration, by the integration of goods and capital markets, or by the sensitivity of domestic life to economic transactions elsewhere – *economic* globalization dates at least from the mid-19th century. Indeed, in some respects it advanced further then than it has in recent years.[7] If part of the motivation of interest in issues of global justice is the thought that the extension

[4] The pivotal works are Robert O. Keohane and Joseph S. Nye, Jr. (eds.), *Transnational Relations and World Politics* (Cambridge: Harvard University Press, 1972); Robert O. Keohane and Joseph S. Nye, *Power and Interdependence: World Politics in Transition* (Boston: Little, Brown, 1977). Also, see the last chapter (on normative issues) in Robert O. Keohane, *After Hegemony: Cooperation and Discord in the World Political Economy* (Princeton: Princeton University Press, 1984).

[5] These phenomena resist easy summary. An inventory would include dramatic growth in international trade and investment, increased integration of goods and capital markets, the articulation of transnational regimes for trade, finance and development, the proliferation of non-governmental organizations and a series of changes in the organization of cultural life that have diminished the social significance of the boundaries of at least the advanced industrial states.

[6] This is, among other things, a self-criticism, since one of the central themes of Charles Beitz, *Political Theory and International Relations*, rev. ed. (Princeton: Princeton University Press, 1999) (1st ed. 1979) was that the growth of economic interdependence after World War II had transformed international relations in such a way that it had become appropriate, for the first time, to worry about international distributive justice. This exaggerated the novelty of the postwar changes.

[7] For example, in the openness of labor markets and in the share of international capital flows destined for developing economies [Kevin H. O'Rourke and Jeffrey G. Williamson, *Globalization and History: The Evolution of a Nineteenth-Century Atlantic Economy* (Cambridge: MIT Press, 1999)]. O'Rourke and Williamson demonstrate that high levels of integration of commodity, capital, and labor markets were achieved by the late-19th century and that these forms of globalization produced very significant domestic economic and political consequences.

of the division of labor across national boundaries gives rise to a new class of ethical concerns, then one must recognize that these concerns have been with us much longer than we sometimes believe.

It is also a mistake to think of recent philosophical attention to global justice as something new. It is new, considered in relation to Anglo-American political philosophy in the decades after World War II, but it is not new if one takes a longer view. I said earlier that Wight's judgment of the tradition of international thought was too severe. I am not sure which writers he had in mind – perhaps the line of international jurists following Grotius. But he must not have considered the works of philosophers from David Hume and Adam Smith to John Stuart Mill and Henry Sidgwick who took up such topics of global interest as the ownership of resources, foreign trade, labor migration, and more broadly, the acceptable uses of imperial power.[8] Contemporary interest in global justice is not so much a new direction in political philosophy as a reframing and expansion of a subject with a neglected history. We can hope that a by-product of the revival of interest in the subject will be a philosophically-informed understanding of this history.

THE MEANINGS OF COSMOPOLITANISM

An artifact of the growth of global political theory has been a reassertion of the idea of the cosmopolitan. This is hardly surprising, of course, since, whatever else it involves, a cosmopolitan perspective is, at least, a perspective that seeks to encompass the whole world. But cosmopolitanism is sometimes regarded, not only as a point of view, but also as a substantive moral and political doctrine that can be expected to yield distinctive prescriptions for policy. This can lead to misunderstanding.

When I first thought about global justice it seemed to me that most views could be classified under one of three general conceptions. These were political realism, the morality of states, and cosmopolitanism.[9] The first two were present in modern and contemporary

[8] Henry Sidgwick's *Elements of Politics*, 2nd ed. (London: Macmillan, 1897), Chapters. 15–18, contains four substantial chapters devoted to moral issues in foreign policy, interestingly including free trade and immigration.

[9] These three conceptions are distinguished in Beitz, *Political Theory and International Relations*, Introduction, Conclusion, and *passim*. For doubts and second thoughts about the basic distinction, see the Afterword in the 1999 reissue.

international thought, not so much as systematic philosophical positions than as families of extensionally-similar views; cosmopolitan views could be found as well but were less well represented. I interpreted political realism as a kind of skepticism, so if we confine ourselves to moral positions, in effect a dichotomous choice was posed: statism or cosmopolitanism. This simple distinction had expository value, but, if there was ever doubt, it is now clear that neither side of the dichotomy represents a single, coherent position.

In describing a "morality of states," I had in mind the conception of the international realm found in the writings of 18th-century international jurists like Christian Wolff and E. de Vattel (the latter in a work whose title, literally translated, is *The Law of Peoples)*. This is the idea of a "society of states" – perhaps the most familiar result of applying the domestic analogy to the international order. The idea has three related elements: the principal bearers of rights and duties are states rather than persons; they are obligated to follow a system of norms analogous to those that apply among individuals in the state of nature; and the value of equality is expressed in a principle requiring states to treat each other as equal moral persons.[10] There is no question that conceptions of this general form have been influential in the modern history of international thought. For that matter, some such conceptions are influential today.

But the normative elements of this idea need a defense, and when we ask how they might be defended we find that the conception of a morality of states fragments into a series of discrete and potentially incompatible positions. For example, there is one form of the view in which considerations of international order are taken to be fundamental. There is a second form in which the state's character as a self-governing political community is basic. There is a third form in which political states, or anyway some of them, are seen as embodiments of social or national identity groups, in which participation is taken to be an important value for their members. There are other forms as well. All of these conceptions are interpretations of the morality of states, but because they motivate the identification of the basic units differently, they generate theories with different normative contents. Reflection about the doctrine of self-determination, for example, would make this clear.

---

[10] See E. de Vattel, *Le droit des gens* [The Law of Nations], trans. Charles G. Fenwick (Washington: Carnegie Institution, 1916), Volume III, Introduction, Sections 2–6, and II, Chapters 1, 3, and 5.

My main interest, however, is the cosmopolitan side of the dichotomy. The adjective "cosmopolitan" can be applied to many kinds of things – for example, to schemes of world political order and conceptions of individual cultural identity. I will comment on a third idea, which I will call "moral cosmopolitanism." Its crux is the thought, to borrow Thomas Pogge's phrase, "that every human being has a global stature as the ultimate unit of moral concern."[11] As this suggests, moral cosmopolitanism is a perspective on the justification of some range of practical choices. Pogge's phrase captures two essential features of this perspective: it is individualistic and inclusive. But obviously more needs to be said. For example, it needs to be specified whether the subject-matter of moral cosmopolitanism is all of morality or only the morality of social institutions and practices. It also needs to be explained how the recognition of every human being as a "unit of moral concern" is supposed to bear on moral reasoning: it might be, for example, that each person's interests or prospects are to be taken into account equally in deliberation about how to act or that each person should be treated as having equal standing as an addressee of justification. On each point, the second alternative seems to me to yield a more plausible interpretation of the view than the first, but I cannot argue it here.

The force of moral cosmopolitanism is clearest when we consider what it rules out: cosmopolitanism stands opposed to any view that limits the scope of justification to the members of particular types of groups, whether identified by shared political values, communal histories, or ethnic characteristics. It also stands opposed to any view that allows the justification of choices to terminate in considerations about the non-derivative interests of collective entities such as states or social groups.[12] If one takes the morality of states to posit that state boundaries are limits to the scope of justification, then cosmopolitanism is plainly incompatible with it.

---

[11] Thomas W. Pogge, *World Poverty and Human Rights* (Cambridge: Polity Press, 2002), p. 169. Also see Charles Beitz, "Cosmopolitan Liberalism and the States System," in Chris Brown (ed.), *Political Restructuring in Europe* (London: Routledge, 1994), p. 124.

[12] Samuel Scheffler, *Boundaries and Allegiances* (Oxford: Oxford University Press, 2001), p. 112; Simon Caney, "Review Article: International Distributive Justice," *Political Studies* 49 (2001), p. 977.

Trouble appears when we ask, not what moral cosmopolitanism rules out, but what it requires, for then the view seems to be far less determinate.[13] For example, moral cosmopolitanism is agnostic about the content of global political justice: it does not commit itself for or against the proposition that there should be a sovereign global authority. There is no automatic inference from cosmopolitanism about moral justification to cosmopolitanism about institutions. The question is how to account for this practical indeterminacy.

No doubt some of it is epistemic, reflecting the defectiveness of our knowledge about the empirical premises required to reach conclusions about how institutions should be arranged from the abstract requirement to include everyone within the scope of moral concern. But the more basic point is that cosmopolitanism is not a complete moral conception: it leaves open too many questions. An indication of this is that both utilitarianism and a globalized contractualism count as cosmopolitan theories. But this is only the beginning. There is no distinctively cosmopolitan position about how we should understand a person's good, how the prospects of different individuals should be aggregated, or how and whether aggregative judgments should be qualified by non-consequentialist constraints and permissions.

These areas of theoretical indeterminacy mean that a wide range of normative positions might count as cosmopolitan. In particular, positions that have practical consequences similar to those of the more progressive forms of the morality of states would count if they obey the foundational requirement to take every person as a unit of moral concern (I will give an example below).[14] I do not mean to endorse such views, only to observe that they can be constructed so as to satisfy the cosmopolitan requirement about justification. Whether we should be attracted to such a view is a substantive question in political ethics. The bare idea of the cosmopolitan is too protean to settle it.

Some people have distinguished between two forms of cosmopolitanism: Samuel Scheffler discriminates between the "extreme"

---

[13] In this respect cosmopolitanism is like political equality, well described by Giovanni Sartori as a "protest ideal" which operates primarily as a basis for criticizing certain institutional arrangements rather than as a basis for choosing any particular one [Giovanni Sartori, *The Theory of Democracy Revisited* (Chatham: Chatham House, 1987), Part 2, pp. 337–338].

[14] See text accompanying note 23.

and the "moderate," Simon Caney, between the "radical" and the "mild," and David Miller, between the "strong" and the "weak."[15] These distinctions are intended in part as antidotes for the excessive simplicity of the basic distinction between cosmopolitanism and statism, but I suspect they may still be too coarse-grained. The fundamental problem is that we find ourselves confronted with an array of apparent reasons for action,[16] some originating in considerations about local attachments and affiliations, some in differences of structure and purpose found at different levels of social organization, some in considerations about the legal and economic structure of the global political economy and that structure's impact on human well-being, and some in facts about the well-being of individuals considered in abstraction from their spatial locations and group memberships. We need a better grasp of the content of these apparent reasons and of the processes by which reasons of these kinds might be integrated when it is necessary to make judgments about how to act. The result may be something like "moderate" or "extreme" cosmopolitanism, but more likely it will be some third conception, more richly described, that we have not yet clearly anticipated.

Cosmopolitanism and World Poverty

All of this is unhappily abstract. Let me illustrate by considering how a recognition of the potential diversity of reasons for action might influence thinking about two dimensions of global justice: first the economic, then the political.

I begin with the question of responsibility for the relief of global poverty. Beginning in the 1970s, philosophical disagreement about

---

[15] Scheffler, "Conceptions of Cosmopolitanism," pp. 114–115; Caney, "Review Article: International Distributive Justice," pp. 975–976; David Miller, "The Limits of Cosmopolitan Justice," in David R. Mapel and Terry Nardin (eds.), *International Society* (Princeton: Princeton University Press, 1998), p. 166. I drew attention to the possibility of conflict between cosmopolitan and nonderivative sectional values – I now think in a slightly Delphic way – in Charles Beitz, "Cosmopolitan Ideals and National Sentiment," *The Journal of Philosophy* 80 (1983), pp. 591–600.

[16] "Apparent reasons for action" – reasons that suggest themselves to us in practical reasoning, before they have been subjected to a process of critical inspection [see Thomas Scanlon, *What We Owe to Each Other* (Cambridge: Harvard University Press, 1998), p. 65].

this has revolved around two questions. The first, prompted by the publication of Peter Singer's influential paper about famine relief,[17] is about the demandingness of reasons of beneficence – that is, about the degree of sacrifice in the satisfaction of one's own interests one is required to undertake in order to improve the situations of destitute persons with whom one has no special relationship. The second is whether there are reasons other than those of beneficence to contribute to the relief of poverty in the world today, and if so, what forms of action one is committed to by these reasons.

The first question implicates deep issues in ethical theory that are still disputed.[18] But with respect to the second, I believe there has been movement. We can see this in the view of international distributive justice found in John Rawls's book, *The Law of Peoples*. His view contains a puzzle. Rawls holds that, strictly speaking, there is no such thing as international distributive justice. Individual states, which he takes to be the basic agents in the global normative order, are not obligated to achieve and maintain any definite global distribution of wealth. It is not only that there is no duty to bring about satisfaction of a global difference principle; there is no duty to bring about satisfaction of *any* global distributive requirement that lacks what Rawls calls a "target" and a "cut-off."[19]

Yet Rawls also holds the following three positions. First, he affirms that well-off societies have duties to assist other societies to escape the burdens that oppress them and he believes that under some circumstances these duties might require international transfers of wealth.[20] Second, in remarks about human rights, he argues that

[17] Peter Singer, "Famine, Affluence, and Morality," *Philosophy and Public Affairs* 1 (1972), pp. 229–243.

[18] Though at an increasingly sophisticated level; see, e.g., Liam Murphy, *Moral Demands in Nonideal Theory* (Oxford: Oxford University Press, 2000). This book illustrates how the attempt to resolve problems that arise in the international context can produce contributions to moral and political theory of quite general interest.

[19] John Rawls, *The Law of Peoples* (Cambridge: Harvard University Press, 1999), Section 16. For an explanation of the significance of these features, see Leif Wenar, "The Legitimacy of Peoples," in Pablo De Greiff and Ciaran Cronin (eds.), *Global Justice and Transnational Politics* (Cambridge: MIT Press, 2002), pp. 65–67.

[20] However, he is skeptical that outside financial assistance can help a society to develop the capacity to satisfy its people's needs in the absence of internal change. He writes, for example, that "merely dispensing funds will not suffice to rectify basic political and social injustices (though money is often essential)" and that "throwing funds at [a burdened society] is usually undesirable" (Rawls, *The Law of Peoples*, pp. 108–109, 110).

people have basic rights to subsistence and that a government that fails to honor its people's basic rights may make itself vulnerable to justified external interference. Third, he observes that the Law of Peoples as formulated is incomplete: it needs to be supplemented by principles to regulate organized international collaboration – for example, standards for fair trade – and to ensure "that in all reasonable liberal (and decent) societies people's basic needs will be met."[21] Each position yields a reason why citizens in rich countries should support policies aimed at helping at least some poor societies to improve the living standards of their people. Rawls does not understand these as reasons of distributive justice, but he does not appear to regard them as reasons of beneficence either. The puzzle is to say what kinds of reasons they are.

I do not know how to answer this question, beyond observing that, in Rawls's terms, any explanation would most likely start from the special character of the public reason of the Society of Peoples. But if we step outside of Rawls's own terms of reference, surely the more natural way to express the point would be to say that the international realm has its own, distinctive form of distributive justice whose principles differ in content and foundation from those that apply within individual societies. Perhaps, as Miller puts it, principles of global justice are noncomparative whereas principles of social justice are comparative.[22] The substantive question is why one should believe that structural differences between the international and the domestic realms generate reasons for action that differ in this way.

[21] Rawls, *The Law of Peoples*, p. 38; see also p. 37 and Sections 15–16. With respect to international cooperative organizations (such as might manage the trade regime), he writes, "should these cooperative organizations have unjustified distributive effects between peoples, these would have to be corrected, and taken into account by the duty of assistance" (Rawls, *The Law of Peoples*, p. 43). He does not say how a baseline might be established to identify "unjustified distributive effects."

[22] Miller, "The Limits of Cosmopolitan Justice," p. 171. It would be reasonable to wonder how Miller's conception of non-comparative justice at the global level differs from beneficence. In introductory comments, he gives as an example of a "weak cosmopolitan" distributive obligation what might be interpreted as a duty of beneficence (p. 167). However, in the substance of the discussion, he refers to the non-comparative principle that establishes an obligation to contribute to the satisfaction of people's vital interests as a principle of justice. Elsewhere, he distinguishes explicitly between considerations of humanity and considerations of justice and holds that under certain circumstances there can be obligations of international justice (specifically, "in cases where people's basic rights were put at risk and it was not feasible for their own national state to protect them") [David Miller, *On Nationality* (Oxford: Clarendon Press, 1995), p. 108].

The answer does not appear to depend on whether one accepts or rejects moral cosmopolitanism. Or rather: the view that global and local distributive justice differ in the way I have described is not ruled out by the cosmopolitan requirement that the scope of justification must be global. Whether we should accept the view is more likely to depend on two kinds of judgment, one normative and the other broadly historical. The normative issue concerns the significance of the fact that domestic-level political orders are coercive in a way that the global order does not seem to be. A possible view, defended by Michael Blake and suggested in a different form by Ronald Dworkin, is that the institutions of domestic society face a higher burden of justification because they constitute a collectively-imposed coercive scheme. On such a view, it might be said, any acceptable justification at the domestic level would have to include a condition requiring distributive inequalities to be kept within some limit; the justification of the global order, on the other hand, because it is not coercive in the same way, need not include any similar condition.[23] The scope of justification is global but the standards of justification respond to variations in the characteristics of the institutions to be justified. (Plainly, there is more to be said on this point.)

The historical issue concerns the assignment of causal responsibility for chronic poverty. One position, taken by Rawls, is that the sources of poverty are largely to be found at the domestic level, so that any enduring improvement must come about through local changes that outsiders are not usually in a position to effect.[24] Another position, taken by Pogge, is that the global order perpetuates and may exacerbate existing global poverty.[25] He argues that because this order has been imposed by the governments of rich countries, they and their people have a duty, deriving from the duty not to harm, to reform the global order and perhaps to compensate for its damaging effects.

[23] I apologize for the crude formulation. See Michael Blake, "Distributive Justice, State Coercion, and Autonomy," *Philosophy and Public Affairs* 30 (2001), pp. 257–296; Ronald Dworkin, *Law's Empire* (Cambridge: Harvard University Press, 1986), pp. 195–202.

[24] These domestic-level sources include "the political culture, the political virtues and civil society of the country, its members' probity and industriousness, their capacity for innovation, and much else. Crucial also is the country's population policy ...." He adds: "But ... the duty of assistance is in no way diminished" (Rawls, *The Law of Peoples*, p. 108).

[25] Pogge describes a variety of mechanisms that bring about this result (Pogge, *World Poverty and Human Rights*, Chapter 6).

In characterizing this as a historical issue, I do not mean that it lacks philosophical elements. One might wonder, for example, whether the causal mechanisms through which poverty is perpetuated in the existing global order count as "harming" in the sense necessary to generate a duty of redress. One might also wonder about the proper allocation of moral responsibility in cases where global-level and domestic-level causes interact to perpetuate deprivation. For now I leave these questions aside. The point is that the resolution of the historical dispute does not depend on whether one accepts or rejects moral cosmopolitanism. It depends on one's understanding of the relationship between participation in the international economy, on the one hand, and domestic poverty and income inequality, on the other. These matters are complex and there is a good deal that philosophers could learn about them from economic historians and development economists.

On the other hand, the details of a cosmopolitan theory of global distributive justice will certainly depend on historical considerations. Here I can only give one illustration, combined with a plea for closer attention in the future. Until recently, discussions of global distributive justice were framed as if the most important practical consequence of taking justice seriously would be a requirement to advocate large increases in inter-country transfer payments. One may have imagined these on the model of foreign development assistance or as no-strings-attached grants to poor country governments.[26] Either way, it is now clear that this is a mistake: a confusion of a part for the whole. This should have been clear earlier as well, if only because a similar mistake can occur in the domestic context. Writing about institutions for distributive justice, Rawls himself noted that the aim was to design the social system so that, so far as possible, whatever distributions were produced by its normal operation would be acceptable. Direct income transfers were to be relied upon to guarantee a suitable social minimum, but this was a backstop for

---

[26] I adopted the first model in Beitz, *Political Theory and International Relations*. In my defense, I observed that aid and international economic reforms had to be considered as supplementary to a largely indigenous process of economic development (p. 173, note 82). For the second model, see Brian Barry, "International Society from a Cosmopolitan Perspective," in David R. Mapel and Terry Nardin (eds.), *International Society* (Princeton: Princeton University Press, 1998), pp. 153–156.

circumstances in which markets failed.[27] Analogously, we might say that a theory of global distributive justice should concern itself primarily with the basic structure of international society – that is, the economic, political and legal institutions and practices that influence the global distribution of advantages. International transfers (for example, foreign aid programs) also influence this distribution, but by any measure they are less significant than other forces which are potentially open to political manipulation, such as private capital flows, the rules of the trade regime, and the system of international property rights. Principles of global distributive justice pertain to all of these.

Global Political Justice

The subject of political justice – that is, the justice of a society's provisions for making political decisions – is the oldest and arguably the most familiar element of the political theory of the state. In historical perspective the subject of distributive justice is a relative newcomer. So it might seem strange that in the recent growth of interest in global justice, this order has been reversed.

This may be because it is unclear how the subject of global political justice should be conceived. This is not such a problem at the domestic level: in any reasonably developed state, there is a structure of coercive institutions with a capacity to make political decisions and to enforce them by limiting people's liberty. This structure includes both an allocation of control over decision-making and some constraints on the use of state power to carry out political decisions. Principles of political justice regulate both aspects of the structure.

The problem is that there is no analogous structure at the global level: no sovereign executive power, no legislature, no effective police capacity. Moreover, there is a general, although hardly a unanimous, disposition to believe that a state-like structure encompassing all existing states is unachievable in the foreseeable future and would be

[27] John Rawls, *A Theory of Justice*, rev. ed. (Cambridge: Harvard University Press, 1999), Section 43. See also Richard Krouse and Michael MacPherson, "Capitalism, 'Property-Owning Democracy' and the Welfare State," in Amy Gutmann (ed.), *Democracy and the Welfare State* (Princeton: Princeton University Press, 1988), pp. 78–105.

undesirable even if it could be achieved. So at first glance it is not clear that there is any subject for global political justice to be about. And even if one discerns a subject, it is not clear how to proceed, since models of political justice familiar from the domestic context do not straightforwardly apply.

But it would be a mistake to be misled by this. Global and regional processes of public decision-making ("regimes," in the jargon of political science) are in some respects well developed already and under favorable circumstances can be expected to develop further. In parallel with these regimes, as my colleague Anne-Marie Slaughter has observed, we find transnational networks of state officials also performing global governance functions.[28] The decisions reached through these processes can have important consequences for those affected by them. Of many possible examples, consider the intellectual property agreement (TRIPS) of 1994 and rules of the world trade regime allowing the rich countries to maintain restrictive agricultural trade preferences which effectively deny access to their domestic markets to cheaper-cost providers in poor countries. In both cases, rules prejudicial to the prosperity of many poor societies were arrived at through rule-making processes in which effective control was distributed very unequally and which lacked mechanisms making them accountable to those affected. These examples involve rule-making processes, but there are equally severe problems of accountability in most international administrative and regulatory organizations. The problems are even more acute in transnational governance networks.

Here, the force of cosmopolitanism is to compel the question whether we have reason to hold international and transnational regimes and institutions responsible to standards of political justice similar to those that apply to the institutions of the state. Is there any sense in the thought that global institutions should be democratic? To some people it seems obvious that they should be, whereas to others, it is a kind of category mistake even to raise the question. The problem is simultaneously philosophical and institutional. The philosophical aspect is to distinguish the various kinds of reasons that explain why democratic forms are desirable at the domestic level and to judge whether and how these reasons are affected when the subject changes to governance beyond the state. The institutional aspect is to

[28] Anne-Marie Slaughter, *A New World Order* (Princeton: Princeton University Press, 2004).

imagine what the range of realistically achievable alternative political arrangements is like at the global level, and to understand how they would likely operate in view of the incentives their procedures would establish. To illustrate: it seems to me that a plausible account of the justifying grounds of democratic institutions in liberal societies would have to take account of at least three kinds of considerations. These institutions should recognize the equal public status of citizens; they should afford procedural opportunities for individuals to protect their important interests against neglect or invasion by the state; and they should establish a political environment conducive to informed, effective deliberation by citizens about the political choices facing them.[29] Now it is not obvious that all of these considerations arise at the global level or, if they arise, that their consequences for the design of institutions are the same. If not, then the appropriate model of global political justice may not be the model of democracy in any familiar form.

With a few exceptions, philosophers have not engaged these problems seriously.[30] In my view they represent an urgent challenge for the future. Or perhaps I should say for the present: Reflection about reform of global governance is well advanced in other venues, both academic and political, almost never with the benefit of the moral clarity that might be contributed by an articulate philosophical conception of global political justice. That is too bad, not so much because moral clarity is a virtue (though it is), as because there is some chance, when ideas are in flux, that the intervention of political philosophers could make a difference for the better.

CONCLUSION

When the organizers invited me to present this paper, they suggested I discuss what they called "the state of the debate about global justice." I soon realized this was ambiguous, because the idea of "global justice," considered as the name of a subject of philosophical interest, has both a broader and a narrower sense. The phrase might be used as it is in the

---

[29] I borrow here from Charles Beitz, *Political Equality* (Princeton: Princeton University Press, 1989), Chapter 5.

[30] The exceptions include David Held, *Democracy and the Global Order* (Cambridge: Polity Press, 1995); James Bohman, "International Regimes and Democratic Governance," *International Affairs* 75 (1999), pp. 499–514; Allen Buchanan and Robert O. Keohane, "Governing the Preventive Use of Force," *Ethics & International Affairs* 18 (2004), pp. 1–22.

title of this conference, as an inclusive label for the normative problems that arise in political life beyond the state. Or it might be used more narrowly, to refer to the global requirements of *justice*, conceived as a special class of reasons for action that apply primarily to the institutional structure of political and economic life. I have tried to limit myself to the narrower of these two senses and have not been able to comment about many other problems whose claim on our attention is undeniable. These include the morality of war, the grounds of sovereignty and the meaning of international toleration, the theory of human rights, the permissibility of humanitarian intervention, emigration and immigration, self-determination, and much else.

Problems like those I have listed and those I have discussed are inherently difficult. The difficulty is compounded by the fact that the problems themselves are often not well defined and, leaving aside the morality of war, we lack well-established traditions of thought to guide reflection. This can be frustrating and sometimes discouraging. But from a more detached perspective, what matters is that philosophers engage with the subject at all. For the result is that practical issues that had been treated as uninteresting and peripheral can be appreciated for their genuine moral significance. Once appreciated, these issues do not go away. I do not believe there is any more urgent preoccupation for political philosophy today than to work out a better theoretical understanding of these matters of global justice. So the fact that they are now, unavoidably, before us should be encouraging: it is a sign of progress.

Department of Politics
Princeton University
130 Corwin Hall
Princeton, NJ 08540, USA
E-mail: cbeitz@princeton.edu

THOMAS POGGE

REAL WORLD JUSTICE

(Received 14 May 2004; accepted in revised form 3 June 2004)

ABSTRACT. Despite a high and growing global average income, billions of human beings are still condemned to lifelong severe poverty with all its attendant evils of low life expectancy, social exclusion, ill health, illiteracy, dependency, and effective enslavement. We citizens of the rich countries are conditioned to think of this problem as an occasion for assistance. Thanks in part to the rationalizations dispensed by our economists, most of us do not realize how deeply we are implicated, through the new global economic order our states have imposed, in this ongoing catastrophe. My sketch of how we are so implicated follows the argument of my book, *World Poverty and Human Rights*, but takes the form of a response to the book's critics.

KEY WORDS: causal explanation, development economics, global resources dividend, harm, human rights, inequality, justice, negative duties, world poverty, WTO

Can normative theories about global justice benefit from empirical theories? This is a rhetorical question – no one seriously argues that we should think about global justice in ignorance of the facts. And the question is also a bit tendentious, prodding us philosophers (heads in the clouds or buried in sand) to pay more attention to the real world as presented, most relevantly, by development economists.

I agree that many philosophers working on global justice know too little about the real world, but I also believe that we should absorb the theories delivered by economists with a great deal of caution. A prominent concept in economics is that of *homo economicus*, an individual who, single-mindedly and rationally, seeks optimally to satisfy his preferences. Such imaginary creatures are not good approximations of persons in the real world. But, as various studies have shown, they do approximate pretty well the kind of people we find in business schools and economics departments – people who cannot comprehend how it could possibly make sense to tip a waiter in a place one does not intend to revisit.

Insofar as they approximate the ideal type *homo economicus*, the work economists do – what they study and how they study it – will be driven by their career goals. These goals will rarely be served by propagating falsehoods and fallacies. But they will be served by propagating truths that are supportive, in preference to truths that are subversive, of the position and policies of those in power. While economists like to present themselves as disinterested scientists, they function today more typically as ideologists for our political and economic "elites" – much like most theologians did in an earlier age. For a nice illustration of this, just look at *The Economist* (March 11, 2004), which gives rather absurd arguments for the claims that global inequality is not increasing and that, in any case, global inequality and poverty are "not a question of justice." Or look at the work of development economists, from Amartya Sen to the Chicago School, which is overwhelmingly focused on relating the persistence of severe poverty to local causes – bad governance, sexist culture, geography, and much else – while leaving unstudied the huge impact of the global economic order on the incidence of poverty worldwide. Unfortunately, in this domain we cannot just learn and benefit from the theories of the experts. We must think for ourselves and, as best we can, become experts.

With this preamble, let me proceed to lay out the empirically informed view on global justice I have been defending. In an attempt to render this exercise interesting to those familiar with my work, I present my view in the form of a response to some of its critics.

1. The Central Claim

In a recent book,[1] I have claimed that we – the more advantaged citizens of the affluent countries – are actively responsible for most of the life-threatening poverty in the world. The book focuses on the 15 years since the end of the Cold War. In this period, billions of people have suffered greatly from poverty-related causes: from hunger and malnutrition, from child labor and trafficking, from lack of access to basic health care and safe drinking water, from lack of

[1] Thomas W. Pogge, *World Poverty and Human Rights: Cosmopolitan Responsibilities and Reforms* (Cambridge: Polity Press, 2002).

shelter, basic sanitation, electricity, and elementary education.[2] Some 18 million people have died prematurely each year from poverty-related causes, accounting for fully one third of all human deaths. This 15-year death toll of 270 million is considerably larger than the 200-million death toll from all the wars, civil wars, genocides and other government repression of the entire 20th century combined.[3]

---

[2] Among 6133 million human beings (2001), about 799 million are undernourished [UNDP, *Human Development Report 2003* (New York: Oxford University Press, 2003), p. 87]; 880 million have no access to basic medical care [UNDP, *Human Development Report 1999* (New York: Oxford University Press, 1999), p. 22]; 1000 million lack access to safe drinking water (UNDP, *Human Development Report 2003*, p. 9); 1000 million lack adequate shelter and 2000 million have no electricity [UNDP *Human Development Report 1998* (New York, Oxford University Press, 1998), p. 49]; 2400 million lack basic sanitation (UNDP: *Human Development Report 2003*, p. 9); and 876 million adults are illiterate (UNDP, *Human Development Report 2003*, p. 6). Some 250 million children (aged 5–14) do wage work outside their family, 8.4 million of them in the "unconditionally worst" forms of child labor, "defined as slavery, trafficking, debt bondage and other forms of forced labor, forced recruitment of children for use in armed conflict, prostitution and pornography, and illicit activities" [International Labour Organisation, *A Future without Child Labour* (Geneva: International Labor Office, 2002, www.ilo.org/public/english/standards/decl/publ/reports/report3.htm)]. Females and people of color are heavily overrepresented in all these horrifying statistics (UNDP, *Human Development Report 2003*, pp. 310–330).

[3] This includes World War Two (1939–45: 50 million), repression and mismanagement under Mao (1949–75: 46 million), Stalin's repression (1924–53: 20 million), World War One (1914–18: 16 million), the Russian Civil War (1917–22: 9 million), the devastation visited on Congo Free State (1886–1908: 5 million), the post-war expulsion of Germans from Eastern Europe (1945–47: 3 million), KMT repression (1928–37: 3 million), the Korean War (1950–53: 2.8 million), the Vietnam War (1960–75: 2.5 million), North Korean repression (since 1948: 2 million), the Biafra/Nigeria civil war (1966–70: 2 million), Pakistani repression in Bangla Desh (1971: 2 million), the Cambodia genocide (1975–78: 1.6 million), the civil war in the Sudan (since 1983: 1.5 million), the recent wars in the Congo (since 1998: 1.5 million), the Afghan wars (1979–2001: 1.4 million), the wars and civil wars in Rwanda and Burundi (1959–95: 1.2 million), the Armenian Genocide (1915–23: 1 million), the Mexican Revolution (1910–20: 1 million), the sanctions against Iraq (1990–2003: 1 million), the civil wars in Somalia (since 1991: 1 million), the Iran/Iraq war (1980–88: 0.9m), the partition of India (1947: 0.5 million), Suharto's coup in Indonesia (1965–66: 0.5 million), the civil war in Angola (1975–95: 0.5 million) and 259 other mega-death events of violence and repression. See http://users.erols.com/mwhite28/war-1900.htm for the figures and the relevant literature supporting them.

Some critics maintain that these problems are peanuts compared to the bad old days when a large majority of humankind was poor.[4] In 1820, they tell us, 75% of humankind were living below the World Bank's "$1/day" poverty line, while today this percentage is only 20%. (This poverty line is defined in terms of the purchasing power that a monthly income of $32.74 had in the year 1993.[5] In 2004, this line corresponds to the purchasing power of $500 *per year* in the United States.[6]) According to these critics, what is remarkable about world poverty is how very little of it there still is today.

I disagree. For one thing, it is quite inappropriate to use percentages for the comparison. The killing of a given number of people does not become morally less troubling the more world population increases. What matters morally is the *number* of people in extreme poverty. In 1820, this number was about 750 million (75% of about one billion).[7] In 1998, this number was nearly 1200 million.[8] Since 1820, the number of extremely poor people has thus increased by over 50%, while the number of people living below the World Bank's more reasonable "$2/day" poverty line has tripled.[9] Moreover, severe poverty was quite hard to avoid in 1820, because even the average purchasing power of incomes worldwide barely reached the World Bank's higher poverty line. Today, by contrast, the average purchasing power of incomes worldwide is well over 10 times that level, and severe poverty is entirely avoidable. We are not avoiding it only because of the fantastic increase in inequality.[10]

---

[4] Notably Gerald Gaus, "Radio Interview on Pogge's *World Poverty and Human Rights*" on *Ideas and Issues* (WETS-FM), 19 January 2003 (www.etsu.edu/philos/radio/gaus-wphr.htm); and Mathias Risse, "Do We Harm the Global Poor?," presentation at *Author Meets Critics* session at the Eastern Division Meeting of the American Philosophical Association, 30 December 2003 (http://ksghome.harvard.edu/~.mrisse.academic.ksg/papers_Philosophy.htm).

[5] Shaohua Chen and Martin Ravallion: "How Did the World's Poorest Fare in the 1990s?," *Review of Income and Wealth* 47 (2001), p. 285.

[6] See www.bls.gov/cpi/home.htm.

[7] See www.census.gov/ipc/www/worldhis.html.

[8] Chen and Ravallion: "How Did the World's Poorest Fare in the 1990s?" p. 290; cf. www.worldbank.org/research/povmonitor for later figures.

[9] To 2812 million (Chen and Ravallion, "How Did the World's Poorest Fare in the 1990s?," p. 290); see www.worldbank.org/research/povmonitor.

[10] The ratio in average income between the fifth of the world's people living in the highest-income countries and the fifth living in the lowest income countries "was 74

My main claim is then that, by shaping and enforcing the social conditions that foreseeably and avoidably cause the monumental suffering of global poverty, we are *harming* the global poor – or, to put it more descriptively, we are active participants in the largest, though not the gravest, crime against humanity ever committed. Adolf Hitler and Joseph Stalin were vastly more evil than our political leaders, but in terms of killing and harming people they never came anywhere near causing 18 million deaths per year.

Most of my readers believe that this claim is obviously mistaken, if not preposterous. Perhaps for this reason, they pay little attention to the structure and details of the case I am building. Instead, they present various general conjectures about what my mistake may be. They suggest that I am making *conceptual* mistakes by re-labeling as harm what are really failures to aid and protect.[11] They suggest that I am *factually* wrong about the causal explanation of severe poverty or confused about the counterfactuals to which I compare the world as it is.[12] They suggest that I am *morally* wrong by presenting as minimal certain moral requirements that are actually excessively demanding.[13] These criticisms are worth addressing, and I will

---

to 1 in 1997, up from 60 to 1 in 1990 and 30 to 1 in 1960. [Earlier] the income gap between the top and bottom countries increased from 3 to 1 in 1820 to 7 to 1 in 1870 to 11 to 1 in 1913" (UNDP: *Human Development Report 1999*, p. 3; see also p. 38). The trend is no more encouraging when one compares the incomes of households worldwide via purchasing power parities: Over a recent five-year period, "world inequality has increased … from a Gini of 62.8 in 1988 to 66.0 in 1993. This represents an increase of 0.6 Gini points per year. This is a very fast increase, faster than the increase experienced by the United States and United Kingdom in the decade of the 1980's. … The bottom 5% of the world grew poorer, as their real incomes decreased between 1988 and 1993 by 25%, while the richest quintile grew richer. It gained 12% in real terms, that is it grew more than twice as much as mean world income (5.7%)" [Branko Milanovic, "True World Income Distribution, 1988 and 1993: First Calculation Based on Household Surveys Alone," *The Economic Journal* 112 (2002), p. 88, see www.blackwellpublishers.co.uk/specialarticles/ecoj50673 pdf].

[11] Gaus: "Radio Interview on Pogge's *World Poverty and Human Rights*;" Alan Patten, "Remarks on Pogge's *World Poverty and Human Rights*" at Author Meets Critics session at the Eastern Division Meeting of the American Philosophical Association, 30 December 2003.

[12] Gaus, "Radio Interview on Pogge's *World Poverty and Human Rights*"; Debra Satz, "Comments on Pogge's *World Poverty and Human Rights*" at Author Meets Critics session at the Eastern Division Meeting of the American Philosophical Association, 30 December 2003.

[13] Patten, "Remarks on Pogge's *World Poverty and Human Rights*."

address many of them in the context of explaining the main lines of argument in the book.

2. Positive Duties

Before doing this, I should dispose of one misunderstanding. My book seeks to show how existing world poverty manifests a violation of our *negative* duties, our duties not to harm. To show this, I leave positive duties aside. I do not assert that there are no positive duties, or that such duties are feeble. Rather, I avoid claims about positive duties so as to make clear that my case does not depend on such claims. My focus is solely on duties not to harm as well as on duties to avert harms that one's own past conduct may cause in the future.

Duties of this last kind – to avert harms that one's past conduct may cause in the future – do not fit well into the conventional dichotomy of positive and negative duties. They are positive insofar as they require the agent to do something and also negative insofar as this requirement is continuous with the duty to avoid causing harm to others. One might call them intermediate duties, in recognition also of their intermediate stringency. My focus is exclusively on negative and intermediate duties, and thus on harm we are materially involved in causing rather than on all the harm people suffer.

This focus is motivated by the belief that negative and intermediate moral duties are more stringent than positive ones. For example, the duty not to assault people is more stringent than the duty to prevent such assaults by others. And, having assaulted another, the attacker has more reason to ensure that his victim's injuries are treated than a bystander would. Suggesting these views in the book, I do assume something about positive duties after all. But this is meant to be a very weak assumption, accepted not merely by libertarians but by pretty much all, except act-consequentialists. I do *not* assume that any negative or intermediate duty is more stringent than all positive duties. Rather, I assume that negative and intermediate duties are more stringent than positive duties *when what is at stake for all concerned is held constant*.[14] I go to some length to stress that I do *not* believe the absurdity some critics[15] have attributed to me: namely that *any* negative duty, including the duty to refrain from doing some

[14] Pogge, *World Poverty and Human Rights*, p. 132.

[15] Notably Satz, "Comments on Pogge's *World Poverty and Human Rights*."

small harm, is more stringent than *every* positive duty, including the duty to rescue thousands of children.[16]

Now if negative duties (not to harm) and intermediate duties (to avert harms that one's past conduct may cause in the future) are indeed more stringent than positive duties, then it could be misleading to appeal only to positive duties when duties of the other two kinds are also in play. Consider a corporation polluting a river with dire consequences for the health of many. One might ask this corporation, along with other businesses in the region, to help reduce that problem through donations toward purchasing pollution control equipment and toward paying for medical treatment of those sickened by the pollution. This sort of request may be politically opportune. But it also misleadingly suggests that the polluting corporation is morally in the same boat as the other potential donors: helping out for a good cause, pursuant to an imperfect positive duty of occasional charity. In fact, these two points are related. What makes such a plea in the positive-duty idiom politically opportune (when it is so) typically is precisely the misleading suggestion that its addressees have no negative and intermediate duties to forestall the harm they are being asked to help mitigate.

One may well think that being misleading is a very small price to pay for political success against the catastrophic problem of world poverty. But, for better or worse, it does not seem that we are actually facing this choice. The appeal to positive duties has been well presented by Peter Singer, Henry Shue, Peter Unger, and others.[17] If citizens in the affluent countries were minimally decent and humane, they would respond to these appeals and would do their bit to eradicate world poverty. If they did this, my argument would be of much less interest and importance, and I might not see the need to elaborate it at such length. As it is, I see it as my best chance to

---

[16] I repeatedly warn against this misunderstanding in formulations such as this: "I hope I have made clear enough that this is not presented as a strict, or lexical, hierarchy: It is generally acknowledged that a higher moral reason can be outweighed by a lower, if more is at stake in the latter" (Pogge, *World Poverty and Human Rights*, p. 240, note 207; see also p. 132 and p. 241, note 216).

[17] Peter Singer, "Famine, Affluence and Morality," *Philosophy and Public Affairs* 1 (1972), pp. 229–243; Henry Shue, *Basic Rights: Subsistence, Affluence, and U.S. Foreign Policy* (Princeton: Princeton University Press, 1980); and Peter Unger, *Living High and Letting Die: Our Illusion of Innocence* (Oxford, Oxford University Press, 1999).

contribute to ending or reducing the immense deprivations we affluent are now inflicting upon the global poor.

I also see my argument as essential to an accurate portrayal of how we affluent citizens of the rich countries are morally related to those deprivations. Yes, we are able to alleviate them, and, seeing how cheaply this can be done, we surely have positive duties to do so. But because we are also implicated, with many others, in shaping and enforcing the social institutions that produce these deprivations, and are moreover benefiting from the enormous inequalities these unjust institutions reproduce, we have much more stringent duties to seek to reform these social institutions and to do our fair share toward mitigating the harms they cause.

3. An Ecumenical Approach to Demonstrating Harm

Let us now look at the arguments of the book. The case I seek to build is broadly ecumenical. I am trying to convince not merely the adherents of some particular moral conception or theory – Lockeans or Rawlsians or libertarians or communitarians, for example. Rather, I am trying to convince the adherents of *all* the main views now alive in Western political thought. This ambition makes the task much harder, because I must defend my conclusion on multiple fronts, fielding parallel arguments that address and appeal to diverse and often mutually incompatible moral conceptions and beliefs.

This ecumenical strategy has been confusing to some who complain that I am unclear and inconsistent about the baseline relative to which the global poor are supposedly harmed by existing institutional arrangements.[18] They are right that I do not provide a single consistent such baseline. But they are wrong to see this as a flaw. If I want to convince readers with diverse ideas about morality and justice, then I must support my conclusions with diverse arguments. And these may have to appeal to diverse baselines. A state-of-nature baseline is relevant to a reader with Lockean or Nozickian views. But a Rawlsian will reject such a baseline, insisting that the existing distributional profile should be compared to the profiles achievable under alternative feasible institutional arrangements. To satisfy

[18] Notably Satz, "Comments on Pogge's *World Poverty and Human Rights*," and Patten, "Remarks on Pogge's *World Poverty and Human Rights*."

readers of both kinds, I need to give different arguments to them, each with a different baseline. This is more work, to be sure. But the pay-off is that my case cannot justifiably be dismissed as dependent on some partisan moral premises or theory which readers may feel free to reject.

The ecumenical strategy is broadest and most explicit in the final chapter, which argues for a global resources dividend (GRD). My first step there is to show that our world is pervaded by what, following Tom Nagel,[19] I call "radical inequality":

(1) The worse-off are very badly off in absolute terms.
(2) They are also very badly off in relative terms – very much worse-off than many others.
(3) The inequality is impervious: It is difficult or impossible for the worse-off substantially to improve their lot; and most of the better-off never experience life at the bottom for even a few months and have no vivid idea of what it is like to live in that way.
(4) The inequality is pervasive: It concerns not merely some aspects of life, such as the climate or access to natural beauty or high culture, but most aspects or all.
(5) The inequality is avoidable: The better-off can improve the circumstances of the worse-off without becoming badly off themselves.

I go on to assume that most of my readers demand more than the fact of radical inequality between us and the global poor as proof that we are *harming* them. I also assume that different readers differ on the question of what is missing. To satisfy more readers, I present *in parallel* three second steps of the argument, each of which shows in a different way that the existing radical inequality involves us in harming the global poor. All three strands of the argument lead to the conclusion that today's massive and severe poverty manifests a violation by the affluent of their negative duties: an immense crime in which we affluent citizens of the rich countries (as well as the political and economic "elites" of most poor countries) are implicated.

[19] Thomas Nagel, "Poverty and Food: Why Charity Is Not Enough," in Peter Brown and Henry Shue (eds.), *Food Policy: The Responsibility of the United States in the Life and Death Choices* (New York: The Free Press, 1977).

4. Engaging Historical Conceptions of Social Justice

In one strand of the argument I invoke the effects of a common and violent history. The present world is characterized not only by radical inequality as defined, but also by the fact that "the social starting positions of the worse-off and the better-off have emerged from a single historical process that was pervaded by massive grievous wrongs."[20] I invoke these historical facts specifically for readers who believe that it matters morally how radical inequality has evolved. Most of the existing international inequality in standards of living was built up in the colonial period when today's affluent countries ruled today's poor regions of the world: trading their people like cattle, destroying their political institutions and cultures, and taking their natural resources. In 1960, when the colonizers finally left, taking what they could and destroying much else, the inequality in *per capita* income between Europe and Africa had grown to 30:1, and vast inequalities existed also in education, health-care, infrastructure, and legal and political organization. These inequalities greatly disadvantaged Africans in their dealings with governments and corporations of the affluent countries. This disadvantage helps explain why the Europe/Africa inequality in *per capita* income has since risen to 40:1. But even if *per capita* income had, since 1960, increased a full percentage point more each year in Africa than in Europe, this inequality would still be 20:1 today and would be fully erased only early in the 24th century.

Readers attracted to historical-entitlement conceptions of justice disagree about the conditions an historical process must meet in order for it to justify gross inequalities in life chances. On this point, I can once more afford to be ecumenical. The relevant historical crimes were so horrendous, so diverse, and so consequential that no historical-entitlement conception could credibly support the conclusion that our common history was sufficiently benign to justify even the radical inequalities in starting positions we are witnessing today.

In short, then, upholding a radical inequality counts as harming the worse-off when the historical path on which this inequality arose is pervaded by grievous wrongs. "A morally deeply tarnished history must not be allowed to result in *radical* inequality."[21] This is the moral rationale behind Abraham Lincoln's 40-acres-and-a-mule

[20] Pogge, *World Poverty and Human Rights*, p. 203.
[21] Pogge, *World Poverty and Human Rights*, p. 203.

promise of 1863, which of course was quickly rescinded. And it is the rationale for saying that we are not entitled to the huge advantages we enjoy from birth over the global poor, given how these inequalities have been built up.

Some critics may seem to address this strand of the argument when they point out that the radical inequality between Europe and Africa might have come about even without colonialism.[22] Perhaps Europe could have "taken-off" even without slavery and stolen raw materials, and perhaps the resulting inequality would then have been equally great. In the absence of conclusive proof that, without the horrors of European conquest, severe poverty worldwide would be substantially less today, Risse suggests, we are entitled to keep and defend what we possess, even at the cost of millions of deaths each year (I wonder if he would make the same argument against the 40-acres-and-a-mule proposal).

As a response to the first strand of the argument, this complaint is irrelevant. The first strand addresses readers who believe that the *actual* history *is* relevant. These readers will say: "Yes, if things had transpired as in Risse's hypothetical, then the citizens of the affluent countries might not, by upholding the radical inequality, be harming the global poor. But this has no bearing on whether such upholding of radical inequality constitutes harm in the *actual* world with its *actual* history."

Still, Risse's complaint resonates with other readers who believe that it is permissible to uphold an economic distribution if merely it *could* have come about on a morally acceptable path. It is such readers that the second strand of my argument addresses. To be sure, *any* distribution, however skewed, *could* have been the outcome of a sequence of voluntary bets or gambles. Appeal to *such* a fictional history would "justify" *anything* and would thus be wholly implausible. John Locke does much better, holding that a fictional history can justify the status quo only if the changes in holdings and social rules it involves are ones that all participants could have rationally agreed to. He also holds that in a state of nature persons would be entitled to a proportional share of the world's natural resources. He thus makes the justice of any institutional order depend on whether

---

[22] Notably Risse, "Do We Harm the Global Poor?"

the worst-off under it are at least as well off as people would be in a Lockean state of nature with a proportional resource share.[23] Locke held, implausibly, that this condition was fulfilled in his time, claiming that "a King of a large fruitful territory [in the Americas] feeds, lodges, and is clad worse than a day Laborer in England."[24] I argue that this condition is *not* fulfilled for the global poor today who, living below even the day laborers in Locke's England, are coercively denied "enough and as good"[25] of the world's natural resources without having access to an equivalent substitute.

Readers inclined to a Lockean conception disagree about the relevant state-of-nature baseline that determines how bad the worst social starting positions imposed by a just social order may be. On this question I can once more be ecumenical. However one may want to imagine a state of nature among human beings on this planet, one could not realistically conceive it as producing an enduring poverty death toll of 18 million annually. Only a thoroughly organized state of civilization can sustain horrendous suffering on such a massive scale.

Catering to Lockeans, the second strand of my argument invokes the uncompensated exclusion of the worse-off from a proportional share of global resources: The present world is characterized not merely by radical inequality as defined, but also by the fact that "the better-off enjoy significant advantages in the use of a single natural resource base from whose benefits the worse-off are largely, and without compensation, excluded."[26] The better-off – we – are *harming* the worse-off insofar as the radical inequality we uphold excludes the global poor from a proportional share of the world's natural resources and any equivalent substitute.

The point I was making about Locke is quite similar to one Debra Satz puts forth in a tone of criticism. For Locke, she says, "property rights, however acquired, do not prevail in the face of desperate need" because "everyone has an original pre-appropriation claim-right to an adequate subsistence from the resources of the world."[27] This is correct, although the poor can really have a

---

[23] See Pogge, *World Poverty and Human Rights*, pp. 16, 137–139, and 202–203, for a fuller reading of Locke's argument.

[24] John Locke, "An Essay Concerning the True Original, Extent, and End of Civil Government" [1689], in Peter Laslett (ed.), *John Locke: Two Treatises of Government* (Cambridge: Cambridge University Press, 1960), §41, see §37.

[25] Locke, *Two Treatises of Government*, §27, §33.

[26] Pogge, *World Poverty and Human Rights*, p. 202.

[27] Satz, "Comments on Pogge's *World Poverty and Human Rights*," p. 16.

claim only to a proportional resources share, not to adequate subsistence, because there may simply not be enough to go around. But why does Satz speak in this context of a "*positive* 'property right' of the needy in the means of subsistence"?[28] What *are* positive as opposed to negative property rights? Does Satz want to say that we affluent have merely a positive duty toward the needy? This would suggest that our property rights do prevail after all – that our assets are ours though we ought to give away some. But Satz correctly presents Locke as rejecting this picture: We affluent have *no* rights to property, however acquired, in the face of the excluded. Rather, *they* have a right to what we hold. When we prevent them from exercising this right – when we deprive them of what is justly theirs – then we violate this original right of the poor and we harm them. In this way it is a violation of a *negative* duty to deprive others of "enough and as good" – either through unilateral appropriations or through institutional arrangements such as a radically inegalitarian property regime.[29]

Let me sum up the first two strands of the argument. These strands address readers for whom the justice of the present economic distribution or of present economic arrangements turns on their actual or imaginable history. I conclude that such conceptions of justice cannot justify the status quo. One may try to justify the coercively upheld radical inequality today by appeal to the historical process that *actually* led up to it. But this appeal fails because the actual historical process is massively pervaded by the most grievous wrongs. Alternatively, one may try to justify this coercively upheld radical inequality by appeal to some morally acceptable *fictional* historical process that *might* have led to it. On Locke's permissive version of this account, some small elite may appropriate all, or almost all, of the huge cooperative surplus produced by modern social organization. But such an elite must not enlarge its share even further by reducing the poor below the state-of-nature baseline so that this elite's share of the cooperative surplus is actually more than 100% and the share of the poor correspondingly less than zero. As it is, the citizens and governments of the affluent states are violating this negative duty when

[28] Satz, "Comments on Pogge's *World Poverty and Human Rights*," p. 16.
[29] This is argued at length in Pogge, *World Poverty and Human Rights*, Chapter 5.

we, in collaboration with the ruling cliques of many poor countries, coercively exclude the global poor from a proportional resource share and any equivalent substitute.

5. Engaging Broadly Consequentialist Conceptions of Social Justice

Most contemporary theorists of justice endorse neither of these historical views. Instead, they hold that an economic order and the economic distribution it shapes should be assessed by its foreseeable effects against the background of its feasible alternatives. Thus Rawls considers a domestic economic order to be just if it produces fair equality of opportunity across social classes and no feasible alternative to it would afford better prospects to the least advantaged.

The third strand of my argument addresses such broadly consequentialist conceptions which invoke the effects of shared social institutions. The present world is characterized not only by radical inequality as defined, but also by the following facts:

> There is a shared institutional order that is shaped by the better-off and imposed on the worse-off. This institutional order is implicated in the reproduction of radical inequality in that there is a feasible institutional alternative under which so severe and extensive poverty would not persist. The radical inequality cannot be traced to extra-social factors (such as genetic handicaps or natural disasters) which, as such, affect different human beings differentially.[30]

When these further facts obtain, so I claim, then the better-off – we – are *harming* the worse-off insofar as we are upholding a shared institutional order that is *unjust* by foreseeably and avoidably (re)producing radical inequality.

Now there are many different such broadly consequentialist conceptions of justice which judge an institutional order by comparing its distributional effects to those its feasible alternatives would have. These conceptions differ along three dimensions. They differ in how they characterize the relevant affected parties (groups, persons, time-slices of persons, etc.). They differ about the metric for assessing relevant effects (social primary goods, capabilities, welfare, etc.). And they differ about how to aggregate relevant effects across affected parties. Once again, my response to such diversity is ecumenical. I am trying to specify very minimal conditions of justice that are widely

---

[30] Pogge, *World Poverty and Human Rights*, p. 199.

accepted. Most broadly consequentialist theorists agree that a national economic order is unjust when it leaves social and economic human rights unfulfilled on a massive scale even while there is a feasible alternative order under which these human rights would be much better realized. Most theorists would demand more, of course. But I need no more for my purpose, because our global economic order does not even meet the very weak requirements that form the common core of the various broadly consequentialist theories of economic justice defended today.

Keeping in mind this background as well as the remarks on positive duties in Section 2, we can now address various misreadings of my account of human rights. I understand human rights, within the context of broadly consequentialist conceptions of justice, primarily as weighty moral claims on social institutions. An institutional order is human-rights violating when it foreseeably gives rise to greater insecurity in access to the objects of human rights (physical integrity, freedom of movement, adequate nutrition, etc.) than would be reasonably avoidable through an alternative feasible institutional design. Moral claims *on* social institutions are also, indirectly, moral claims *against* those who participate in designing and upholding these social institutions: Such agents, too, are violating human rights by imposing an institutional order under which access to the objects of human rights is foreseeably and avoidably insecure for some or all participants. I hold that most of the avoidable global underfulfillment of human rights today can be traced back to the design of the global institutional order: Had the avoidance of severe poverty been a priority in the redesign this order has undergone in the early 1990's, then most of that current global underfulfillment of human rights could have been averted.

Can an individual or collective agent violate human rights directly, for example through torture – irrespective of whether there is an institutional order and, if so, of whether this order is just or unjust? I have been reluctant to answer this question affirmatively because I believe that the common use of the expression "human rights" is restricted to crimes that are in some sense official in character. I have been criticized for this reluctance on the ground that it is surely no worse to participate in the imposition of an institutional scheme under which people get tortured than to torture people directly (holding constant what is at stake for the agents and their victims). I completely agree with this substantive point. My reluctance was based not on any comparative moral judgment, but on common usage. Still, I do not object to calling ordinary crimes of torture, rape, etc., human rights violations. In any case, this terminological issue is irrelevant to my work, which is focused specifically on human rights violations committed by means of imposing institutional arrangements that foreseeably produce greater serious insecurity in access to the objects of human rights than would be reasonably avoidable.

Can an individual or collective agent violate human rights passively, by failing to protect people threatened by violence or starvation even when this could be done safely, easily, and at low cost? Human rights are in principle enforceable, so the answer can be affirmative only in cases where it is morally permissible for some other agent to use some coercive means to force the relevant individual or collective to protect the people under threat. In addition, the right to be protected must be general and important enough to qualify as (part of) a human right. Finally, there are two terminological issues to consider. As pointed out, I have been reluctant to apply the language of human rights to ordinary crimes such as a private citizen's refusal to toss a life preserver to a drowning swimmer. Moreover, with regard to passive failures to protect that are official in character, I have proposed that we classify them as *official disrespect* for human rights, but not as human rights *violations*, in order to recognize the moral significance of the passive/active distinction.

I adduce three reasons in support of my plea. One is common usage. The notion of a human rights violation has an active ring and is thus not a fitting label for someone's failure to protect others when she had no role in causing their urgent need for such protection.

It might seem desirable to stretch common usage so as to include certain failures to protect under this notion. But such a move might well be counterproductive with respect to that large number of human beings who – though they know about hunger and torture abroad and do not doubt that, with a bit of research, they could contribute to an effective protection effort – never do anything toward protecting foreigners in great distress.

Moreover, in the world as it is, we can make a more forceful appeal to these people without stretching language. Conceding that they are not human rights violators for passively ignoring even the most vital needs of others, we can still point out that nearly all of them are human rights violators through their uncompensated participation in the imposition of a global institutional order that, foreseeably and avoidably, reproduces a huge excess in human rights underfulfillment. In our world, most of the avoidable underfulfillment of human rights would be avoided if the global institutional order imposed by the affluent countries (in collaboration with many political elites in the developing world) were not so grievously unjust.

It is hard to deny that reasonably privileged citizens of the rich democracies share some responsibility for the global institutional order which their governments are shaping and upholding. But one can question whether this order is human-rights violating. If it is not, then participation in its imposition cannot constitute a human-rights violation either.

I believe, and will argue in the next section, that the present global institutional order is human-rights violating in that the underfulfillment of human rights is foreseeably much greater under this order than it would be under various feasible modifications thereof. If this is true, then it follows that the existing global order is unjust by the lights of all broadly consequentialist conceptions of social justice that recognize human rights as minimal constraints on the justice of social institutions: this order is unjust by foreseeably giving rise to a greater underfulfillment of human rights than would be reasonably avoidable. Uncompensated participation in the imposition of this order can then be said to be *harming* those whose human rights remain unfulfilled by helping to impose upon them unjust social institutions that contribute to their predicament.

In most ordinary contexts, the word "harm" is understood in an historical sense – either diachronically (someone is harmed when she is rendered worse-off than she was at some earlier time) or subjunctively (someone is harmed when she is rendered worse-off than she would have been had some earlier arrangements continued undisturbed). As we have seen, the second strand of my argument, operating on Lockean terrain, conceives harm in this ordinary way and then conceives justice in terms of harm: Prevailing economic arrangements and the present economic distribution are shown to be unjust in virtue of the fact that they harm many by forcing them below any credible state-of-nature baseline. It is worth stressing, then, that the third strand of my argument, catering to broadly consequentialist conceptions of social justice, does not, *pace* Satz,[31] conceive justice and injustice in terms of an independently specified notion of harm. Rather, this third strand

[31] Satz, "Comments on Pogge's *World Poverty and Human Rights*."

relates the concepts of *harm* and *justice* in the opposite way, conceiving harm in terms of an independently specified conception of social justice. On my ecumenical response to broadly consequentialist conceptions of social justice, we are *harming* the global poor if and insofar as we collaborate in imposing *unjust* social institutions upon them; and social institutions are certainly unjust if and insofar as they foreseeably give rise to large-scale avoidable underfulfillment of human rights.

Moreover, *pace* Patten,[32] this third strand of my argument is not addressed to libertarians, who indeed reject any non-historical, broadly consequentialist assessment of social institutions. Libertarians are addressed by the first and, to some extent, by the second strand. To be sure, the third strand, like the two others, is meant to support the conclusion that the immense catastrophe of world poverty manifests not merely the affluents' failure to fulfill their positive duties, but also, and more importantly, their massive violation of their negative duties. But the moral significance of this conclusion can be appreciated far beyond the confines of the libertarian school. Nearly everyone in the affluent countries would agree that our moral duty not to contribute to the imposition of conditions of extreme poverty on people and our moral duty to help protect people from harm in whose production we are implicated in this way are each more stringent than our moral duty to help protect people from harm in whose production we are not materially involved.[33]

As I try to implement the third strand of my argument, specifically for a human right to basic necessities, it involves three main tasks. I seek to show that it is, among broadly consequentialist conceptions, a minimal and widely acceptable demand of justice on all national institutional schemes that these must be designed to avoid life-threatening poverty insofar as this is reasonably possible. I then seek to show that this demand of justice applies not merely to any domestic institutional arrangements, but to the global order as well. And I must then show, thirdly, that there are feasible alternatives to the existing global institutional order under which life-threatening poverty would be wholly or largely avoided.

[32] Patten, "Remarks on Pogge's *World Poverty and Human Rights*."

[33] These comparisons, once again, hold constant the cost or opportunity cost of the required conduct to the duty bearers as well as the reduction in harm it brings to the beneficiaries.

Task one is easy. There simply is no broadly consequentialist conception of social justice in the field that purports to justify, within one national society, radical inequality of the kind the world at large displays today. To be sure, Patten is right to point out that some libertarians (Robert Nozick) do purport to justify such extreme inequalities. But they do this by appeal to historical conceptions of social justice; and I have sketched my response to such justifications in the preceding section.

Task two involves a highly complex argument to which I cannot possibly do justice here.[34] So let me here concentrate on Task three, on which my critics have focused most of their attention.

6. The Causal Role of the Global Institutional Order in the Reproduction of Severe Poverty

Many critics believe that I see the global institutional order as *the main* cause of world poverty. And they respond that, in light of the incompetence, corruption, and oppression prevalent in so many poor countries, this claim is simply not credible or, at the very least, unsupported by empirical evidence. They are wrong on both counts.

Let us begin with a quick general reflection on causes. In the simplest cases, multiple causes *add up* to produce an effect. Thus the smoke in a bar is the sum of the smoke released by all the smokers. In the case of world poverty, however, the relation among causes is more complex in at least two ways. One complexity is that the different causes of poverty, such as global institutional factors and national policies, influence one another's effects.[35] How harmful corrupt leaders in poor countries are, for example, is strongly influenced by whether the global order recognizes such leaders, on the basis of effective power alone, as entitled to sell us their country's resources, to borrow in its name, and to use the proceeds to buy the means of internal repression.

Given this special complexity, it is not correct to identify my assertion that *most* severe poverty worldwide was and is avoidable through global institutional reform with the claim that the existing global institutional order is *the main* cause of world poverty. My

[34] See Pogge, *World Poverty and Human Rights*, Chapter 4, and Thomas W. Pogge, "The Incoherence between Rawls's Theories of Justice," *Fordham Law Review* 72(5) (2004), pp. 1739–1759.

[35] Discussion of the other complexity begins six paragraphs down.

assertion is perfectly compatible with the claim (which I also endorse) that most severe poverty worldwide was and is avoidable through better national policies and better social institutions in the poor countries. To put it simplistically, the interaction between the two sets of causal factors is not so much additive as multiplicative. The worse each set of factors is, the more it also aggravates the marginal harmful impact of the other.

But if, as development economists like to stress, most severe poverty worldwide was and is avoidable through better national policies and better social institutions in the poor countries, does this not show that our global institutional order is morally acceptable as it is? Am I not, as Patten put it,[36] demanding too much from ourselves, given that the ruling elites in the poor countries could also eradicate much poverty?

Now it is true that many of these elites are incompetent, corrupt, and oppressive. Failing, as badly as we are and often worse, to honor their negative duties not to harm, they are indeed responsible for most severe poverty worldwide. But this is quite compatible with the advantaged citizens in the rich countries also being responsible for most severe poverty worldwide. For it is equally true that most such poverty was and is avoidable through a better global institutional order. Given this basic symmetry, we cannot accept Patten's judgment that *we* should not be required to stop *our* contribution until *they* are ready to stop *theirs*. If this were right, then it would be permissible for two parties together to bring about as much harm as they like, each of them pointing out that *it* has no obligation to stop so long as the other continues.

The situation is roughly analogous to that of two upstream factories releasing chemicals into a river. The chemicals of each factory would cause little harm by themselves. But the mixture of chemicals from both plants causes huge harm downstream. In this sort of case, we must not hold each factory owner responsible for only the small harm he would be causing if the other did not pollute. This would leave unaccounted-for most of the harm they produce together and would thus be quite implausible. In a case of this kind, provided each factory owner knows about the effluent released by the other and can foresee the harmful effects they together produce, each owner bears responsibility for his marginal contribution, that is, for as much of the harm as would be avoided if he alone were not discharging his chemicals. Each factory owner is then responsible for most of the harm they jointly produce.

---

[36] Patten, "Remarks on Pogge's *World Poverty and Human Rights*."

Despite this symmetry in my causal account, my critics nonetheless have a point when they accuse me of explanatory globalism[37] (in analogy to the explanatory nationalism of which I am accusing the majority of development economists[38]). This accusation is accurate in that I *focus* much more on global than on national factors. I do this, because these are the factors that my readers and I are morally responsible for and because, not unrelatedly, these factors are grossly neglected by development economists of all stripes, by the media, and by the citizens of the affluent countries for whom I am writing.

And I have another reason for paying more attention to the causal role of global factors in the reproduction of massive severe poverty. This further reason depends on the second special complexity I mentioned earlier, which is that the causes of world poverty also influence one another. As the global institutional order *is shaped* by the political leaders of the most powerful countries, who in turn are selected and shaped by their domestic institutional arrangements, so the global institutional order powerfully *shapes* the national regimes especially of the weaker countries as well as the composition, incentives, and opportunities of their ruling elites. For example, corrupt rule in poor countries is made much more likely by the fact that our global order accords such rulers, on the basis of effective power alone, the international resource and borrowing privileges just described.[39] These privileges provide strong incentives to potential predators (military officers, most frequently) to take power by force and compel even the most well-intentioned rulers, if they want to maintain their hold on power, to allow such potential putschists corruptly to divert state revenues. The global order thus exerts a strong influence upon the weaker and poorer countries, which makes them considerably more likely to have corrupt and oppressive national regimes. Not all of them will have such regimes, of course, but many of them will, as is well-illustrated by Nigeria and many other developing countries in which the resource sector accounts for a large fraction of GDP.[40] This

---

[37] This accusation is due to Patten: "Remarks on Pogge's *World Poverty and Human Rights*," though he uses the less fitting term "explanatory cosmopolitanism."

[38] See Pogge, *World Poverty and Human Rights*, Section 5.3.

[39] See Pogge, *World Poverty and Human Rights*, Sections 4.9, 6.3, 6.4.

[40] See Ricky Lam and Leonard Wantchekon, "Dictatorships as a Political Dutch Disease" (www.library.yale.edu/socsci/egcdp795.pdf); Leonard Wantchekon, "Why Do Resource Dependent Countries Have Authoritarian Governments?" (www.yale.edu/leitner/pdf/1999-11.pdf, 1999).

is one *more* reason to focus on global factors – especially on those that affect the quality of national regimes in the poorer countries.

Let us now look at the evidence I have for believing that severe poverty is largely avoidable through global institutional reforms. Because the effects of sweeping reforms are harder to assess, I discuss in some detail several small reforms and their likely effects. In the WTO negotiations, the affluent countries insisted on continued and asymmetrical protections of their markets through tariffs, quotas, anti-dumping duties, export credits, and subsidies to domestic producers, greatly impairing the export opportunities of even the very poorest countries. These protections cost developing countries hundreds of billions of dollars in lost export revenues.[41] Risse believes these protections will be phased out. Let us hope so. Still, these protections certainly account for a sizable fraction of the 270 million poverty deaths since 1989.

7. Moderate and Feasible Reforms of the Global Institutional Order

Are there other feasible reforms of the existing global order through which severe poverty could be largely or wholly avoided? The reform I discuss in most detail involves a small change in international property rights.[42] In accordance with Locke's inalienable right to a proportional share of the world's resources or some adequate equivalent, this change would set aside a small part of the value of any natural resources used for those who would otherwise be excluded from a proportional share. I show how this GRD could comfortably raise 1% of the global social product specifically for poverty eradication. And I outline how these funds could be spent so as to provide strong incentives toward better government in the developing countries.

The proposed GRD in the amount of 1% of the global product would currently raise about $320 billion annually, or 86 times what all affluent countries combined are now spending on basic social services in the developing world. What sort of impact would this money have? Consider health care. The WHO Commission on Macroeconomics and Health, chaired by Jeffrey Sachs, has put the

41 See Pogge, *World Poverty and Human Rights*, Section IV.

42 See Pogge, *World Poverty and Human Rights*, Chapter 8.

cost of providing basic medical care in the developing world at $62 billion annually and has estimated that this initiative alone would prevent about 8 million deaths from poverty-related causes each year.[43] Another $20 billion could go to incentivize research into the so-called neglected diseases which, because they affect mostly the poor, are grossly under-researched thus far: hepatitis, meningitis, dengue fever, leprosy, sleeping sickness, Chagas disease, river blindness, leishmaniasis, Buruli ulcer, lymphatic filariasis, bilharzia, malaria, tuberculosis, and pneumonia. There would be money to give every human being access to clean water and electricity. There would be money for free nutritious meals in schools that children could attend free of charge (thanks to the International Monetary Fund, many schools in developing countries are now charging attendance fees). There would be money to subsidize micro-lending which has been highly effective in recent decades even while charging interest rates of around 20%. And there would be money to relieve the crushing debt burden – often accumulated under wholly undemocratic regimes – that is weighing down many of the poorest countries.[44]

Critics have worried about domestic cooperation. But how many governments would refuse the offer to spend large amounts of money in their country? Consider India, which has about 30% of the world's poor and currently receives about $1.7 billion annually in all kinds of official development assistance from all rich countries combined. Under the reform, some 96 billion dollars of GRD funds could be

---

43 *The Economist* (22 December 2001), pp. 82–83.

44 An especially dramatic example of this perverse consequence of the international borrowing privilege is played out in Rwanda:

> Perhaps there was no better reflection of the world's shabby treatment of post-genocide Rwanda than the matter of the debt burden incurred by the Habyarimana government. The major source of the unpaid debt was the weapons the regime had purchased for the war against the RPF, which had then been turned against innocent Tutsi during the genocide. ... incredibly enough, the new government was deemed responsible for repaying to those multilateral and national lenders the debt accrued by its predecessors. The common-sense assumption that Rwanda deserved and could not recover without special treatment and, that the debt would have been wiped out more or less automatically, had no currency in the world of international finance. Instead of Rwanda receiving vast sums of money as reparations by those who had failed to stop the tragedy, it in fact owed those same sources a vast sum of money. [International Panel of Eminent Personalities, *Rwanda: The Preventable Genocide*, 7 July 2000 (www.visiontv.ca/RememberRwanda/Report.pdf), Sections 17.30 and 17.33].

spent there, greatly benefiting also India's pharmaceutical industry, its agricultural sector, its construction firms, its minimum wage level, its unemployment rate, and its tax intake. India's politicians would be extremely eager to cooperate in securing India's share of the GRD funds.

The GRD, though it re-channels money from the consumers of resources to the global poor, is not, pace Satz,[45] a form of aid. It does not take away some of what belongs to the affluent. Rather, it modifies conventional property rights so as to give legal effect to an inalienable moral right of the poor. For libertarians, this is the right not to be deprived of a decent start in life through a grievously unjust historical process. For Locke, this is the pre-institutional right not to be excluded, without equivalent substitute, from a proportional share of the world's resources. For broadly consequentialist theorists of justice, this is the right not to have imposed upon one an institutional order that is unjust by virtue of the fact that under this order, foreseeably and avoidably, many human beings cannot meet their most basic needs.

Alan Patten claims that mine is just an exercise in re-labeling. But by assuming that I must really be calling for aid and assistance, he is begging the question I raise. Our moral failure in the face of world poverty is a mere failure to aid only if we really are morally entitled to the huge advantages we enjoy, from birth, under present institutional arrangements. And this is exactly what I am denying – by appeal to how our advantages arose historically, by appeal to Locke's resource-share criterion, and by appeal to the massive life-threatening poverty to which the existing global institutional order foreseeably and avoidably exposes the majority of humankind.

Patten worries that if the rich countries were to implement my proposals, they and their citizens would be unfairly disadvantaged *vis-à-vis* the elites of many poor countries who would continue to refuse to shoulder their fair share of the cost of eradicating global poverty.[46] The details of the GRD proposal show that no country could avoid the levy on resource uses without incurring even greater surcharges on their exports (and possibly imports as well). Still, Patten is right that some politically privileged people in poor countries (and some economically privileged people in rich countries!) will

---

[45] Satz, "Comments on Pogge's *World Poverty and Human Rights*."

[46] Patten, "Remarks on Pogge's *World Poverty and Human Rights*."

manage to contribute less than their fair share to the eradication of world poverty. What is baffling is how Patten can deem this unfairness a sufficient reason to release us from our duty to contribute.

I suspect he is once more tacitly assuming here that our relevant duty is a duty to aid and that the literature on fair sharing of the burdens of positive duties is therefore relevant. Perhaps one may indeed refuse to contribute one's fair share to a morally urgent aid project on the ground that others similarly placed successfully avoid contributing theirs. But appealing to this thought again assumes what I dispute: that the status quo involves us in violating only *positive* duties toward the global poor. Once it is accepted that we are violating our negative and intermediate duties toward the poor, Patten's postulated permission seems absurd. One may not refuse to bear the opportunity cost of ceasing to harm others on the ground that others similarly placed continue their harming. Thus, in particular, we are not entitled to go on inflicting harm upon the global poor on the ground that others (preditorial elites in the poor countries) are also continuing. Likewise, we may stop some from harming third parties, and compel some to mitigate harms they have caused, even when we are unable so to stop and to compel all who do harm in a similar way. Thus, in particular, we are no more barred from setting up a GRD by the fact that some of the affluent would unfairly escape its effects than we are barred from setting up a criminal-justice system by the fact that some crimes and criminals are unfairly neither prevented, nor deterred, nor punished. Yes, some will get away with murder or with enriching themselves by starving the poor. But this sad fact neither permits us to join their ranks, nor forbids us to reduce such crimes as far as we can.

Centre for Applied Philosophy and Public Ethics
Australian National University
Canberra ACT 0200
Australia
E-mail: tp6@columbia.edu

DAVID MILLER

AGAINST GLOBAL EGALITARIANISM*

(Received 14 May 2004; accepted in revised form 3 June 2004)

ABSTRACT. This article attacks the view that global justice should be understood in terms of a global principle of equality. The principle mainly discussed is global equality of opportunity – the idea that people of similar talent and motivation should have equivalent opportunity sets no matter to which society they belong. I argue first that in a culturally plural world we have no neutral way of measuring opportunity sets. I then suggest that the most commonly offered defences of global egalitarianism – the cosmopolitan claim that human lives have equal value, the argument that a person's nationality is a morally arbitrary characteristic, and the more empirical claim that relationships among fellow-nationals are no longer special in a way that matters for justice – are all defective. If we fall back on the idea of equality as a default principle, then we have to recognize that pursuing global equality of opportunity systematically would leave no space for national self-determination. Finally, I ask whether global inequality might be objectionable for reasons independent of justice, and argue that the main reason for concern is the inequalities of *power* that are likely to emerge in a radically unequal world.

KEY WORDS: cosmopolitanism, culture, equality of opportunity, global justice, national self-determination, power

I

In this article I want to set out some reasons why equality should not play a foundational role in our thinking about global justice. Much recent political philosophy has, I believe, been mesmerised by the idea of equality, to the extent that it is often taken for granted that all valid principles of distributive justice must be egalitarian in form. Although this is an error, there are good reasons for giving equality a central place in thinking about *social* justice, justice applied to the basic structure of self-governing political communities, of which

* I am very grateful to Gillian Brock and Kok-Chor Tan for their helpful comments on an earlier draft of this article.

nation-states are the main examples in the contemporary world.[2] It is sometimes taken for granted that principles of justice that apply within such communities must also apply to the world as a whole, albeit with a different set of institutions to put the principles into practice. Global justice is simply social justice stretched outwards across national borders, and insofar as the latter can be captured by a suitably tailored principle of equality, this same principle can be used to define justice at a global level.

In arguing against this position, I should not be taken to mean that we should not be concerned about global inequality. As everybody knows, the extent of global inequality, whether measured in terms of per capita incomes or more sophisticated measures of human advantage and disadvantage such as those proposed by Amartya Sen, is both striking and shocking, and this is relevant to our thinking about global justice in a number of ways. If, for instance, we think that everyone's basic human rights include a right to a minimal level of material subsistence, which for many millions of people currently remains unfulfilled, then the scale of global inequality will determine how much those who live in rich countries would have to sacrifice to fulfil this right – the greater the inequality, the less significant, in human terms, would the resource transfers be for the rich. Or again, large economic inequalities between nations almost inevitably determine the outcome of international negotiations, trade deals and so forth, with the result that richer nations are able to set terms of interaction that work to their further advantage. For these and other reasons, we may well conclude that a just world would also be a world with far less inequality in it than ours. But here our concern with equality is derivative, not foundational. Global inequality matters because of its effects, or because of what it tells us about the costs of achieving justice, but not because it is intrinsically unjust.

Ridding ourselves of global egalitarianism would enable us to focus our attention more directly on global injustice and how to respond to it, for instance on what is to be done about the ongoing widespread violation of basic human rights, or on how to induce states to agree on measures to stop the wholesale destruction of the natural environment. In abandoning global equality, we would not be giving up on a radical political agenda – far from it. We would,

[2] Central, but not exclusive. See my defence of a pluralistic conception of social justice in David Miller, *Principles of Social Justice* (Cambridge: Harvard University Press, 1999), Chapters 2 and 11.

though, be abandoning a utopian vision of a world in which, as one commentator has put it, "a child growing up in rural Mozambique would be statistically as likely as the child of a senior executive at a Swiss bank to reach the position of the latter's parent" (this is the equality of opportunity version of global egalitarianism, which I will discuss shortly).[3] My main objection to this view is that it is based on a mistaken principle, not that it is politically utopian, but I also think that making equality our aim at the global level will push justice so far out of reach that most people would abandon the effort to achieve it. This may, I conjecture, explain why eminent philosophers like Charles Beitz and Thomas Pogge, both of whom originally defended a broadly Rawlsian version of global egalitarianism, have subsequently lowered their theoretical sights without reneging on their practical radicalism – Beitz now preferring to stress the derivative rather than intrinsic arguments for greater global equality, Pogge hinging his case for global economic transformation on the principle of non-violation of human rights.[4] Neither philosopher, to my knowledge, has explicitly abandoned global egalitarianism. They prefer to underline how far it is possible to travel politically starting from less contentious premises. Others, however, continue to espouse global principles of equality, even though much of their argument about global justice turns out in practice to rest on other premises, such as the human right to subsistence.[5] So the underlying issue remains unresolved, and worthy of serious attention.

Since my aim here is primarily critical, I shall not set out at any length the alternative, non-egalitarian, conception of global justice

---

[3] Darrel Moellendorf, *Cosmopolitan Justice* (Boulder: Westview Press, 2002), p. 49.

[4] See Charles Beitz, "Does Global Inequality Matter?" in Thomas Pogge (ed.), *Global Justice* (Oxford: Blackwell Publishers, 2001), pp. 106–122; Thomas Pogge, *World Poverty and Human Rights* (Cambridge: Polity Press, 2002). Both had argued in earlier publications for the global application of Rawlsian principles of distributive justice – see Charles Beitz, *Political Theory and International Relations* (Princeton: Princeton University Press, 1979), Part III; and Thomas Pogge, *Realising Rawls* (Ithaca: Cornell University Press, 1989), Part III.

[5] See, for instance, Simon Caney, "Cosmopolitan Justice and Equalizing Opportunities," in Thomas Pogge (ed.), *Global Justice* (Oxford: Blackwell Publishers, 2001), pp.123–144; Simon Caney, "Global Equality of Opportunity and the Sovereignty of States," in Anthony Coates (ed.), *International Justice* (Aldershot: Ashgate, 2000), pp.130–149; Moellendorf, *Cosmopolitan Justice*, Chapter. 4; Kok-Chor Tan, *Toleration, Diversity, and Global Justice* (University Park: Pennsylvania State University Press, 2000), Chapter 7.

that I favour. But, in brief, I see it as having three main requirements: the obligation to respect basic human rights world-wide; the obligation to refrain from exploiting vulnerable communities and individuals; and the obligation to provide all communities with the opportunity to achieve self-determination and social justice.[6] This is not a complete conception, because it needs to be filled out with principles indicating how the accompanying responsibilities should be allocated, given that very often there are several agents (e.g., richer states) capable of discharging them.[7] But I introduce the requirements in order to indicate what a conception of global justice that does not demand that individuals should be made equal along some dimension might look like. To compare it with global egalitarianism, we need to specify the latter in greater detail, and to this task I now turn.

II

To assess global egalitarianism, we must avoid loose definitions such that any policy or institution whose effect is to benefit the world's poor or to narrow the gap between rich and poor counts as egalitarian. Such policies and institutions may be supported from a number of different perspectives, so our willingness to endorse them cannot be counted in favour of global egalitarianism specifically. Instead, I want to restrict global egalitarianism to those principles that present equality in some respect between individual people across the world as having intrinsic value. One important subset of these principles will be principles of egalitarian *justice*: principles holding that global equality between individuals along some dimension – resources or opportunities, say – is required by justice. My main focus will be on such principles. But since it is possible to value equality for reasons independent of justice, I also want to explore whether there might be a case for global egalitarianism that takes this form.

It follows, to underline the point just made, that policies aimed at securing human rights worldwide, or policies that give priority to

[6] This conception is spelt out more fully in David Miller, "Justice and Global Inequality," in Andrew Hurrell and Ngaire Woods (eds.), *Inequality, Globalization, and World Politics* (Oxford: Oxford University Press, 1999), pp. 187–210; and in David Miller, "National Self-Determination and Global Justice," in David Miller (ed.), *Citizenship and National Identity* (Cambridge: Polity Press, 2000), pp. 161–179.

[7] On this issue, see David Miller "Distributing Responsibilities," *Journal of Political Philosophy* 9 (2001), pp. 453–471.

people whose material standard of living is very low, are not in themselves egalitarian policies, although of course they can be pursued as one part of an egalitarian strategy. They are not egalitarian because their goal is not to achieve equality as such along any dimension. Of course in a world in which human rights were universally protected, people would be equal in that respect, but this is consistent with some having more than others along the dimensions that the rights capture. Thus if people have a right to a subsistence income, protecting that right is consistent with allowing significant inequalities of income above the subsistence level. This is a familiar point, but it is worth repeating given that so much writing on global justice seems to slide back and forth between egalitarian principles and others whose underlying logic is very different.

The version of global egalitarianism that I shall examine in greatest detail is *global equality of opportunity*. This has been defended by several authors, and is in any case one of the more plausible contenders in the field. It holds that people of similar talent and similar motivation should have the same life chances (in particular access to educational and job opportunities and the rewards they bring) no matter which society they were born into. This is less demanding than the principle that people should have the same opportunities regardless of their talents, since it allows that differences of ability may affect people's life chances, and it can be seen as a global version of John Rawls' principle of "fair equality of opportunity."[8] Although we are some way from achieving fair equality of opportunity in domestic contexts, it is far from being a utopian aspiration, and it has had some effect on public policy. So in choosing to assess global equality of opportunity, I hope to have selected a version of global egalitarianism that is not obviously a straw man.

So what, more specifically, does global equality of opportunity require? Does it require, to begin with, that people with the same talent and motivation should have *identical* opportunity sets no matter which society they are born into? This seems to be the implication of Moellendorf's statement, cited earlier, that "a child growing up in rural Mozambique would be statistically as likely as the child of a senior executive at a Swiss bank to reach the position of the latter's parent." But surely such a requirement would be too strong. It would, for instance, require unlimited rights of migration coupled with

[8] John Rawls, *A Theory of Justice* (Cambridge: Harvard University Press, 1971), Sections, 12, 14, 46.

unrestricted admission to citizenship, given that some positions, such as chief executive of *Credit Suisse*, or President of the United States of America, presuppose membership of particular societies. Moreover, even leaving aside the difficulty of being able to apply formally for certain positions, the child from rural Mozambique would be less fluent in German, French or Italian than his Swiss counterpart, and on that ground alone less likely to succeed in the competition to become a Swiss banker.[9] So unless advocates of global equality of opportunity envisage a borderless world in which everyone speaks Esperanto, it is more plausible to interpret the principle as requiring *equivalent* opportunity sets. It would be satisfied provided the child from rural Mozambique had the same chance to attain an executive post in a bank somewhere, perhaps in Mozambique itself, with the same salary and other benefits as the position aimed at by the (equally talented and motivated) child of a Swiss banker.

By taking this specific case, we can understand what it would mean for two opportunity sets to be equivalent but not identical. But now consider more fully how we might apply this idea. In order to decide whether two opportunity sets are equivalent, we have to apply some kind of metric, and the metric we use can either be finer-grained or broader-grained. In the case just discussed, we found that the broader-grained metric "opportunity to become chief executive of a national bank" was preferable to the finer-grained "opportunity to become chief executive of a Swiss bank." We don't think that the Mozambiquean child is disadvantaged in any significant way by having a lesser opportunity to head a Swiss bank so long as he has a greater opportunity than the Swiss child to head a similar bank in Mozambique. So let us now consider, more generally, how fine-grained or broad-grained our metric of equality should be. If we make it too fine-grained, then we will get lots of meaningless results like the one just mentioned – equalities and inequalities that just do

[9] This issue is raised by Bernard Boxill in "Global Equality of Opportunity and National Integrity," *Social Philosophy and Policy* 5 (1987), pp. 143–168. Boxill discusses the implications of cultural diversity for global equality of opportunity without distinguishing as sharply as I would wish between culture's role in defining "success" and culture's role in motivating people to strive for success, however defined. In the present discussion I am bracketing the issue of motivation by defining equal opportunity as opportunity for people of similar talent and motivation. It may well be the case that children in rural Mozambique are not taught to aspire to be bank executives, but for purposes of argument I am assuming that we have a child with the appropriate motivation, and asking under what circumstances such a child could be judged to have equal opportunities with his or her Swiss counterpart.

not matter because they are too specific to engage our ethical attention. But if we try to make it as broad-grained as possible, then we run into controversy about how, if at all, different components of our metric should be evaluated relative to one another.[10]

Let me attempt to make this clearer through an example. Suppose we have two relatively isolated villages, broadly similar in size and general composition. Suppose that village *A* has a football pitch but no tennis court, and village *B* has a tennis court but no football pitch. Do members of the two communities have equal opportunities or not? In the morally relevant sense I think that they do: football pitches and tennis courts seem to fall naturally into the broader category "sporting facilities," and measured in terms of this metric the two communities are more or less equally endowed. It would seem morally perverse for members of *B* to complain of injustice by using "access to football pitches" as the relevant metric. But now suppose also that village *A* possesses a school but no church, and village *B* possesses a church but no school. Can we still say that people in these two villages enjoy equal opportunities? I think almost all of us would say that they do not. We think that the opportunities provided by a school and a church are just different, that if someone were to suggest a metric such as "access to enlightenment" in terms of which the two villages should be judged as equally endowed, this would just be a piece of sophistry. It is also worth noticing that while most of us would judge that the villagers in *A* were better off by virtue of having a village school, those who thought that having a church was more important would *also* resist the idea that there was some overarching metric in terms of which the two villages could be judged. They would not think that the religious deprivation suffered by people in *A* could somehow be compensated for by their educational advantages.

[10] Replying to Boxill's concern about cultural diversity, Simon Caney suggests the following: "Global equality of opportunity requires that persons (of equal ability and motivation) have equal opportunities to attain an equal number of positions of a commensurate standard of living" ("Cosmopolitan Justice and Equalizing Opportunities," p. 130). This, however, is simultaneously too narrow and too vague. It is too narrow in focussing exclusively on opportunities to attain jobs; and it is too vague when it uses the metric "a commensurate standard of living" to compare them. What does this mean? Does it refer simply to salary, perhaps adjusted to take account of differences in purchasing power? Or does it mean "standard of living" in a much wider sense, in which case we would need to know how the different components that make up someone's life are to be weighed against each other? For a penetrating critique of Caney's view, see Gillian Brock, "The Difference Principle, Equality of Opportunity, and Cosmopolitan Justice" (unpublished).

Now the question is: how are we able to judge that in the football pitch/tennis court case there is no significant inequality between *A* and *B*, whereas in the school/church case there is significant inequality? The answer must be that we have cultural understandings that tell us that football pitches and tennis courts are naturally substitutable as falling under the general rubric of sporting facilities, whereas schools and churches are just different kinds of things, such that you cannot compensate people for not having access to one by giving them access to the other. The cultural understandings tell us that the broader-grained "access to sporting facilities" is a better metric than the finer-grained "access to football pitches" while the finer-grained "access to schools" is a better metric than the broader-grained "access to enlightenment" which I suggested is what someone would need to invent if they wanted to argue that the two villages were equally endowed in the second case.

If we look at how this question is answered within nation-states – in other words at how the general idea of equal opportunity is cashed out in terms of more concrete forms of equality, then what we find is that a number of specific types of resource and opportunity are singled out as significant, and these are not regarded as substitutable. Included in the list would be personal security, education, health care, mobility, and so on. Finer-grained distinctions within these categories are not regarded as relevant. So, for instance, while it is regarded as an essential part of the educational package that every child should have the opportunity to learn foreign languages, it is not regarded as a source of inequality if one school offers Russian and another offers Italian. Mobility opportunities might mean underground trains for some people and rural buses for others, and so forth. At the same time, any attempt to use a broader-grained metric – to suggest, for instance, that poorer health facilities could be compensated by better educational facilities when opportunities are measured – would be strongly resisted. The public culture marks education and health out as different kinds of goods, in respect of each of which citizens should have equal opportunities.

What happens if we try to carry this understanding of equality across to the global level? We run into serious difficulties created by the fact that we can no longer rely upon a common set of cultural understandings to tell us which metric or metrics it is appropriate to use when attempting to draw cross-national opportunity comparisons. We face difficulties both within the familiar categories and across them. If education, for instance, takes different forms in different places, how can we judge whether a child in country *A* has better or worse educational opportunities than a child in country *B*? And even if we can make judgements of that kind, how can we decide whether it is appropriate or inappropriate to merge specific metrics into more general ones? Suppose, for instance, that we can find a measure of education such that people in Iceland plainly have better educational opportunities than people in Portugal, but that people in Portugal equally plainly have superior leisure opportunities than people in Iceland (sunny beaches, swimming pools, etc.). Is it legitimate to say that people in one of these places are better off (in a global sense) than people in the other, or can we say only that according to metric *E* Icelanders are better off while according to metric *L* the Portuguese are better off, and nothing beyond this?

Global egalitarians faced with this challenge will probably respond that the most urgent cases are cases of *gross* inequality where no reasonable person could doubt that the resources and opportunities available to members of *A* are superior to those available to members of *B*. We are not primarily concerned about Iceland/Portugal comparisons, but about comparisons between, say, any one of the current European Union member-states, and any sub-Saharan African country. And to make such comparisons we need only refer to measures such as the United Nations Human Development Index (HDI), defined in terms of capacities such as life expectancy and literacy that are regarded as basic across all cultures. Two things are worth noting about this response. First, by taking countries at the opposite ends of the development scale, and using the components of the HDI as our metric, it may indeed be possible to conclude that the set of opportunities open to a typical citizen of Niger, say, is strictly smaller than the set open to a typical citizen of France – there is no basic dimension along which the former has greater opportunities than the latter. But this does not mean that in general we are in a position to make such inter-societal comparative judgements, either within the group of rich societies or within the group of poor societies, and so although we might be able to identify the most egregious forms of inequality, we remain unable to specify what *equality* (of opportunity) would mean. Second, we can agree that the existence of societies scoring very low on the HDI is a global injustice without agreeing about *why* it is an injustice – whether by virtue of the *inequality* between rich and poor societies, or simply by virtue of the absolute level of deprivation experienced by most members of the poorest societies. Our moral responses to the global status quo are over-determined, and so we can agree in practice about what needs to be done most urgently to promote global justice without having to formulate explicitly the principles that lie behind this judgement.

I want to end this section by stressing that the problem I have identified is not a technical problem of measurement: it is not that we lack the data that would enable us to compare societies in terms of the opportunities they provide for work, leisure, mobility, and so forth. It is essentially the problem of saying what equality of opportunity *means* in a culturally plural world in which different societies will construct goods in different ways and also rank them in different ways. The metric problem arises not just because it is hard to determine how much educational opportunity an average child has in society *A*, but because the meaning of education, and the way in which it relates to, or contrasts with, other goods will vary from place to place. We can only make judgements with any confidence in extreme cases; and in those cases, what seems at first sight to be a concern about inequality may well turn out on closer inspection to be a concern about absolute poverty or deprivation, a concern which suggests a quite different general understanding of global justice.

III

In response to the argument I have advanced in Section II, would-be global egalitarians might suggest switching to a different conception of egalitarian justice – for instance to *global equality of resources*. I believe that such proposals will also fall victim to the problem of finding a suitable metric for measuring equality or inequality, and in the case of equality of resources I have tried elsewhere to demonstrate this.[11] But rather than run through the list of possible candidates for a global principle of egalitarian justice, I want to ask a more basic question, namely why should we be looking for such a principle in the first place? What makes us suppose that global justice demands that people should have equal shares of some *X*, whether the *X* be opportunities, or resources, or welfare, or something else?

It is sometimes suggested that global egalitarianism is entailed

[11] Miller, "Justice and Global Inequality," pp. 191–193.

by the general moral outlook that has come to be called "cosmopolitanism." So we need to look carefully at what "cosmopolitanism" means when it is presented as a moral doctrine with no specific political implications – its defenders are at pains to insist that moral cosmopolitanism does not entail political cosmopolitanism, understood as a theory of world government.[12] The most straightforward account is given by Brian Barry, who holds that cosmopolitanism combines three elements: that individual human beings have (ultimate) value; that each human being has *equal* moral value; and that the first two clauses apply to all human beings.[13] The significance of this can best be appreciated by seeing what it rules out: first, attaching ultimate value to collective entities such as states or nations; second, weighting the value of people differently according to features such as race, sex, or nationality; third, attaching no moral value at all to some people – excluding them entirely from the moral universe. So cosmopolitanism will exclude, for example, racist doctrines that hold that the welfare of white people simply matters more than the welfare of blacks; or certain nationalist doctrines that hold that it is a matter of moral indifference what happens to people who do not belong to our national community.

But, what, more positively, does cosmopolitanism entail? Here its defenders are quick to point out that it can embrace many different substantive moral doctrines. For instance, it is consistent with a form of universal utilitarianism that tells us to enter the happiness of every human being with an equal weighting into the utilitarian calculus and to design policies and institutions accordingly. But it is also consistent

[12] For instance Charles Beitz writes:

"Cosmopolitanism need not make any assumptions at all about the best political structure for international affairs; whether there should be an overarching, global political organization, and if so, how authority should be divided between the global organization and its subordinate political elements, is properly understood as a problem for normative political science rather than for political philosophy itself. Indeed, cosmopolitanism is consistent with a conception of the world in which states constitute the principal forms of human social and political organization...." [Charles Beitz, "International Relations, Philosophy of," in Edward Craig (ed.), *The Routledge Encyclopaedia of Philosophy* (London: Routledge, 1998), Volume 4, p. 831].

[13] Brian Barry, "Statism and Nationalism: a Cosmopolitan Critique," in Ian Shapiro and Lea Brilmayer (eds.), *Nomos: Global Justice* (New York: New York University Press, 1999), pp. 35–36. A similar account of cosmopolitanism is offered in Thomas Pogge, *World Poverty and Human Rights*, pp. 169–170.

with a doctrine of human rights that tells us simply that there are ways in which every human being must and must not be treated. It is consistent with global equality of opportunity, or global equality of resources, each of which manifests a different way of recognizing the equal value of human beings. But it does not require these, or any other form of global egalitarianism.

Why is this? Cosmopolitanism, as I have presented it here, and as its defenders present it, is a thesis about value, or about what is sometimes called "moral concern." It says that the fate of human beings everywhere should in some sense count equally with us. Global principles of equality, on the other hand, are principles intended to govern the design of our institutions. They require that we should establish institutions that provide people everywhere with equal amounts of some good – resources, opportunity, etc. Such principles are action-guiding – they specify how we should behave as individuals, voters, and so forth. Claims about value and claims about how agents should act are distinct, and there can be no entailment from one to the other.

An example may help to drive this point home.[14] Suppose a child goes missing and there are fears for her safety. This is equally bad no matter whose child it is, and there are some agents, for instance the police, who should devote equal resources to finding the child in all cases. But there are other agents whose reasons for action will depend on their relationship to the child. If the child is mine, then I have a strong reason, indeed an overwhelming reason, to devote all my time and energy to finding her. If the child comes from my village, then I have a stronger reason to contribute to the search than I would have in the case of a child from another community. Of course if I have information that might help find that distant child, then I should give it to the police at once. It is not that I lack any responsibilities to the distant child. But nearly everyone thinks that I have a much greater responsibility to my own child, or to one I am connected to in some other way. The important point is that this is perfectly consistent with the view that it is equally bad, equally a matter of moral concern, when any child goes missing.

It might be said in reply here that if claims about the equal value of human beings have no implications for how we should act, they become redundant. All moral claims must in some way or other guide

[14] I borrow this from David Miller, "Cosmopolitanism; A Critique," *Critical Review of International Social and Political Philosophy* 5 (2002), pp. 80–85.

our behaviour. But this is acknowledged in the example just given. The value of the distant child is registered in my obligation to supply relevant information to the police. In a similar way, the cosmopolitan premise means that we cannot be wholly indifferent to the fate of human beings with whom we have no special relationship of any kind. There is something that we owe them – but cosmopolitanism by itself does not tell us what that something is, and certainly does not tell us that we owe them some form of equal treatment. So cosmopolitans who go on to argue that their cosmopolitan convictions are best expressed through practical doctrines such as the doctrine of human rights, or global equality of opportunity, need to add a substantive premise about what we owe to other human beings as such – a premise that, to repeat, is not contained in the idea of cosmopolitanism as such. Some independent reason has to be given why cosmopolitan concern should be expressed by implementing the particular conception of global justice favoured by any particular author.[15]

So let me now consider a different attempt to justify global egalitarianism, one that begins from the premise that principles of justice are principles of equal treatment – they are principles that require us not to discriminate on morally irrelevant grounds such as (in most instances) a person's race or sex. Equality of opportunity, for instance, is taken to be a valid principle of justice within nation-states, but, so it is argued, a person's nationality is an irrelevant feature when we are considering what opportunities they should have, so the principle should be given a global application. As the argument is often put, nationality is a "morally arbitrary" feature of persons in the same way as their hair colour or the social class of their parents.

[15] It also follows from this that "cosmopolitanism" may not be a very helpful concept in distinguishing between different approaches to global justice. If we remain with the general definition given in the text, then almost everyone who writes on the subject will fall under the cosmopolitan umbrella. Some authors provide stronger and therefore more discriminating definitions – for instance Beitz distinguishes "cosmopolitan liberalism" and "social liberalism" as competing approaches to the philosophy of international relations, saying of the former that it "accords no ethical privilege to state-level societies" and that it "effectively extends to the world the criteria of distributive justice that apply within a single society" [Charles Beitz, "Social and Cosmopolitan Liberalism," *International Affairs* 75 (1999), pp. 519–520]. I have commented on this tendency for conceptions of cosmopolitanism to slide between weaker and stronger versions in "Caney's 'International Distributive Justice': A Response," *Political Studies* 50 (2002), pp. 974–977, replying to Simon Caney, "International Distributive Justice," *Political Studies* 49 (2001), pp. 974–997.

So they are owed equal treatment as a matter of justice no matter which society they belong to.

Once again, we need to look carefully at how this argument moves from premise to conclusion, and when we do we find that it relies on a crucial equivocation about what it means for some feature of a person to be morally arbitrary. In one sense, a person's nationality might be described as morally arbitrary because in the great majority of cases the person in question will not be morally responsible for her national membership – people are simply born into a nation and acquire the advantages and disadvantages of membership as they grow up regardless of their choice. In this spirit, Caney writes that "people should not be penalized because of the vagaries of happenstance, and their fortunes should not be set by factors like nationality and citizenship."[16] Here "nationality and citizenship" are assimilated to other features for which people cannot be held morally responsible – Caney mentions "class or social status or ethnicity" – and the implicit assumption is that if someone is not morally responsible for possessing a certain feature, then unequal treatment on the basis of that feature cannot be justified.

But "morally arbitrary" may also be used to signal the conclusion of the argument as opposed to its premise. Here a morally arbitrary feature of persons is a feature that should not be allowed to affect the way they are treated – it is a morally irrelevant characteristic, something we are bound to ignore when deciding how to act towards them. Obviously, if nationality is a morally arbitrary feature in this second sense, then inequalities of treatment based on national belonging are unjustified; this follows by definition. What needs to be shown is why we should regard nationality as morally arbitrary in this second sense.

In order to link the two senses of moral arbitrariness – the argument's premise and its conclusion – we need a substantive principle. Here is a likely candidate: if two people are differentiated only by features for which they are not morally responsible (arbitrariness in sense 1), then it is wrong that they should be treated differently (arbitrariness in sense 2). This principle would certainly do the job,

[16] Caney, "Cosmopolitan Justice and Equalizing Opportunities," p. 125. See also "Nationality is just one further deep contingency (like genetic endowment, race, gender, and social class), one more potential basis of institutional inequalities that are inescapable and present from birth" (Pogge, *Realizing Rawls*, p. 247).

but unfortunately it is quite implausible. We can see this by thinking about people who have different *needs*, where these needs are not the results of actions for which their bearers are morally responsible (think, for instance, of people who have been handicapped from birth). Need differences are morally arbitrary in sense 1, but they are not morally arbitrary in sense 2. Virtually everyone thinks that people with greater needs should be given additional resources, whatever precise characterisation of the moral duty involved they prefer to give.

So we have yet to be given a reason why it is wrong if people are better or worse off on account of their national membership. Why regard nationality as a morally irrelevant characteristic like hair colour rather than a morally relevant characteristic like differential need? The fact that in some sense it is "happenstance" that I belong to this nation rather than to any other does not settle the question, for the reason just given. It is equally "happenstance" that somebody should be born with a physical handicap. There has to be a *substantive* argument for the irrelevance of nationality, not merely a formal argument that trades on the ambiguity of "arbitrariness."

What might the substantive argument be here? Well, the argument that nationality *should* be allowed to count in determining what opportunities are open to people depends on characterising national belonging in a certain way. It relies on the claim that people who form national communities have special relationships to one another that they do not have to people elsewhere, relationships that in practice give rise to global inequalities. So one may try to counter this by pointing out how relationships across the globe are becoming more like relationships within nations: people are increasingly caught up in economic interactions that are global in scope, environmental problems tend to spill across national borders, transnational political institutions are becoming ever more significant, and so forth. In other words, nationality should be treated as morally irrelevant because it no longer *describes* a significant form of relationship between people.

These observations are very much to the point insofar as we are thinking about global justice and what it should mean, especially if we take the view (as I do) that what justice requires us to do for other people depends crucially on the relationships in which we stand to them.[17] Changes in the economic and political configuration of the world, and indeed in its physical characteristics insofar as these impact on human welfare, should indeed change our practical conception of global justice. But it does not follow that we should run straight into the arms of global egalitarianism. To do this would presuppose that we are already in a world in which nationality no longer constitutes *any* set of special relationships that are morally relevant. Such a presupposition seems implausible. Despite the globalising tendencies noted above, the great majority of people continue to identify strongly with their national community, most significant political decisions are taken at nation-state level, and nations to a greater or lesser extent constitute themselves as mutual benefit schemes in which people who suffer from certain types of loss – disability, ill-health, unemployment, and so forth–are compensated by those who enjoy better fortune. To show that all of this is morally irrelevant when assessing the opportunity sets enjoyed by people belonging to different national communities would require a great deal of argument. It is not enough to point out that new international relationships supervene upon these longer-standing national ones.

To conclude this section, I have tried to defeat three grounds on which global equality, in some form, might be defended as a requirement of justice. The first ground is that global equality is entailed by a general cosmopolitan claim about the equal value of human beings. I argued that there was no such entailment. The second ground was the claim that national boundaries, like other boundaries between people, were morally arbitrary and therefore irrelevant to justice. I pointed out that this depended on a crucial equivocation about moral arbitrariness. The third ground was that relationships among fellow-nationals were no longer special in a morally relevant sense. Unlike the first two grounds, this does provide a substantive argument of the right kind in favour of global equality, but I suggested it was implausible: despite much-feted aspects of globalisation, national membership still has features that appear to have considerable moral significance. So, in the absence of further arguments in its favour, there seems to be no positive reason why we should regard equality of opportunity, or some other principle of this form, as a requirement of global justice.

[17] See my general argument to this effect in David Miller, "Two Ways to Think about Justice," *Politics, Philosophy and Economics* 1 (2002), pp. 5–28.

IV

Even if the positive arguments used to defend global egalitarianism are all defective, it might be said, cannot we still rely on the idea that equality is our default principle – the principle that we use to allocate resources and opportunities when we lack any good reason to discriminate, for instance when we have no information at all about the people among whom the allocation is going to be made?[18] Perhaps there is no strong reason why the child in rural Mozambique should have the same opportunities as the offspring of a Swiss banker. But, on the other hand, why should she not, assuming we are able to determine, or at least influence, the relevant opportunity sets? This throws the burden of proof back on those who are willing to permit global inequality, especially inequality between national communities. They are challenged in their turn to give positive reasons why global inequality may be morally defensible, so as to defeat the idea of equality as the fallback position, the principle we should use in the absence of reasons to discriminate.

In earlier essays I appealed to the value of national self-determination as a reason of this kind.[19] Democratically governed nations, I argued, are likely to make policy decisions that affect the resources and opportunities available to future generations of their own members, so that even if we were to imagine starting out from a baseline of equality, that equality will immediately be broken as political and cultural differences between nations find expression in the policies that they pursue.[20] To preserve equality we would have continually to transfer resources from nations that become relatively better-off to those that become worse-off, undermining political responsibility, and in a sense undermining self-determination too, insofar as this involves choosing between alternative futures and receiving the costs and benefits that result from such choices. But this argument has been challenged on the grounds that it makes individuals in the present suffer as a result of the decisions (including the mistakes) of their predecessors. Although it is widely accepted that individuals may fairly become worse off as a result of choices that

---

[18] I have discussed the idea of equality as a default principle in Miller, *Principles of Social Justice*, pp. 233–236.

[19] Miller, "Justice and Global Inequality," and Miller, "National Self-Determination and Global Justice."

[20] This argument is also made in John Rawls, *The Law of Peoples* (Cambridge: Harvard University Press, 1999), Section 16.

they make themselves, how can this be extended to policy decisions taken collectively before their birth?[21]

This challenge raises questions about collective responsibility and its limits that I have tried to address elsewhere,[22] so here I want only to take up one particular issue, namely the parallel that is sometimes drawn between collective inheritance and individual inheritance. Equality of opportunity, like other egalitarian theories, is clearly hostile to the current practice of individual inheritance. If we wanted to pursue it consistently, we would tax all inherited wealth at 100% and provide each child with a capital grant (or its equivalent) of the same value when he or she reached maturity. Practical difficulties aside, such schemes are possible because we can identify a specific moment of inheritance at which the egalitarian principle is applied. That is, we can allow individuals freely to pursue the opportunities that their equal inheritance provides, and to become unequal in the process, so long as they do not attempt to pass on material benefits to their children, thereby undermining the scheme. But now consider what the collective analogue to this scheme would have to look like, if we wanted to preserve equality of opportunity at global level. Although we often talk about people as belonging to discrete generations, each of which passes certain benefits on to its successor, in one important sense this is a fiction: the real picture is one of continual population replacement. So if we imagine once again a world in which each nation starts out from a baseline of equality, we cannot allow nations to make autonomous decisions over the course of one generation – 30 years, say– and then apply an international tax-and-transfer regime that restores equality for the next generation. For in the meantime, all those reaching maturity in nations which pursue wealth-creating policies will be materially advantaged relative to those reaching maturity in nations with other goals. The only way to ensure continuing equality of opportunity over time would be to nullify political self-determination entirely in all those areas that

[21] For this challenge, see for instance Cecile Fabre, "Global Egalitarianism: An Indefensible Theory of Justice?" in Daniel Bell and Avner De-Shalit (eds.), *Forms of Justice* (Lanham: Rowman and Littlefield Publishers, 2003), pp. 315–330; Beitz, "Social and Cosmopolitan Liberalism," pp. 526–528; and Pogge, *Realizing Rawls*, pp. 252–253.

[22] In David Miller, "Holding Nations Responsible," *Ethics* 114 (2003–2004), pp. 240–268; and in David Miller, "National Responsibility and International Justice," in Deen Chatterjee (ed.), *The Ethics of Assistance: Morality and the Distant Needy* (Cambridge: Cambridge University Press, 2004), pp. 123–143.

impact on individual opportunity sets, which in reality would mean virtually everywhere. In other words, an equal opportunity world would have to be a world in which all policy decisions that made a significant impact on the life-chances of individuals were taken by a central authority. The systematic pursuit of global equality of opportunity would not merely constrain national self-determination, but would undermine it altogether.

There is of course an alternative to the scenario I have just painted. This is to allow nations to continue to determine their own futures, including the sets of opportunities available to their members, but then to require them to allow free access to anyone who wants to join (to ensure "fair equality of opportunity" in Rawls' sense, this would need to be accompanied by policies that nullified the cost of moving across national borders). But it is easy to see that this would also undermine self-determination, in any world that we can realistically envisage. For decisions about admission to citizenship are inseparable from other decisions about the kind of society one wants to build. Some nations setting out on a path of rapid economic growth may welcome all-comers, or at least everyone who possesses marketable skills. Other nations with demanding environmental objectives may pursue policies aimed at reducing population growth among their existing members to zero – policies which would obviously be undermined if significant number of immigrants were permitted to enter. Yet other nations may want to preserve linguistic or religious aspects of their public culture, implying selection on these grounds among potential candidates for membership. An unlimited right to free movement would pre-empt policy choices of this kind, and in a different way hollow out the idea of national self-determination.

One could, of course, respond to this by saying "So much the worse for national self-determination." But recall that in this section of the article I am exploring the idea that global equality might be defended as a default option, not as a principle with a strong independent justification. If one had strong reasons for favouring global equality of opportunity, say, then one might well decide that national self-determination should go by the board in the name of global justice. But in the previous two sections I tried to show, first, that global equality of opportunity may be impossible to define, and second, that the arguments that have so far been given in its defence are defective. All we are left with, then, is the idea that in the absence of reasons to discriminate, we should treat people equally. Provided, however, you attach *some* value to the idea that, in a culturally diverse world, political communities should be able to determine their own futures, we have a good reason to allow departures from global equality.[23] And this is sufficient to defeat global egalitarianism, when the latter is taken merely to be the default position.

V

So far I have been looking critically at global equality as a principle of global justice. But as I mentioned at the outset, equality can also be valued for reasons that are not directly reasons of justice. More precisely, equality can be valued because inequality is seen as a *source* of injustice, without being unjust in itself; and it can be valued for reasons that are quite independent of justice. This idea in its general form has been explored in an important article by Tim Scanlon, and more recently insightfully applied to the global context by Charles Beitz.[24]

Let me, then, survey some reasons for objecting to global inequality that do not turn on the now-discredited idea of egalitarian justice. The first, and probably the most powerful, is that material inequalities broadly conceived will naturally translate into inequalities of power, which then become a source of ongoing global injustice.[25] This can happen in a number of fairly obvious ways. When

[23] As I shall point out in the next section, valuing self-determination also gives us a reason to *limit* global inequality. I assume here that an ethically acceptable nationalism must treat self-determination as a universal value. So, on the one hand, national communities must have the opportunity to set their own priorities in terms of economic policy, environmental policy, population policy and so forth, even though such collective choices will inevitably generate inequality along particular dimensions over time. On the other hand, these decisions may not deprive other national communities of opportunities for self-determination by, for example, creating global economic conditions in which their choices are almost completely constrained by the demands of economic survival. This need for a balance may justify transferring some powers – say over economic and environmental issues – upwards to international bodies. Valuing self-determination does not mean accepting national sovereignty in its traditional sense.

[24] T. M. Scanlon, "The Diversity of Objections to Inequality," Lindley Lecture, University of Kansas, 1996, now reprinted in T. M. Scanlon, *The Difficulty of Tolerance: Essays in Political Philosophy* (Cambridge: Cambridge University Press, 2003), pp. 202–218; Beitz, "Does Global Inequality Matter?"

[25] See also Debra Satz, "International Economic Justice," in Hugh LaFollette (ed.), *The Oxford Handbook of Practical Ethics* (New York: Oxford University Press, 2003), pp. 636–637.

rich countries or rich corporations interact economically with communities or individuals who are very much poorer, they can set the terms of exchange and/or employment very much in their own favour, simply because they are far better placed to withdraw from the exchange than are those they exploit. This phenomenon has been widely documented, and all that I need to emphasize here is that the principle of justice that is violated by such interactions is not a strongly egalitarian one. To protest when workers in third world countries are employed in sweatshop conditions by powerful corporations, one does not have to believe that these workers ought to enjoy the same terms and conditions, or have the same opportunities, as their counterparts in the developed world. The injustice at stake is more rudimentary.

Next, gross inequality between nations makes it difficult if not impossible for those at the bottom end of the inequality to enjoy an adequate measure of self-determination, unless one imagines, counterfactually, that rich nations' interest in self-determination concerns only their own internal affairs, and not what happens in the world outside. In reality we know that inequalities in wealth and military power place severe constraints on the policies that weaker nations can pursue. So if our vision of a just world includes the idea that each nation should have a fair opportunity to pursue the particular goals that its members value most – the international equivalent of the domestic idea of toleration – then we are bound to be disturbed by inequalities on the current scale.

Finally, large inequalities in wealth and power also make it difficult to achieve what we might call "fair terms of co-operation" internationally. Given that there are a number of areas in which nation-states need to co-operate with one another to their mutual advantage–environmental policy is perhaps the most obvious–the distribution of costs and benefits in the agreement that emerges is likely to be determined largely by the relative bargaining power of the various parties. If rich countries refuse to co-operate altogether, poor countries have few sanctions that they can deploy to bring the recalcitrants back to the negotiating table. The refusal of the US to sign the Kyoto agreement is a clear instance of this phenomenon. Since we cannot place the parties behind a veil of ignorance, procedural fairness in practice requires that they should stand to gain or lose roughly the same amount when co-operation succeeds or fails, and large inequalities make this condition impossible to satisfy.

In a domestic context, there are two possible ways of tackling inequality as a source of injustice: reduce the inequality, or prevent it from having unjust consequences. We employ a battery of measures designed to prevent inequalities of wealth, in particular, from creating injustice, ranging from the regulation of employment contracts, through limitations on the inheritance of wealth, to restrictions on the political uses of money. It is not so easy to envisage global analogues of such measures. So in this respect we may have more reason to worry about global inequalities than about domestic ones. Of course, for the very same reasons that large global inequalities pose a threat to justice, they are also difficult to counteract. It is difficult to envisage rich states agreeing to narrow the gap in wealth and power between themselves and poor states. Perhaps the most hopeful prospect is of a world in which rich states, or blocks of rich states, compete with each other on roughly equal terms, and thereby also check one another's power *vis-à-vis* third parties. But rather than speculate further along these lines, I want to turn to two other reasons we might have for combating inequality, again drawing inspiration from domestic analogies.

One such reason is the value of what we may call *equality of status* or alternatively *social equality*. This is the idea of a set of social relationships within which people regard and treat each other as fundamentally equal, despite specific differences between them, and it is valuable because of the quality of the relationships in question: where it exists nobody has reason to feel subservient or deferential and on the other hand nobody has cause to be haughty or condescending.[26] Now, whatever one thinks about this idea, it might seem that it can only apply within a bounded society and not to the world as a whole. On the other hand, since travel and communication have broken down perceptual barriers between societies, we do appear increasingly to be living in a world in which people are likely to compare their own positions with those of people in wealthier societies, and may find the comparison humiliating or degrading. Thus it seems that there may be a global version of equality of status, and that this would give us reason to be concerned about large inequalities, especially of wealth and income, along dimensions that give rise to perceived status differences.

[26] I have explored this more fully in David Miller, "Equality and Justice," *Ratio* 10 (1997), pp. 222–237 and in Miller, *Principles of Social Justice*, Chapter 11.

Although there is something to this argument, I am inclined to be sceptical. Equality of status is important among people who are in daily contact with one another, and who share a common way of life. Insofar as people belong to smaller communities and associations which form their main focus of identity, relationships between these sub-groups matter less than how people are treated within them, since it is there that they will gain the sense of self-esteem that comes from being treated as an equal (or not as the case may be). Rawls makes this argument in the section of *A Theory of Justice* where he is responding to the objection that a society governed by the difference principle may still give rise to what he calls "excusable envy":

> we tend to compare our circumstances with others in the same or in a similar group as ourselves, or in positions that we regard as relevant to our aspirations. The various associations in society tend to divide it into so many noncomparing groups, the discrepancies between these divisions not attracting the kind of attention which unsettles the lives of those less well placed.[27]

If this argument applies domestically, it seems it should apply with greater force still internationally, since for most people national boundaries mark out salient spheres of comparison and non-comparison. Admittedly international society lacks one feature which Rawls sees as counterbalancing material inequalities, namely equal citizenship: there is no common public sphere in which global citizens encounter one another as equals. On the other hand, cultural differences between societies make it less likely that people will be drawn into comparing themselves with each other along a single dimension such as material wealth. We might aspire to an international version of Michael Walzer's "complex equality," where people in different societies derived their self-esteem in part from their society's success in living up to its own standards, whether materialistic or anti-materialistic. I suggest this not in order to defend the existing global order, since extremes of poverty prevent national projects of all kinds from being pursued, but as a way of thinking about what social equality might mean in a culturally plural world.

Finally, equality is sometimes defended because of its connection to the idea of *fraternity*: if we want people to live together in close, solidaristic relationships, then we should ensure that they live in much the same material conditions. Fraternity on a global scale might seem an impossibility: however a weaker version of the same claim is that if we want a world in which people are willing to

[27] Rawls, *A Theory of Justice*, pp. 536–537.

co-operate and to settle their differences peacefully, then this must also be a world in which material inequalities are not too great. In support of this, one might cite arguments made in recent years that the ultimate source of international terrorism is the material gulf that exists between the affluent West and the position of nations in the Middle East and elsewhere, giving rise to anger and resentment that manifests itself in hatred of all things Western.

Once again, my response to this argument is somewhat sceptical. What international co-operation requires is indeed not fraternity, but mutual respect between political communities who recognize their differences but also realise that they need to work together in a number of policy areas. And the precondition for this is not equality, but the absence of serious injustice. In other words, we have first to establish what justice requires in international contexts, and having done that we can then set down the conditions under which international co-operation is likely to prove feasible. To assume that the relevant principle of justice here is some form of substantive equality is to beg all the questions raised in earlier sections of this article. In my alternative account of global justice, the main bases for international co-operation would be respect for human rights world-wide, measures to prevent the international exploitation of political communities and smaller groups, and adequate opportunities for political self-determination for all peoples. One might want to add to this the redress of historic injustice: envy and resentment may be less a function of inequality *per se* than of a perception that societies that are currently poor owe their position to past domination and exploitation. Such perceptions are not always accurate, but where they are, they are likely to pose a serious obstacle to mutual respect and future co-operation between the parties involved.[28]

To conclude, once we have disentangled the issue of global inequality from questions about global justice, and in particular the deprivation suffered by people living in poor societies, we may still be concerned about the effects of large inequalities. But these concerns will be derivative, and will centre mainly on differences of *power* between rich and poor countries, and the likely effects of these on global justice in the future. If we could prevent the conversion of material advantage into political domination, there would be nothing

[28] For an approach to historic redress that emphasises this forward-looking consideration, see Janna Thompson, *Taking Responsibility for the Past: Reparation and Historical Injustice* (Cambridge: Polity, 2002). I have discussed Thompson's position in "Inheriting Responsibilities" (unpublished).

inherently reprehensible about global inequality, and we might regard it as an inevitable feature of a culturally diverse world. Unfortunately, as I suggested earlier, blocking that conversion is likely to prove difficult if not impossible in practice. So we *should* continue to worry about the extent of global inequality, but not for the reasons touted by the global egalitarians whose views I have been discussing.

Nuffield College, Oxford
New Road
Oxford, OX1 1NF
UK
E-mail: david.miller@nuffield.ox.ac.uk

MATHIAS RISSE

WHAT WE OWE TO THE GLOBAL POOR

(Received 14 May 2004; accepted in revised form 3 June 2004)

ABSTRACT. This essay defends an account of the duties to the global poor that is informed by the empirical question of what makes countries rich or poor, and that tends to be broadly in agreement with John Rawls's account in *The Law of Peoples*. I begin by introducing the debate about the sources of growth and explore its implications for duties towards the poor. Next I explore whether (and deny that) there are any further-reaching duties towards the poor. Finally, I ask about the moral foundations for the duties to the poor of the sort that earlier parts argue there are.

KEY WORDS: duties to the global poor, global justice, institutions, John Rawls, poverty

1. Introduction

In September 2000, the United Nations General Assembly committed governments to eradicating extreme poverty.[1] Endorsing several specific development goals, this historical document was called the "Millennium Declaration," and has since become a reference point for development efforts across the globe. Two years later, the High-Level Panel on Financing for Development, charged with exploring possibilities for financing these goals, submitted its report, known as the "Zedillo Report" (after its chairman, former Mexican President Ernesto Zedillo). Its first recommendation was that:

[1] Many thanks for helpful comments or discussion of this material to Abena Asare, Charles Beitz, Eric Cavallero, Michael Ignatieff, Simon Keller, Hélène Landemore, Thomas Pogge, Sanjay Reddy, Ani Satz, Leif Wenar, Members of the Faculty Seminar of the Center for Ethics and the Professions at Harvard University, and audiences at a panel on "Political Philosophy and Development Economics" (held during the convention of the Pacific Division of the American Philosophical Association in Pasadena, March 2004), and at the conference on "The Theory and Practice of Equality" (Harvard University, April 2004). Thanks to Lant Pritchett, Ricardo Hausmann, and Dani Rodrik for conversations about development. The original title of this study was "What Do we Know about What Makes Societies Rich or Poor, and Does it Matter for Global Justice: Rawls, Institutions, and Our Duties to the Global Poor." That title gives a good preview of what is to come.

[E]very developing country needs to set its economic fundamentals in order. No country can expect to achieve equitable growth, or to meet the International Development Goals,[2] unless it focuses on building effective domestic institutions and adopting sound policies including: Governance that is based on participation and the rule of law, with a strong focus on combating corruption; disciplined macroeconomic policies; a public expenditure profile that gives priority to investment in human capital, especially basic education and health, the rural sector, and women; a financial system that intermediates savings to those capable of investing efficiently, including microfinance borrowers, women, and the rural sector; a funded, defined-contribution pension system that will promote saving in the short run and, supplemented by a tax-financed scheme to assure a minimum pension, will secure adequate, universal pensions in the long run; capacity building focused on developing a positive institutional environment progressively more able to implement the policies listed above; protection of property rights and a regulatory environment that effectively protects workers' rights and the environment.

So before making any other recommendations, the report stressed the importance of domestic institutions for economic growth (while at the same time also giving us an excellent account of what institutions the commission thought counted most).

Emphasis on institutions also appears in John Rawls's *The Law of Peoples*. Rawls insists that

the causes of the wealth of a people and the forms it takes lie in their political culture and in the religious, philosophical, and moral traditions that support the basic structure of their political and social institutions, as well as in the industriousness and cooperative talents of its members, all supported by their political virtues. I would further conjecture that there is no society anywhere in the world – except for marginal cases – with resources so scarce that it could not, were it reasonably and rationally organized and governed, become well-ordered.[3]

Based on this view, Rawls rejects redistributive duties among peoples beyond duties of assistance to "burdened" societies, non-aggressive societies lacking appropriate traditions, resources, or technology. That duty seeks to enable societies to develop their own institutions and thus shape their development. Such duties may well be daunting: one cannot

---

[2] The Millennium Goals (to be reached by 2015) are: to cut in half the proportion of people living in extreme poverty; to achieve universal primary education and gender equality in education; to accomplish a three-fourths decline in maternal mortality and a two-thirds decline in mortality among children under five; to reverse the spread of HIV/AIDS and to assist AIDS orphans; to improve the lives of 100 million slum dwellers. See the United Nations website for a progress report: http://www.un.org/millenniumgoals/index.html. For the Zedillo report, see http://www.un.org/reports/financing/.

[3] John Rawls, *The Law of Peoples* (Cambridge: Harvard University Press, 1999), p. 108.

easily "assist" others with institution-building, and presumably many societies will qualify for assistance. However, economic inequalities across societies as such are, for Rawls, a matter of moral indifference.[4]

The background to the Zedillo Report's emphasis on institutions is the macro-economic debate about why some societies are poor and volatile and others wealthy and stable – a debate that goes back at least to Adam Smith's *Wealth of Nations*. I hope to show that the most promising answer to this question not only lends support to the above-quoted passage from the Zedillo Report, but also illuminates and supports Rawls's position on global justice. Moreover, unless that answer prevails, Rawls's account is implausible, since then there would be much pressure to acknowledge duties beyond assistance in institution-building. Section 2 introduces the debate about the sources of growth and explores its implications for duties towards the poor. Section 3 begins to apply these insights to *The Law of Peoples* and explores whether (and denies that) there are any further-reaching duties towards the poor. Finally, Section 4, expanding on *The Law of Peoples*, asks about the moral foundations for the duties to the poor of the sort that Section 3 argues there are. In a nutshell, then, this essay defends an account of the duties to the global poor that is informed by the empirical question of what makes countries rich or poor, and that tends to be broadly in agreement with Rawls's in *The Law of Peoples*.[5]

---

[4] Rawls, *The Law of Peoples*. Well-ordered societies are liberal or decent peoples. Liberal peoples have "a reasonably just constitutional democratic government that serves their fundamental interests; citizens combined by what Mill calls 'common sympathies;' and finally, a moral nature" (p. 24). Decent societies meet basic requirements of "political right and justice and lead its people to honor a reasonable and just law for the Society of Peoples" (pp. 59 – 60). Many considerations bearing on what well-ordered societies owe burdened societies coincide with those bearing on what developed countries owe developing countries. While there are differences because "well-ordered" societies are defined in terms of their political nature, whereas "developed" societies are defined in terms of their economic level, I treat these questions as roughly interchangeable for purposes of exploring what duties societies have towards each other. Yet one important question not fitting in here is whether the global order as such harms developing (burdened) societies. I discuss this question in Risse, "Does the Global Order Harm the Poor? Some Reflections" (unpublished). I write crudely about developed/industrialized/rich societies (or countries) in opposition to developing societies/countries, but this simplicity should do no harm.

[5] The reason why empirical matters are central for assessing what the global poor are owed is this: many agree that there is a duty to support the global poor, with disagreement remaining about the nature of this duty (normative question). Once such a duty is in place, we must ask more precisely about its content, which draws on

2. Theories of Growth and Duties to the Poor

2.1

Development economics is a young discipline with ongoing disagreements. It will be useful to introduce some of them because the view developed later depends on the success of one such view. One important disagreement is about how to define "poverty." Should it be understood absolutely or relatively? Should it be defined in terms of consumption expenditure or through a set of conditions that one cannot aggregate into any single index? A second disagreement is about whether development should aim at economic growth ("growth solves other problems eventually"), or pursue different goals (see UN Human Development Indicators). A third is whether there is a recipe for development as captured, say, by the neo-liberal "Washington Consensus," or whether local factors determine success, and a fourth is about whether development needs more money or wiser spending of funds that, given such spending would actually be sufficient. The disagreement crucial for us is yet another, a disagreement of a rather theoretical kind, namely about the sources of growth.

Economists and historians have long debated what makes countries rich or poor. This debate has recently gained sophistication through econometric techniques that allow for the testing of broad hypotheses about the causes of growth against cross-country data. Three major views have emerged:

---

the question of what makes countries wealthy (empirical). (By "nature" of the duty I mean whether it is a positive or negative duty, and by "content" I mean whether it is a duty to transfer resources, assist in building institutions, etc. A positive duty requires us to do something good for somebody else, whereas negative duties require not to do something bad.) What it makes sense to impose as a duty must be influenced by what makes countries do well. The content of the duty, in turn, affects its scope and limits (normative). At any rate, it should be plausible that sensible views on what societies owe to each other must be informed by views on what determines growth. If geography is economic destiny, it is implausible to claim that some countries are poor because others impose an economic system that harms them. Yet then the moral arbitrariness of geography generates a positive duty to help them. If growth depends on domestic institutions, development aid should take the form of support in building institutions, rather than resource transfer. If geography trumps, we may be able to say that "it is the fault of developed countries that certain institutions are in place now" (they derive from colonialism), but that does not entail that "it is their fault that developing countries are *poor*." If institutions trump, the inference holds. So, indeed, what determines the wealth of nations bears on what societies owe to each other.

Geography: Growth is primarily determined by factors such as location, climate, endowment of resources (including soils), disease burden, and thus agricultural productivity, quality of human resources, and transportation costs.[6]

Integration: Growth is primarily determined by world market integration.[7]

Institutions: Prosperity depends on the quality of institutions, such as stable property rights, rule of law, bureaucratic capacity, appropriate regulatory structures to curtail at least the worst forms of fraud, anti-competitive behavior, and graft, quality and independence of courts, but also cohesiveness of society, existence of trust and social cooperation, and thus overall quality of civil society.[8]

One may find it odd to ask which theory "wins," since any country's prosperity will depend on many factors, including those championed

---

[6] See Jared Diamond, *Guns, Germs, and Steel: The Fates of Human Societies* (New York: Norton, 1999); John Gallup, Jeffrey Sachs, and Andrew Mellinger, "Geography and Economic Development," National Bureau of Economic Research Working Paper w6849 (1998); and Jeffrey Sachs, "Tropical Underdevelopment," National Bureau of Economic Research Working Paper w81119 (2001).

[7] See Jeffrey Frankel and David Roemer, "Does Trade Cause Growth?" *American Economic Review* 89 (1999), pp. 379–399; and Jeffrey Sachs and Andrew Warner, "Natural Resource Abundance and Economic Growth," National Bureau of Economic Research Working Paper 5398 (1995). Policy makers from World Bank, IMF, WTO, and OECD frequently argue that integration into the world economy is the way to prosperity.

[8] See Douglass North, *Institutions, Institutional Change, and Economic Performance* (Cambridge: Cambridge University Press, 1990); David Landes, *The Wealth and Poverty of Nations: Why Some Are So Rich and Some So Poor* (New York: Norton, 1998); Robert Hall and Chad Jones, "Why Do Some Countries Produce So Much More Output per Worker Than Others?" *Quarterly Journal of Economics* 114 (1999), pp. 83–116; Daron Acemoglu, Simon Johnson and James Robinson, "Botswana: An African Success Story," in Dani Rodrik (ed.), *In Search of Prosperity: Analytical Narratives on Economic Growth* (Princeton: Princeton University Press, 2003) pp. 80–123; Dani Rodrik, Arvind Subramanian and Francesco Trebbi, "Institutions Rule: The Primary of Institutions over Geography and Integration in Economic Development" (http://ksghome.harvard.edu/~.drodrik.academic.ksg/papers.html). The importance of domestic institutions is also discussed in the 2003 *World Economic Outlook*, Chapter 3, which includes a good review of the recent literature and an illustration of the importance of institutions: calculations show (p. 106) that an improvement of institutional development from its current average to that of developing Asia implies an 80% increase in per capita income for Sub-Saharan Africa: from \$800 to over \$1400. (For measuring institutional quality, see p. 119, Appendix 3.1.)

by these theories, mixed with history and human choices. Also, factors relevant for growth affect each other. Countries with stable institutions can more easily integrate their economies globally, and successful integration facilitates their maintenance. Landlocked countries and those far from markets have difficulties in trading. Absence of debilitating epidemics favors stable institutions, but institutions also advance capacities to control diseases. Resource abundance, by contrast, can foster rent-seeking institutions ("*resource-curse*"). Not only do these factors influence each other, but prosperity itself, the *explanandum*, affects factors that supposedly cause it. It may be *because* a country is wealthy that it has good institutions, benefits from trade, or can control diseases, rather than vice versa. Such feedback makes it hard to determine the "deep" causes of prosperity. Still, questions about deep causes that are not themselves the outcome of feedback processes are meaningful, and econometrics investigates how much of the variation in cross-national incomes geography, integration, and institutions can respectively explain.

2.2

As a matter of professional hazard philosophers underestimate the relevance of empirical questions for normative inquiries, to the detriment of our discussions and of the impact of political philosophy outside philosophical circles. Our professional training makes us see normative problems where often the crucial questions are empirical. One drawback of enlisting empirical research is that philosophical studies will mostly quote its contributions, instead of doing the work to establish them. While it is with such regret that I introduce a claim about the growth-debate (and concede right away that my arguments, to the extent that they depend on the stance I am about to embrace are subject to revision in light of possible changes in what the available empirical evidence suggests), we obviously must go where the questions take us.[9]

[9] Although we are here assuming a stance in an empirical debate that is far from closed, that stance should be plausible enough to warrant an investigation of its normative implications. At the same time, possible empirical advancements would leave at least the arguments in Sections 3 and 4 largely unchanged (i.e., the arguments against further-reaching duties beyond the duties to support in institution-building and the arguments assessing why there is any duty of assistance to begin with). I say "largely" because the arguments would then obviously have to be reformulated in a manner that does not presuppose anymore that the content of the duty to the poor is support *in institution-building*.

Among the views above, the *institutional* view seems most promising. It was only recently that econometric work showed that institutional quality is truly causal. It is hard to show that institutions are genuinely causal for growth, rather than vice versa. It is tempting to suggest that growth causes good institutions, not vice versa, or that institutions could arise only because of favorable geographical factors. The challenge is to show that institutions are genuinely causally efficacious.[10] It was even more recently that econometric results suggested that the causality of institutions was crucial. A key contribution, building on much other work, is work by Dani Rodrik, Arvind Subbramanian, and Francesco Trebbi, which shows that institutions trump everything else[11]: once institutional effects are determined, integration has nothing left to explain, and geography very little. Moreover, institutional quality significantly affects market integration and vice versa, and geography affects the quality of institutions. It is mostly channeled through their impact on institutions that geography and market integration matter without undermining the causal efficacy of institutions.[12]

Before we continue to work with this view ("the institutional stance"), we must be aware of its limitations, especially the following two. First, social sciences can only explain what the world has been

---

[10] To explain: a simple linear regression model looks like this: $y = \beta_0 + \beta_1 x + u$. That is, we are explaining a function y (the dependent variable) in terms of a function x (the independent or explanatory variable), for instance, prices of houses in terms of their square footage. Function u is the error term, while β_0 is an additive constant and β_1 is a coefficient. To be sure that x explains y, we must be sure that there is no other variable z "hidden" in the error term correlated with x and that thus explains the allegedly explanatory variable. If there is such a z, we call x an endogenous variable; otherwise it is exogenous. Suppose we want to explain $y =$ economic growth in terms of $x =$ institutional quality. How can we make sure that institutional quality is not itself explained by some z (like geography) hidden in the error term? How can we make sure institutional quality is exogenous, not endogenous? We can do so by choosing a so-called instrumental variable z for x. That is, we look for a z correlated with x and that thus can substitute for x, but is uncorrelated with error term u and thus does not leave the explanatory work for other variables hidden in u. As far as institutional quality is concerned, this was achieved only recently [see Daron Acemoglu, James A. Robinson and Simon Johnson, "The Colonial Origins of Comparative Development: An Empirical Investigation," *American Economic Review* 91 (2001), pp. 1369–1401].

[11] Rodrik, Subramanian, and Trebbi, "Institutions Rule," forthcoming.

[12] Rodrik et al., "Institutions Rule," builds on a significant amount of earlier work, and conduct both robustness tests and discussions of related results, all of which confirms their findings.

like in the past, and hence results of this sort by themselves deliver no immediate policy advice regarding measures that have not been tried yet.[13] Second, these results are statistical in nature and do not reveal much about specific countries. Therefore it is important that a collection of case studies confirms that institutions "that provide dependable property rights, manage conflict, maintain law and order, and align economic incentives with social costs and benefits are the foundation of long-term growth,"[14] and do so by tracing the economic development of different countries. Examples include China, Botswana, Mauritius, and Australia. For illustrative purposes, I briefly discuss Botswana.[15] Botswana is a largely tropical, land-locked country with insignificant agriculture in a geo-politically precarious location. At independence the British left 12 kilometers of roads and a poor educational system. Making headlines for devastatingly high HIV rates, Botswana suffers from high inequality and unemployment. Officially a democracy, it has yet to see a functioning opposition party. 40% of Botswana's output draws on diamonds, a condition that often casts the resource-curse. Still, Botswana is a growth miracle. Between 1965 and 1998, it had an average annual growth rate of 7.7%, and a 1998 average per capita income four times the African average. Rule of law, property rights, and contract enforcement work. The government is efficient, small, and relatively free from corruption. Indigenous institutions, resisting colonization, encourage broad participation and constrain elites. Institutional quality and good policies have allowed for success against the odds.[16]

---

[13] For that reason, reference to these social-science results will in particular not show why we should not now start making massive transfers to the global poor, regardless of whether they contribute to institution building. It will not be until Subsection 4.1 that we will have resources to explain why we should indeed not make such transfers.

[14] See Rodrik (ed.), *In Search of Prosperity*, p. 10.

[15] I do so following Acemoglu et al., "Botswana."

[16] Botswana also shows that development does not reduce to growth: but these results stimulate hope that other things will change too. Another example is Vietnam [see Lant Pritchett, "A Toy Collection, a Socialist Star and a Democratic Dud: Growth Theory, Vietnam, and the Philippines," in Dani Rodrik (ed.), *In Search of Prosperity*, pp. 123–152]. Freeman and Lindauer argue that economic success in Africa depends on institutional quality [see Richard Freeman and David Lindauer, "Why Not Africa?" National Bureau of Economic Research, Working Paper 6942 (1999)]. Van de Walle and Johnston concur [see Nicolas van de Walle and Timothy Johnston, *Improving Aid to Africa* (Baltimore: Johns Hopkins University Press, 1996)].

2.3

Suppose now that there is indeed a duty to help the world's poor to more prosperity – a claim for which I will argue in Section 4. If so, it will be an empirical question of how actually to discharge that duty, and any answer to this question must be informed by our understanding of the sources of prosperity. It is in light of the work just reported that I adopt, as an empirical conjecture with strong support, the view that the content of the duty to aid the global poor includes support in building institutions, and hence that development assistance should include institution-building. Otherwise the content of that duty conflicts with its goal. I will argue in Section 3 that additional redistributive duties (beyond the duty to build institutions) are not part of that duty, but everything I say in this study should be consistent with there being a duty to emergency aid in exceptional cases (such as natural disasters).

Let us explore some implications of this view. According to Douglass North, institutions are the rules of the game in a society or, more formally, are the humanly devised constraints that shape human interaction. In consequence they structure incentives in human exchange, whether political, social, or economic. Institutional change shapes the way societies evolve through time and hence is the key to understanding historical change.[17]

Those constraints benefit societies only if most individuals support the "rules of the game." This is true especially for institutions that cannot be created by governmental fiat (as, say, market-regulating institutions can), such as a constitution guiding generations through political disputes, a legal system enforcing property rights and contracts, but most importantly a culture of trust, shared understandings of what are reasonable benefits from and sacrifices imposed by cooperation, commitment to the common good, and other hallmarks of civil society. Such institutions emerge and persist only with broad

---

[17] See North, *Institutions*, p. 3. Rawls, *The Law of Peoples*, pp. 47–48, defines institutions similarly. One concern about the institutional stance developed with such a broad definition of institutions in the background is that the thesis "economic growth depends critically on institutions" becomes rather unspecific. However, this concern arises with regard to the practical impact of the institutional stance more than within the confines of our current theoretical debate. What matters, for our purposes, about the three views we have introduced is that geography traces growth to environmental influences, whereas institutions traces it to what one society "does with others," and institutions to "what individuals in a given society do with each other."

domestic support. Call the view that especially those institutions requiring broad domestic support matter for prosperity the "*Authenticity Thesis*."[18] This thesis is safe within the confines of the institutional stance: there can be a "stable structure to human interaction" only if most people cooperate. Still, this condition should be made explicit since it is important for what follows. Crucially, often all external aid can contribute absent such institutions is analytical work, identification of internal reform champions, training of future leaders, bureaucrats or professionals, and technical assistance.[19]

---

[18] "Emergence" and "persistence" of institutions must be kept apart more than the account above suggests. It might well be possible for outsiders to force the emergence of a certain set of institutions that would not have otherwise emerged, but then can (and need to be) maintained by the indigenous population. Think of the imposition of democratic structures in Japan at the end of World War II. Still, situations in which outsiders can impose institutions in this manner will tend to be cataclysmic moments, such as the one just mentioned, and thus be rather rare.

[19] Van de Walle and Johnston, *Improving Aid to Africa*, pp. 2–3, argue that institutions in Africa founded on substantial donor support are weak and dependent on outside resources. The 2002 *World Development Report*, *Building Institutions for Markets* elaborates on the theme discussed above, and provides literature references. The World Bank Research Report, *Assessing Aid* finds that financial aid works in good policy environments; improvements in economic institutions and policies are key to a quantum leap in poverty reduction; effective aid complements private investment; the value of development projects is to strengthen institutions and policies so that services can be effectively delivered; an active civil society improves public services; aid can nurture reform even in highly distorted environments – but it requires patience and focus on ideas, not money [World Bank, *Assessing Aid: What Works, What Doesn't, and Why* (Oxford: Oxford University Press, 1998), pp. 2–4]. *Assessing Aid* points out that the following three measures are unlikely to work: large amounts of money; buying reform (i.e., conditional lending not supported by a domestic movement); focusing on individual projects (World Bank, *Assessing Aid*, p. 103). Pogge argues as if one may simply bypass governments (institutional structures) and start a project regardless of domestic support [Thomas W. Pogge, *World Poverty and Human Rights* (Cambridge: Polity Pres. 2002), p. 206]. Yet such projects tend to fall apart as soon as the donor moves out. Van de Walle and Johnston claim that the proliferation of stand-alone projects not tied into a general improvement of infrastructure and institutions is a key weakness of aid to Africa. An earlier influential expression of this view is Tamar Tendler, *Inside Foreign Aid* (Baltimore: Johns Hopkins University Press, 1975). Leif Wenar questions the claim that "small sacrifices bring great benefit" by displaying how difficult it is to determine the effects of contributions to aid efforts, and in the process surveys a considerable amount of empirical literature expressing skepticism about aid (Leif Wenar, "What We Owe to Distant Others," *Politics, Philosophy, and Economics*, forthcoming). Pogge takes up the theme that "world poverty cannot be eradicated by 'throwing money at

While I will argue in Section 4 that there indeed is a duty to assistance in institution building, I am, at this stage, interested in exploring some *prima facie* reasons implied by the institutional stance that speak *against* development assistance as well as, derivatively, against global egalitarianism. These reasons do by no means refute the view that there is a duty of assistance in institution building; they will, however, constrain the duty to assistance, and do so in ways that draw on the fact that it is institutions that the duty to assistance requires us to build, and hence do so on internal grounds. If the institutional stance (plus Authenticity Thesis) holds, we encounter four *prima facie reasons* against development assistance (and, *mutatis mutandis*, humanitarian intervention). The first is that assistance is ineffective: What is needed cannot be "imported." Instead, the task of building, or re-building institutions ("nation-building") is one that must (and can only) evolve from within, as unsatisfactory as that may be from the point of view of good-willed outsiders. The second is a paternalism concern: it is inappropriate for outsiders to shape institutions, since they will inevitably shape them according to their own understanding. The third is that outsiders cannot be blamed if societies fail in creating something they can only create themselves – and thus are not obliged to try. The fourth reason is that the stability of institutions might be undermined if those whose participation maintains them rely on support from the outside. Dependence on outside support, that is, is the enemy of institutions' internal viability.

Each reason must be set aside to justify assistance. One reason for setting all four aside is if, contrary to the statistical support for the institutional view, in particular cases persistent poverty turns on factors that are not adequately captured within an institutional approach. But, as I hasten to add, even to the extent that institutions are crucial, each reason can indeed be overruled: it is in that sense that I introduced these reasons as *prima facie* reasons. Contrary to the first, it may be possible to offer the needed help. ("It is true that one cannot just start working on AIDS or build some schoolhouses in Sub-Saharan Africa; one must also make sure that there is an appropriate medical or educational system to support these efforts, and there can

---

the problem"' (Pogge, *World Poverty and Human Rights*, p. 8). He rejects that claim by reference to the facts that much development aid has been given for strategic reasons, and that only a rather small percentage share was allocated to the least developed countries. However, the 1998 World Bank Report and van de Walle and Johnston are also well aware of these facts – but these facts simply do not refute the claim that Pogge dismisses.

be no such systems without broad domestic support. But there are measures one could take to generate such support." Or even more to the point, disaster relief will often be possible, but does nothing to relieve poverty in the long run.) Contrary to the second, paternalism may be irrelevant, and possibly grotesquely so, in the face of death and starvation (similarly for the fourth reason); and contrary to the third, the reason why bad institutions have emerged in the first place may be outside interference. Yet while each case will require close analysis, it is clear, on the institutional stance, that development is not primarily a matter of transferring resources, and its main challenge is not to convince wealthy Western restaurant patrons to forfeit one dinner a month. Again, I will argue below that there indeed *is* a duty to aid the global poor, to be understood, as we just saw, as a duty of assistance in institution-building, but this duty will have to be understood as constrained by these *prima facie* reasons.[20]

2.4

The institutional stance entails that equality among societies is not, on balance, a goal that we should bring about. For *to the extent* that those reasons remain forceful, they push outsiders not to worry about societies' comparative wealth levels. Even if we say that, "from the viewpoint of equality," such a state of affairs is problematic, and even if in a domestic context we find such an observation sufficient to bring about a change, we will find this reasoning overruled *vis-à-vis* other societies. For *to the extent* that those reasons can be maintained – a matter of degree and variable across societies – we have simply no reason to alter another people's economic situation. For instance, if one society is at welfare level L1 and another at L2 < L1, and if there is nothing anybody from the outside can do to bridge the gap between L2 and L1 because it would require institutional changes that must come from the inside, then there is no obligation to do so, and the gap between L1 and L2 is not one that external actors ought

[20] Views following Peter Singer often speak as if the problems of the world could be solved if only rich Westerners were willing to make that sort of sacrifice [Peter Singer, "Famine, Affluence, and Morality," *Philosophy and Public Affairs* 1 (1972), pp. 229–243; Peter Singer, *One World: The Ethics of Globalization* (New Haven: Yale University Press, 2002), however, shows a considerable awareness of the practical obstacles to such a view].

to close. In particular one can consistently be a domestic egalitarian and not insist on cross-societal equality.

Cosmopolitans might resist this view. Following Thomas Pogge, I take cosmopolitans to think that individuals are the unit of moral justification, that all individuals matter equally, and that all individuals should matter equally *to* everybody.[21] Such cosmopolitans might object that individuals cannot be held liable for their institutional affiliations: after all, they were simply born into more or less functional institutional frameworks, just as they were born male or female. Put differently: the institutions into which individuals are born are just as much beyond their control as are their society's geographical circumstances. Therefore, blocking claims to socio-economic equality by reference to the importance of institutions would mean to hold individuals responsible for matters that are generally beyond their control.

However, claims to socio-economic equality could obviously not always be honored by allowing individuals from less developed societies to join more developed societies. Instead, they would have to be honored by attempts to build institutions of high quality for those individuals *where they are*. And this takes us straight back to the four reasons against development assistance that, as I just argued, also suggest that equality across societies is not morally required. Cosmopolitanism may require that individuals' *needs* must be met, regardless of where they live, but that view is consistent with the view that inequality *per se* is not morally problematic. I submit that the institutional stance entails that cosmopolitans should not take their position to entail claims to socio-economic equality. Moreover, contrary to Loren Lomasky, "classical liberalism" is consistent with state boundaries that are less porous than the boundaries between the states composing a federal structure.[22]

However, the claim that inequality as such across societies is not morally problematic is consistent with the claim that *excessive*

---

[21] Pogge, *World Poverty and Human Rights*, p. 169.

[22] See Loren Lomasky, "Towards a Liberal Theory of National Boundaries," in David Miller and Sohail Hashmi (eds.), *Boundaries and Justice* (Princeton: Princeton University Press, 2001), pp. 55–79. The term "classical liberalism" should be clear enough for our purposes, but see p. 75, to see what he means by it. One may argue against all this, though, that peoples (plural!) as such have claims to equal treatment to such an extent that they have claims to economic equality regardless of institutional performance and of issues of individual responsibility. That sort of collectivist stance, however, just strikes me as independently implausible.

inequalities of the sort that we observe in the world at this stage *are*. The argument so far, that is, has really not shown anything beyond the claim that demand for equality *per se* is unwarranted. I suspect, however, that much of what seems morally problematic about excessive inequalities is that some people live in abysmal poverty while others live in luxury. That sort of concern would cease to apply once all societies possess quality institutions, and it seems like a plausible empirical conjecture that the actual amount of inequality (at least on a purchasing-power-parity basis, rather than an exchange-rate basis) will decrease once that is so. Internationally, that is, I suspect that many concerns commonly expressed in egalitarian terms really are concerns of the "sufficientarian" sort. Domestically, the justifiability of law will constrain socio-economic inequalities considerably, but I believe that no argument is available that requires global socio-economic inequalities to be constrained to a similar extent. Sections 3 and 4 will offer some considerations in support of this view.

If this view on domestic versus global inequalities is correct, remaining inequalities might, and I believe would, still be problematic from a point of view of rationality, rather than from a moral point of view: a world with massive inequalities is likely to be an unstable world, even if domestic institutions are of high quality. So for that reason, it would still be in everybody's interest to prevent global inequalities from being excessive even though equality as such across societies is not morally required. Enlightened self-interest, I believe, does more work here than moral considerations.[23]

3. INSTITUTIONS, *THE LAW OF PEOPLES*, AND THE LIMITS OF DUTIES TO BURDENED SOCIETIES

3.1

So far we have been concerned with exploring the institutional stance as such, as well as some *prima facie* reasons against development

[23] At the same time, it is a bit hard to assess how urgent this instability concern really would be in a world in which quality institutions are pervasive. It seems that people's self-esteem and ambitions are very much shaped by their immediate environment, rather than by other societies [Robert H. Frank, *Choosing the Right Pond: Human Behavior and the Quest for Status* (Oxford: Oxford University Press, 1986), on such themes]. However, it is hard to predict the impact of an ever-more interconnected world on these phenomena (think of widely-transmitted Western Television or widely-shown movies, etc.).

assistance and their implications for the demand for global economic equality. Let us next explore how this discussion illuminates Rawls's *The Law of Peoples*. As Rawls explains, the

> third guideline for carrying out the duty of assistance is that *its aim is to help burdened societies to be able to manage their own affairs reasonably and rationally and eventually to become members of the Society of well-ordered Peoples*. This defines the "target" of assistance. After it is achieved, further assistance is not required, even though the now well-ordered society may still be relatively poor. Thus the well-ordered societies giving assistance must not act paternalistically, but in measured ways that do not conflict with the final aim of assistance: freedom and equality for the formerly burdened societies.[24]

Rawls limits duties to the poor to transitory assistance in institution building, implying that inequalities as such among peoples are morally irrelevant. Our discussion of the debate about growth in Section 2 bears immediately on the assessment of this view. If integration or geography holds, Rawls's account of what societies owe to each other will be hopelessly indefensible. Especially, if geography is true, a society's wealth will depend on factors beyond human control to such an extent that redistributive claims must succeed. So empirical issues bear crucially on the question of what redistributive claims societies have towards each other, and it is only on the institutional stance that what Rawls says in the quote above appears plausible. Of course, as Charles Beitz also emphasizes, the institutional stance does not by itself rule out *further-reaching* duties, and thus we will below have to ask explicitly whether there indeed are such duties.[25]

Defending his account by appeal to David Landes and Sen,[26] Rawls insists, in a passage already quoted above in Section 1, that

> the causes of the wealth of a people and the forms it takes lie in their political culture and in the religious, philosophical, and moral traditions that support the basic structure of their political and social institutions, as well as in the industriousness and cooperative talents of its members, all supported by their political virtues. I would further conjecture that there is no society anywhere in the world – except for

---

[24] Rawls, *The Law of Peoples*, p. 111, italics provided.

[25] Charles Beitz, "Rawls's 'Law of Peoples,'" *Ethics* 110 (2000), provided pp. 690–692.

[26] Landes, *The Wealth and Poverty of Nations*, and Amartya Sen, *Poverty and Famines* (Oxford: Clarendon Press, 1981). According to Sen, famines are not problems of food production, but political and economic disasters. It is by reference to Landes that Rawls asserts there is no need to discuss Beitz's resource distribution principle [see Charles Beitz, *Political Theory and International Relations* (Princeton: Princeton University Press, 1979)].

marginal cases – with resources so scarce that it could not, were it reasonably and rationally organized and governed, become well-ordered.[27]

So Rawls, unfortunately, endorses the institutional stance without making any conceptual space whatsoever for other factors, and it is in virtue of its sheer strength that his view seems so overdrawn. Yet while the institutional stance introduced in Section 2 agrees with Rawls on the importance of institutions, it does make room for other factors and improves the version of that view that Rawls offers. In particular, that stance can address worries deriving from the view that unfavorable locations may make it unduly hard for some to develop successful institutions. For the causal impact of such factors is captured by that stance: Geographical factors affect prosperity through affecting institutions. If geographical factors make it hard to build institutions, the duty to assistance will be more demanding: while such a duty has a goal and a cut-off point, as Rawls insists, how hard it is to reach them depends on the situation. Still, in some cases it may be inappropriate to think of a duty to increase the level of prosperity of the global poor in terms of institution-building to begin with, and the institutional stance developed above is consistent with such cases as well (in virtue of its drawing on statistical generalizations). In some situations the duty of assistance in building institutions will be very demanding, but as we have seen in Section 2, there will also be situations in which no duty applies because what requires doing cannot be done by outsiders. Moreover, it may often be a difficult question to assess whether a duty to support in institution-building applies, but is very demanding, or whether it does not apply because some of the four reasons against assistance hold. At any rate, the framework of Section 2 captures the relevance of geographical factors.

One may object that my argument (like the theories on the sources of growth) is committed to what Pogge calls "*explanatory nationalism,*" fallaciously reducing development indicators to domestic causes.[28] States and individuals, argues Pogge, react to incentives given by the global order, which may affect institutional quality. Inquiries so committed cannot detect the impact of the global order. However, the institutional stance does not commit this fallacy. While the theories of growth above do collect data on a country-by-country basis, this is an organizational device that does in particular not address any *causes* of institutional performance. To the extent that the global order (or an

[27] Rawls, *The Law of Peoples*, p. 108.
[28] Pogge, *World Poverty and Human Rights,* pp. 143–144.

oppressive past) causes bad institutions, this, along with geographical factors, must be considered in the execution of the duty of assistance. So the institutional stance can properly integrate global factors.[29]

3.2

I take it that we have shown by now in particular that, first, support in institution building is generally required *if* anything is (a duty, however, that is constrained by the four *prima facie* reasons against development assistance that we encountered in 2.3), as well as that, second, the institutional stance developed in Section 2 improves on some implausible aspects of the most visible view in favor of that institutional stance on duties, namely Rawls's view in *The Law of Peoples*. However, what has been said so far is consistent with considerations supporting additional redistributive duties once the duty to institution-building is fulfilled (to be sure: this concern is indeed about ongoing redistributive duties, rather than duties in emergencies). This leaves us with two questions. On the one hand, we must ask whether there are indeed such additional duties, and on the other hand, we must explore on what grounds duties to provide such support (and possibly others, depending on how that first question is answered) would arise in the first place. That is, the first question asks about the scope and limits of the duties to burdened societies, whereas the second asks about their moral foundations. We will explore the first question in the remainder of this section, and the second in the next.

We have addressed one consideration that speaks in favor of further-reaching duties towards burdened societies, namely, that geographical factors urge ongoing compensation. Yet on the institutional stance, such factors are best understood not as justifying additional duties, but as making assistance in institution-building more or less demanding. As their causality operates through the difficulty or ease in establishing good insti-

[29] Will Kymlicka is a recent proponent of the view that

> parties to the original position would choose some form of redistributive tax – perhaps a global resource tax – which requires wealthier countries to share their wealth with poorer countries. The goal would be to ensure that all people are able to live a decent life in their country of birth, without having to leave their culture and move to another country to gain access to a fair share of resources. [Will Kymlicka, "Territorial Boundaries: A Liberal-Egalitarian Perspective," in David Miller and S. H. Hashmi (eds.), *Boundaries and Justice* (Princeton: Princeton University Press, 2001), pp. 249–275].

Following the argument of this section, it seems Kymlicka should focus on institution-building and think of such a tax only in purely instrumental terms.

tutions, such factors cannot *also* justify additional demands. It is useful to explore whether there are other such considerations. Rawls offers two arguments intended to show that there are *not:* first, that peoples themselves do not desire wealth, absolutely or comparatively, and thus cannot have redistributive claims; second, that, unlike citizens in well-ordered societies, societies do not exist in an environment in which such claims are valid.[30] Let us discuss both. It will turn out that the second argument succeeds, which suggests that there are indeed no further-reaching duties.

Talking about interests of peoples, Rawls lists protection of territory, security and safety, preservation of free political institutions and "the liberties and free culture of their civil society." As opposed to that, increasing economic strength, like enlarging territory, is a feature of *states*, not peoples.[31] Rawls cannot mean that peoples do not care about wealth because they are not of the sort that *could*; after all, peoples care about territorial integrity. The point must be that it is unreasonable for *citizens* to care about wealth other than in relation to each other, regardless of their absolute level of wealth. For if individuals can reasonably care about wealth otherwise, there will be an *aggregate* sense in which society cares about *its* absolute (not relative) wealth. Yet this claim about citizens seems false. Citizens within justice as fairness want more, rather than less, income and wealth to pursue their conceptions of the good, within a certain range.[32] Peoples

---

[30] Rawls, *The Law of Peoples,* pp. 113–115.

[31] Rawls, *The Law of Peoples*, pp. 27f., 107. While page 28 of *The Law of Peoples* discusses relative and not absolute economic standing, page 34 argues that liberal peoples do not have a conception of the good. These passages themselves do not entail that Rawls thinks that peoples are unconcerned with their *absolute* standing. Wenar, for one, understands him to be arguing that [Leif Wenar, "The Legitimacy of Peoples," in Pablo de Greiff and Ciaran Cronin (eds.), *Global Justice and Transnational Politics* (Cambridge: MIT Press, 2002), pp. 53–76]. If Rawls does not mean this, the objection I am about to make does not apply: but then this whole approach does not explain why there should be no redistributive duties.

[32] Wenar, "The Legitimacy of Peoples," also notes this, but does not criticize it. Pogge also discusses the assumption that peoples only care about being well-ordered [Thomas Pogge, "An Egalitarian Law of Peoples," *Philosophy and Public Affairs* 23 (1994) pp. 195–224]. See Rawls on the necessity of wealth:

> What men want is meaningful work in free association with others, these associations regulating their relations to one another within a framework of just basic institutions. To achieve this state of things great wealth is not necessary. In fact, beyond some point it is more likely to be a positive hindrance, a meaningless distraction at best if not a temptation to indulgence and emptiness. [Rawls, *A Theory of Justice* (second edition) (Cambridge: Harvard University Press, 1999), p. 257–258]

may decline further wealth increases, but that differs from dismissing redistributive duties because peoples are unconcerned about wealth. On the contrary: given the relevance of wealth and income for realizing conceptions of the good, governments should foster growth unless citizens instruct them otherwise. So societies may indeed desire more wealth.

3.3

But do societies exist in an environment in which they can make redistributive claims? Citizens can make such claims as free and equal members of fair systems of cooperation. Yet one might say that they cannot reasonably regard themselves as standing in such relationships with citizens from other societies. There is no background for such claims among societies to be valid. However, no matter how this argument is developed (and such development is obviously needed), it is open to instability concerns. As critics point out,[33] there are increasingly dense international structures that seem to undermine the claim that citizens can reasonably regard themselves domestically but not internationally as engaged in a cooperative system. Relevant international relations include trade liberalization, worker migration, multi-national structures like the European Union and global institutions like the United Nations, World Bank, International Monetary Fund, World Trade Organization, and the International Criminal Court. Individuals themselves stand in economic relationships across the world, including, say, workers in the car industry whose fate turns on attitudes of workers abroad. Globalization weaves together, in highly complex systems, the fates of communities, households, and individuals in distant parts of the world.[34]

Yet this objection fails, or at any rate, the view suggesting that societies exist in an environment in which they cannot make redistributive claims upon each other can be reformulated in such a way that the objection does not apply any longer. What lets citizens make

---

[33] Pogge and Beitz have long insisted that there is a kind of global basic structure; [Beitz, *Political Theory*, Part III, Sections 3 and 4, and Beitz, "International Liberalism and Distributive Justice: A Survey of Recent Thought," *World Politics* 51 (1999), pp. 269–296; Alan Buchanan, "Rawls's Law of Peoples: Rules for a Vanished Westphalian World," *Ethics* 110 (2000), pp. 697–721].

[34] Debra Satz, "Equality of What Among Whom? Thoughts on Cosmopolitanism, Statism, and Nationalism," in Ian Shapiro and Lea Brilmayer (eds.), *Global Justice* (New York: New York University Press, 1999).

redistributive claims on each other is not so much the fact that they share a *cooperative* structure, but instead, as Michael Blake argues, the fact that they share a *coercive* structure.[35] If individuals are jointly subject to a body of law (which is what is meant here by coercive structure), ranging from criminal to civil, one that is constantly enforced by officials, this body of law must be justifiable to each of them in virtue of its interference with their autonomy. Redistribution among them may be necessary for such justification to be possible (especially since what needs justification is in particular a property regime), and it is through this requirement of justifiability that redistributive claims arise. The importance of cooperative structures for *redistributive* claims, I think, is rather limited. To be sure: both cooperative structures and coercive structures are special cases of shared norms, and as such require justification to those subjected to them. However, both sorts of structures require justification *appropriate to their natures*: cooperative structures will have to be justified *qua* cooperative structures, and similarly for coercive structures. Through the justification of the legal body in general and of property law in particular, the justification of coercive structures leads straightforwardly to economic redistribution. The justification of cooperative structures *per se*, however, leads straightforwardly merely to the demands that exchanges be fair and that individuals benefit proportionately from their input into the cooperative system.

So what exerts the real justificatory pressure within a fair system of cooperation, and thus within a given society in particular, is not actually the presence of cooperation *per se*, but the presence of an underlying coercive structure. It is, at any rate, the additional presence of coercive structures that differentiates individuals that share a citizenship from a group of individuals that merely happen to live in the same area and are engaged in cooperative enterprises. For that reason, the view that societies, as opposed to citizens, do not exist in an environment in which redistributive claims can be made can be developed without being open to the objection just developed. The

[35] Michael Blake, "Distributive Justice, State Coercion, and Autonomy," *Philosophy and Public Affairs* 30 (2001), pp. 257–297. Note that the terms "coercive structure" and "cooperative structure" are not used in a mutually exclusive sense. Social institutions are often both cooperative in the sense that they involve collaboration among individuals to their mutual benefit, and at the same time they are coercive by limiting the participants' autonomy. Note also that it is indeed in this "autonomy-constraining" sense that I use the term "coercive" here: in particular, there should be no immediate association with "oppressive" relationships.

point is that the reason why individuals can make such claims upon each other is not the presence of cooperative structures to begin with, and hence the objection, as stated, does not arise any more. That is, no objection to this view can succeed based on the observation that international cooperative structures are, by now, fairly dense as well.[36]

For an illustration of what these considerations amount to in the international arena, consider Basel in Switzerland. Close to both the German and the French frontier, Basel is economically integrated with southern Germany and eastern France. France begins, literally, on the premises of the Basel train station. Yet Switzerland keeps its international political arrangements minimal (and has, in particular, no interest in joining the EU). Intense economic trans-boundary relationships fail to undermine the claim that individuals' primary political identity is, or should be, that of citizens *qua* members of a shared coercive structure (i.e., shared domestic laws). Many laws that hold in Switzerland, of course, are reasonably similar to those that hold in Germany or France, but nevertheless, any enforcement would be by *Swiss* authorities.

Trade relationships put pressure on the creation of larger political entities (See EU), but themselves do not create relevant coercive structures. To be sure, trade relationships, like other cooperative

---

[36] I refer here to "citizens" vs. "non-citizens" and thereby oversimplify the debate. After all, in addition to the citizens living in a country there are also other residents, and their existence, just like questions of immigration, complicates matters. But for our current purposes, I will ignore these complications. The following quote from Christopher Jencks illustrates nicely how the need for justification of domestic policies arises:

> Almost everyone who studies the causes of economic inequality agrees that by far the most important reason for the differences between rich democracies is that their governments adopt different economic policies. (…) A number of rich countries have centralized wage bargaining, which almost always compresses the distribution of earnings. Many rich democracies also make unionization easy, which also tends to compress the wage distribution. Some rich democracies transfer a lot of money to people who are retired, unemployed, sick, or permanently disabled, while others are far less generous. The United States is unusually unequal partly because it makes little effort to limit wage inequality: the minimum wage is low, and American law makes unionization relatively difficult. In addition, the United States transfers less money to those who are not working than most other rich democracies. [Christopher Jencks, "Does Inequality Matter?" *Daedalus*131 (2002) pp, 49–65, 52f]

Jencks here offers a list of economic and legal arrangements that must be justifiable to the citizens of a country (and with regard to which states differ significantly) – but not to anybody else.

structures, domestic or international, are subject to appropriate moral claims, but those would be claims that govern *trade relationships*, or respectively other cooperative structures, and nothing else. I disagree with Beitz, then, that a theory relying on sharp distinctions between the domestic and the international domain is unstable.[37] Domestic egalitarians, at any rate, should base their views on this premise of shared coercive structures (and not cooperative structures, which at any rate would not deliver much by way of egalitarian conclusions, even domestically), and if so, their egalitarianism does not straightforwardly extend to cross-societal inequalities.[38]

Before I discuss some objections to the view just developed, let me say where this view, if successful, leads us. It follows from our discussion that one Rawlsian argument rejecting duties beyond assistance in building institutions succeeds: societies, unlike citizens of well-ordered societies, do not exist in an environment where redistributive claims beyond duties to assistance succeed. There may be other arguments, but the most prominent considerations commonly advanced on behalf of further redistributive claims draw on the importance (and arbitrariness) of geographical factors and transnational economic relationships. Both considerations fail, so lest there are other arguments that this analysis has overlooked, there are no redistributive duties across societies over and above the duty in support of institution-building.

With all this in place, we revisit the claim that inequalities across peoples are a matter of moral indifference. The importance of insti-

[37] Beitz, "Rawls's 'Law of Peoples,'" p. 694.

[38] The Basel example also lends itself to this objection. Suppose that the Swiss economy, for some reason, suffers severe harm, so that many Swiss workers have no reasonable alternative to seeking employment in the neighboring countries. Suppose somebody living in Basel crosses the border each day to work for a French company, and that the company has a policy of paying Swiss workers half what it pays equivalent French workers. Does this not seem unfair, and does it not mean that this Swiss citizen has a morally legitimate claim to compensation from the company? I think he does have such a claim, and it is a claim that he has in virtue of doing the same work for less pay. However, suppose that the relative social status of his French co-workers for their income is higher than his social status in Switzerland. The view above entails that he does not have any legitimate complaint about that, nor does he have a legitimate say in how the French can bequeath or otherwise transfer their money. There is no need for the French laws regulating property to be justifiable *to him*. Whatever claims he has, he has in virtue of being a worker of that company, and the only regulations that must be justifiable to him are those that apply to his role as a worker in that company.

tutions for prosperity itself rendered it plausible that equality across societies does not matter morally. Now we have argued that additional claims justifying a duty of redistribution in addition to assistance in institution building fail. If there are no such redistributive duties, there are no duties aimed at economic equality either. The earlier view on equality across societies emerges strengthened.

3.4

Let me complete this section by discussing, in some detail, a few objections to my way of spelling out the claim that societies do not exist in the kind of environment in which they can make redistributive claims upon each other. One may object in two ways: first, one may argue internally against my argument by insisting that basing a moral distinction between citizens and non-citizens on the existence of shared *coercive* structures is open to the same instability objection that troubled the attempt of basing such a distinction on a shared *cooperative* structure, and hence that this shift in focus will not solve the problem. And second, one may say that this argument at best succeeds at showing that some normative relevance can be attached to shared citizenship *given* that the existence of states is taken for granted – yet what really is at stake (at least as far as cosmopolitan critics are concerned) is just that assumption. Let me elaborate.

According to the first objection, globalization has not only led to the creation of a global network of cooperative relations at odds with national borders, but also given rise to new, transnational and multi-layered forms of rule that national governments share with other governments and with transnational agencies. Sovereignty, as traditionally understood, is being transformed and reconfigured, and has become shared and divided among agencies of public power at different levels. Traditionally, sovereignty was the (at least largely) *unsupervised exercise of authority in a domain*; nowadays sovereignty of states is, in many cases, more closely related to sheer *independence from individual other states*, in a sense in which colonies were dependent on specific states, and it remains to be seen just how this understanding of sovereignty develops. The state is now located at the intersection of global, regional, transnational, and local systems of governance. Much like cooperative structures, coercive structures exist across state boundaries and thus cannot form a basis for identifying what is distinctive about citizenship and hence cannot provide an argument for why there are no redistributive duties across societies.

There are two responses to this objection. The first denies the point of the objection by insisting that coercion of the relevant sort is exercised by states only. John Ruggie captures the point well: "International officials or entities may be endowed with normative authority that comes from legitimacy, persuasion, expertise, or simple utility; but they lack the basis and means to compel."[39] That is, it is admittedly not the case (any longer) that states are the ultimate and sole source of authority exercised on their territory. Still, to the extent that political authority has moved to non-state actors, it has done so only through explicit or implicit approval of states and at any rate still depends on state power for enforcement. International law, in particular, cannot coerce in the sense in which domestic law can (and constantly does), since it generally does not have its own enforcement organs and is parasitic on domestic law and its enforcement organs, even where states have opted always to resolve conflicts between state law and international law in favor of the latter (since that is itself a decision that the state has made).

It will be useful, however, to have a different response to the objection because, on the one hand, at least for some transnational

---

[39] John Ruggie, "American Exceptionalism, Exemptionalism, and Global Governance," in Michael Ignatieff (ed.), *American Exceptionalism and Human Rights* (Princeton: Princeton University Press, forthcoming). See page 27 of the paper as found on Ruggie's webpage in February 2004 (http://www.ksg.harvard.edu/cbg/director.htm) as well as the following related statement in Anne-Marie Slaughter:

> [G]overnance without government is governance without power, and government without power rarely works. Many pressing international and domestic problems result from states' insufficient power to establish order, build infrastructure, and provide minimum social services. Private actors may take up some slack, but there is no substitute for the state. [Anne-Marie Slaughter, "The Real New World Order," *Foreign Affairs* 76 (1997), pp. 183–195]

This is a remark from an author who does by no means wish to insist on the old Westphalian order, but instead, urges us to think of the world order in terms of trans-governmental networks [Anne-Marie Slaughter, *A New World Order* (Princeton: Princeton University Press, 2004)]. Turning around the proposal that sovereignty has been eroded through the increasing importance of transnational organizations and trans-governmental activities of the sort described by Slaughter in *A New World Order*, Abram Chayes and Antonia H. Chayes argue that "the only way most states can realize and express their sovereignty is through participation in the regimes that make up the substance of international life" [Abram Chayes and Antonia H. Chayes, *The New Sovereignty* (Cambridge: Harvard University Press, 1995), p. 27].

structures such as the European Union, this picture is changing: Once the EU has its own police force, it will have its own means of enforcement (the EU, of course, is a rather special case). On the other hand, and more importantly, this objection depends crucially on what precisely counts as "means to compel." Coordination of or resolutions for economic sanctions or moral pressure can, under appropriate circumstances, be rather effective "means to compel" as well, and those draw significantly on non-state actors.

The second response, then, is to grant much of the objection, but to insist that it misses the point. That is, this response grants that there exist genuinely coercive structures not confined to or ultimately dependent on nation states, and that those structures must be justified to those whom they coerce. But consider how the coercive-structures-approach to assessing the distinctness of shared citizenship might support domestic redistribution. The crucial point is that among the shared legal structures that must be justified to all citizens of a given state there are laws regulating acquisition and transfer of property, including business interactions, taxation, labor markets, inheritance and bequest, gifts, etc. "Redistributive" measures emerge naturally *as components of a property regime* justifiable to all participants – where one must not understand "re-distribution" in terms of taking something away from its "real" owner and give it to somebody else: the question is obviously precisely what the ground rules of ownership should be, and hence what sorts of individual appropriation everybody can be expected to tolerate. So it is in the nature of what domestic law regulates that its justifiability straightforwardly involves "redistribution."

Now consider international law. International law addresses questions of transnational concern, including topics such as the position of states, state responsibility, peace and security, the law of treaties, the law of the sea and of international watercourses, the conduct of diplomatic relations, and more recently also international organizations, the environment, air law and outer space activities, deep-sea resources, and the international protection of human rights. In all these cases, however, the justifiability of appropriate international law to those affected by it does not involve redistribution of any sort. If we are concerned with military intervention, for instance, we must formulate conditions under which intervention would be appropriate, or if we are regulating trade relations, we must do so in terms justifiable to all trade partners. None of this, however, involves redistribution, except perhaps by way of rectifying injustices. So while indeed international law coerces as well, what makes it justifiable does, in virtue of its very subject matter, not involve any redistribution, unlike the justifiability of domestic law.

3.5

This leads us straight to the second objection. For it seems that the reason why the justifiability of international law does not involve any redistributive measures is that it takes the existence of states (which are the parties that have implemented international law to begin with) and many aspects of the state system for granted. International law, that is, is not a set of instruments to design or redesign the political surface of the earth from scratch, but instead a set of conventions and other arrangements among political entities whose existence itself it never questions and that it regulates only to a limited extent (by governing the recognition of new states, for instance).

This, then, is where the second objection enters. This objection, recall, insists that the existence of states itself requires justification. What matters in this case is not justification to those who are subject to state authority (which, of course, is a longstanding subject of political thought), but instead, justification to those who are excluded by the state (which is a relative newcomer as a subject of political thought).[40] There are at least two ways of articulating the view that the existence of states itself must be questioned. First, one may say that the exclusion of some (the "foreigners") entailed by the existence

[40] Christopher Morris, in a wide-ranging discussion of the modern state, argues that "states ... are legitimate to the extent that they are just and minimally efficient" [Christopher Morris, *An Essay on the Modern State* (Cambridge: Cambridge University Press, 1998), p. 165]. So the concern here is inward-directed (i.e., towards the citizens of the state), rather than outward-directed (i.e., towards those excluded from the state). As opposed to that, Samuel Scheffler gives much room to discussing the concern that we are about to address, and calls it the "distributive objection" [Samuel Scheffler, *Boundaries and Allegiances* (Oxford: Oxford University Press, 2001)]. The distributive objection is an objection to the existence of so-called associative duties (i.e., duties that arise, in one form or another, through associations) from the point of view of those who are excluded from the group of people among whom these duties apply; that is, it challenges those who defend such a duty to justify it to those who cannot benefit from its existence, and who may in fact be disadvantaged by it. Scheffler contrasts this objection to associative duties with the "voluntarist objection," which arises from the point of view of those who are said to have that kind of duty, but never voluntarily accepted it. The account developed here should also be taken to be a response to the distributive objection. (What is essential for this response is already present in Blake, "Distributive Justice.")

of states with borders is illegitimate coercion. And second, one may say that no group of people has the required sort of entitlement to occupy a piece of the earth at the exclusion of others.

These two arguments belong very much to the folklore surrounding the debates about global justice, and so do their responses. While I will here be able merely to sketch them, I believe these responses are rather robust under scrutiny and elaboration. It seems all the justification states need to prohibit arbitrary and uncontrolled immigration (which is what the first argument asks them to allow) is that they are doing something morally defensible, even morally praiseworthy that in general cannot be maintained if there is no access regulation. What states do that deserves such protection is to provide for their members by maintaining a morally defensible legal framework and social system. Obviously, not all states do this, and if so, this argument will not apply to them. But there surely are states that pass the relevant moral tests, and hence acquire the right to maintain their existence by prohibiting uncontrolled access. It is consistent with this view that states have obligations towards people in need (refugees, asylum-seekers), or that states must offer support in institution-building.

Surely, there is coercion involved in regulating access to states, but only in the Hobbesian sense in which every impediment counts as a deprivation of liberty. And it seems that such coercion is justified along the lines just sketched. It is, in terms of its moral justifiability, not much different from coercion in a domestic context that keeps people from randomly seizing each other's property. Just as individuals within states should be allowed to have property in their lives for them to pursue meaningful projects, so states (i.e., organized groups of individuals) should be as well. Moreover, there is nothing about the presence of this sort of coercion that undermines the *moral equality* of all persons. Contrary to Joseph Carens, then, I think it is rather misleading to compare the existence of states to medieval feudalism.[41]

The second argument (the one questioning the entitlement of states to their territories) offers a successful objection to the existence of states only if one grants a strong notion of the earth being common property of all humanity, a notion so strong that it prohibits any group of individuals from legitimately reserving some parts of the

[41] See Joseph Carens "Aliens and Citizens: The Case for Open Borders," *Review of Politics* 49 (1987), pp. 251–273.

earth for themselves at the exclusion of all others. The guiding intuition that would make us think that the earth is common property is that its resources exist independently of anybody's contribution. It is, however, a big step from acknowledging that to the conclusion that, therefore, no group of human beings can occupy any part of the earth for their exclusive use. This step can only be taken if it is not only the case that the earth as such is common property of humankind, but *each part* of it as well. And it seems that this is more than the original intuition ("it is nobody's accomplishment that the earth is there") can support, especially under the institutional stance on economic prosperity. For the institutional stance allows for a broad range of possibilities for others to enjoy "enough and as good" (to put it in Lockean terms) of the common property since economic success is not immediately tied to possession of raw materials and to geographic location.

3.6

The defense of states involved in this discussion so far is a rather modest one: I have argued that the existence of states without redistributive duties towards each other is morally justifiable to those excluded from them. That by itself does not entail that one would or should *actually support* a state system over alternative world orders, such as Pogge's model of vertically dispersed sovereignty, from standpoints that propose such a choice.[42] So far the discussion has not required us to question the existence of states from that angle. The argument of Section 4, however, will.

4. Why are there Duties to Burdened Societies at all?

4.1

So far we have assumed that duties to the poor exist, and argued first that their content includes support in institution building, and then rejected additional redistributive duties. But *are* there such duties in the first place? Needless to say, much could be (and has been) said by way of exploring the foundations of such duties. I will limit myself to offering reasons within a Rawlsian framework. To put our question in Rawlsian terminology, then: would well-ordered societies in the

[42] Pogge, *World Poverty and Human Rights*, pp. 178–182.

global original position accept duties of assistance to burdened societies? Before I explore this question, however, let me address one concern. One might say that this way of asking the question distorts the ethical issues in a way that prejudices against cosmopolitans. For what really needs to be asked here is what the global poor, *qua* individuals, are owed, and any answer to this question must in turn constrain what global political structures there can be; so answers in terms of domestic institutions will become relevant only if "domestic structures" themselves are consistent with this individualistic outlook. I am conscious of this concern, but I will proceed in a different order from what this objector suggests. I will *first* pursue the question in its Rawlsian form as just introduced, and *then* address the objector by way of formulating the cosmopolitan concern in response to the answer I am about to develop.

There are three reasons why well-ordered societies in the global original position would accept duties of assistance to burdened societies. The first is prudential, the other two moral. As far as prudence is concerned, enlightened self-interest acknowledges that collapsing states spread refugees, involve others in domestic conflicts, or undermine regional stability; that national financial crises are internationally transmitted; that drug-trafficking, illegal immigration, arms trade, trafficking in women, money-laundering, international terrorism, or joint ventures combining several of these must be fought globally; that disease control is a global problem as much as the creation of a sustainable environment, since, say, damage to the ozone layer is damage done to us all; that development delivers gains from trade, from cooperation in science, culture, business, and tourism. Like outlaw states, burdened societies are a global liability.[43]

For the moral reasons, recall that the global original position assembles representatives of well-ordered peoples (no others) to deliberate about principles of *foreign policy* for such peoples. In particular, it is their job to regulate foreign policy of well-ordered peoples *vis-à-vis* other societies. The first moral reason draws on the importance of institutions. We saw that there were reasons why representatives would be unconcerned with assistance beyond building institutions. Yet the significance of institutions for development also pressures deliberators to demand at least such assistance.

[43] Beitz, "Rawls's 'Law of Peoples,'" p. 689, states that the self-interest argument primarily applies to outlaw states. I hope my discussion shows that it also applies to burdened societies.

However, since deliberators know they represent only well-ordered peoples, they may not find the adoption of such a duty strictly compelling. To do so, they must envisage being representatives in an original position in which they do not know whether they represent well-ordered or burdened societies. This device can be consistently added since original positions, for Rawls, clarify duties among parties by not allowing their representatives to know whom they represent (Original position devices, after all, are merely *apparatus*: so what matters is whether the relevant considerations are available within the Rawlsian framework). The same argument applies if individuals, rather than peoples, are represented in the second original position (as proposed by Beitz and Pogge, respectively). For their representatives would understand the importance of institutions. So on the institutional stance, it becomes irrelevant whether individuals or peoples are represented in the original position.

The second moral reason (independent of the first) draws on consistency. Behind the idea of well-ordered societies stands an ideal of personhood. From the legitimacy-directed standpoint of *Political Liberalism*, this is a thin, political notion of personhood envisaging persons as having a capacity for a sense of justice and one for a conception of the good.[44] Rawls accounts for these features in a minimal way, as they are to be explicated by different comprehensive views. Still, these features of personhood must apply to individuals regardless of whether they belong to any society, or which. Within the confines of shared coercive structures the moral esteem in which those powers are to be held imposes special requirements, in particular to develop one's society into a well-ordered society.[45]

But since those powers must be esteemed alike no matter who possesses them, what duties, if any, hold *vis-à-vis* those with whom one does not share coercive structures? If respect for moral powers by itself is strong enough to push for a well-ordered society *among those*

[44] John Rawls, *Justice as Fairness*: *A Restatement*, ed. Erin Kelly (Cambridge: Harvard University Press, 2001), Section 7.

[45] Well-ordered societies possess institutions in which individuals are at least recognized as citizens entitled to the protection of human rights and to a legal system guided by a "common good idea of justice" (Rawls, *The Law of Peoples*, p. 66) and have adopted these institutions based on a picture of personhood. The *liberal* societies among them go further, recognizing "that persons are citizens first and have equal basic rights as equal citizens" (Rawls, *The Law of Peoples*, p. 66), but decent hierarchical peoples part company here. For the present argument, what well-ordered societies have in common suffices.

who share coercive structures, this will be so because it is strong enough to impose a duty to help *anybody* endowed with those powers in the creation of an environment in which they can be exercised in the first place. Impartiality in the respect for persons with these powers demands as much, but it does then demand different measures depending on whether one actually shares coercive structures with another person, or not. This view is only reinforced by the point that an environment in which those moral powers can be exercised is also an environment that triggers economic growth: good institutions are required for both. So consistency in the impartial application of the respect in which the moral powers are held entails a duty to assistance in the absence of shared coercive structures. As Rawls points out, it is the statesman's obligation to ensure that duty will be implemented, by transforming self-interest gradually into affinity.[46]

Now that these arguments are on the table, we can address one question that neither Section 2 nor Section 3 was equipped to address. That question is what element of the argument of this study defeats the view that we should transfer massive amounts of money or other resources to the global poor, *regardless* of whether such transfers can be understood as contributing to institution building? The social science results in section 2 cannot tell us that such transfers do "not make a difference" and thus are ruled out on such grounds: Those results only tell us that, *so far*, good institutions have been the key to economic prosperity, which in turn gives us a reason to think of institution building as included in development assistance. The arguments in Section 3, then, show that, once appropriate institutions have been built, no *further* redistributive duties exist, but they do not show that there is no straightforward duty to transfer money or resources *regardless* of any such cut-off point. What has been missing so far are reasons demonstrating why assistance should be directed at putting people in a position to help themselves.

The arguments just given provide such reasons. This is obvious for the self-interest argument and the consistency argument (the second moral argument), but it is also the case for the first moral argument using the original-position device. For if it is indeed possible to offer support to the global poor in a manner that will eventually put them in a position to take care of themselves, then a duty to do so would, in that original position, be chosen over a duty that prescribes transfers without a cut-off point and without the prospect that, eventually, the

[46] Rawls, *The Law of Peoples*, pp. 112–113.

targets of assistance will be able to take care of themselves. From the standpoint of self-interested parties that find themselves behind the relevant veil of ignorance, a duty that ceases to apply once the target group is in a position to help itself will be easier to defend than a duty that demands a transfer without that transfer being tied to such a condition.

4.2

Yet there is a problem with this completion of our argument. Recall that already in Section 3 we encountered questions about the justifiability of states. At that stage it was sufficient to argue that a system of states without redistributive duties is *morally acceptable* in the sense of being justifiable to those excluded from them. But now that we are operating with an original-position framework we must entertain more radical questions about the political organization of the world. We must ask whether deliberators behind a suitably constructed original position would actually *support* a global order that includes such entities, and hence whether that system would not only be within the scope of what is justifiable, but would be *favored over* alternative organizational models from a vantage point that allows us not to take any organization model (in particular not a system of states) as already given.

The two most promising lines of argument in support of a state system over other forms of political organization are these. The first conceives of states largely as public good providers and argues that, on practical grounds such as efficiency or stability, public goods are best provided in large packages and in territories under unified control (i.e., states). The second argument focuses on the value of self-determination. The crucial components of that view are first, the idea that individuals desire to live in peoples, that is, groups tied by what Rawls, following John Stuart Mill, calls "common sympathies"[47] (i.e., not necessarily by blood-connections), groups that are, and for which individuals desire to be, the primary locus of social, economic, and political structures that persons belong to; and second, the idea that individuals desire for their people to have the right to self-determination, and that, barring unacceptable effects, this right should be granted.[48]

---

[47] Rawls, *The Law of Peoples*, p. 24.

[48] For the self-determination argument, see Avishai Margalit and Joseph Raz, "National Self-Determination," *The Journal of Philosophy* 87 (1990), pp 440–460.

It is hard to assess how strongly these arguments support a state system. Pogge, for one, offers considerations that potentially undermine both. He insists that the existence of states undermines the realization of peace, security, global justice, democracy, the reduction of oppression, and the maintenance of the ecology.[49] If this is true, it suggests that alternative forms of political organization will, on balance, be better at providing public goods, since the existence of states would come at costs that are too high. That same point would undermine the importance of self-determination as well: if a system of self-determining entities creates massive problems, self-determination should not be implemented as a feature of global political organization. It is hard to tell, however, whether these problems arise because of the sheer existence of a system of self-determining entities or because of its local failures, and its general need for reform (i.e., independence of states to be transformed into independence of peoples) – that is, because not all states correspond to well-ordered societies. It would be difficult to come by the relevant knowledge to decide whether the state system needs "reform" or "revolution" since we can only observe this one world. So the question of how strongly these lines of argument (suitably refined, of course) support states seems rather intractable.

4.3

At this stage, looking at Rawls's notion of a realistic utopia will be useful. "Political philosophy," as Rawls explains, "is realistically utopian when it extends what are ordinarily thought to be the limits of practicable political possibility and, in so doing, reconciles us to our political and social condition."[50] He constrains the set-up of his global original position by the condition that it deliver advice that is realistically utopian. That is why the task of the global original position is to deliver principles of foreign policy of well-ordered societies, and not to redesign the global political order: a good deal of the present order, that is, will be kept fixed. One way of motivating this is that otherwise the global original position will be set up in a manner that confronts the parties behind the respective veil of ignorance with intractable questions such as the one we just

[49] Pogge, *World Poverty and Human Rights*, Chapter 7.
[50] Rawls, *The Law of Peoples*, p. 11.

encountered, and therefore will be in no position to deliver any action-guiding advice.[51]

A realistic utopia is relative to a point in time or state of affairs. What is realistically utopian at the beginning of the early 21st century may differ from what is so generations later. Perhaps at some point what counts as a realistic utopia coincides with the most plausible account of global justice. We may have reached that point: I take no stance on that matter. But it does seem that setting up the original position in such a way that self-determination of peoples is valued is necessary for the global original position to pass as realistically utopian *here and now*, at the beginning of the 21st century. Pursuing self-determination of peoples is *utopian* in the sense that, although self-determination is widely desired, many peoples are not yet self-determining. The current state system does not correspond to a system of self-determining peoples. At the same time, pursuing this ideal is *realistically*-utopian in the sense that self-determination of peoples is, *as an ideal*, already embodied in the global order, especially through occupying a central place in important UN-documents.[52]

In the pursuit of that ideal, it might also become clear that, occasionally, or perhaps even on a large scale, political, economic, or cultural reasons urge a transfer of sovereignty (thus of self-determination) to supranational organizations. Within the Rawlsian model, this could be accommodated as a modification and development of an ideal originally aimed at realizing the self-determination of peoples without thereby having to consider such self-determination as final

---

[51] According to this argument, then, the global original position is constrained by epistemic considerations that are themselves motivated on the grounds that that original position is supposed to generate advice. This immediately triggers the concern that the global original position might not be a good device to use to inquire about global justice, or at any rate, that it cannot be *both* such a device *and* a good device to obtain action-guiding advice. This may be true, but the objection I am trying to answer here is that the use of the device of the original position will all by itself entail that a stronger justification of states is required than what we have offered in Section 3 (or put differently, it is the objection that we cannot *both* use that device to determine the moral foundations of the duties to the poor *and* continue to support a system of states). But it seems that this objection can indeed be rebutted in the manner sketched here. The following paragraph in the text will give an answer to the question of how the device of the global original position relates to global justice.

[52] United Nations Charter, Chapter 1, Article 1, Paragraph 2; International Covenant on Economic, Social and Cultural Rights, Part 1, Article 1; International Covenant on Civil and Political Rights, Part 1, Article 1.

once realized. That is, once self-determining, peoples might decide on transferring authority to supranational organizations. I emphasize this point because in particular the existence and development of the EU including its massive eastward expansion in 2004 and possible further enlargements in the near future that might lead to the inclusion of states (in addition to the Baltic states) that were part of the former Soviet Union, should not be taken to conflict with the views defended here. This development seems best understood as driven by the enlightened self-interest of self-determining peoples to begin with. However, as opposed to a global original position constrained by its being committed to the value of self-determination, most models championing alternative ideals (like Pogge's vertically dispersed sovereignty), whatever virtues they may have, are not within the range of what is realistically utopian and thus fail to provide proper guidance to action. This sort of defense of the states (in conjunction with the considerations in Section 3.5 that show how to justify a state to those excluded from it) is, I think, the best we can do: but I also think we can indeed do as much.[53]

A remaining concern about assuming the value of self-determination of peoples in the global original position is that membership in peoples, as Pogge suggests, may be a matter of degree, rather than an all or nothing affair.[54] Therefore, what is problematic is not only (or not so much) the value of self-determination, but the presupposition

[53] As Buchanan, "Rawls's Law of Peoples," points out, individuals do not now generally live in peoples organized by their own governments. Yet that is no objection to the claim that *The Law of Peoples* is a realistic utopia. The first goal towards realizing global justice is to make sure that appropriate groups of common sympathies are organized by governments. *The Law of Peoples* allows both for the formulation of that vision and for the formulation of a vision of how peoples should relate to each other. One may also object that Rawls's account has no larger claims to being a realistic utopia than cosmopolitanism. After all, there is a massive disconnect between peoples and existing states: Getting from existing states to a society of peoples would involve breaking up some states and changing the borders of others. So policy makers today may have little use for *The Law of Peoples* either. However, self-determination is widely acknowledged as a legitimate goal of peoples, with disagreement persisting about the precise circumstances under which it can be brought about against resistance, about the legitimacy of outside help, etc. Cosmopolitan ideals are considerably less well entrenched. The argument presented here, then, is one about how one should set up the global original position. In Section 4.1, I have argued for one addition to the way Rawls sets up that global original position to make sure that duties to burdened societies are properly considered. That addition does not seem to stand in any conflict with the limitations suggested here.

[54] Pogge, "An Egalitarian Law of Peoples."

that individuals neatly fall into peoples. In response, note first that this concern affects the understanding of peoples as tied by *common sympathies* less than that of peoples as tied by blood bonds. Still, sometimes such membership is indeed a matter of degree. The idea that individuals belong to peoples should be regarded as a pragmatic simplification allowing for macroscopic answers to macroscopic questions, admitting more complex considerations in specific cases. In such cases, say, Pogge's proposed vertical dispersion of sovereignty, or other modes, might be appropriate as a local solution, although, by and large, the model of self-determining peoples is still appropriate.

5. Conclusion

We began by asking what we know about what makes countries rich and stable or poor and volatile. According to the best available answer, institutions are crucial for prosperity. While this institutional stance is rather unspecific, it becomes specific enough for our purposes if contrasted with geography and integration. Geography's point is that natural parameters are crucial for wealth, and integration's point is that a society's dealings with others shape its prosperity. Institutions insists that it is what people do with each other within shared institutional frameworks that is crucial for their prosperity. Section 2 argued that this view has implications for the content of our duties to the poor, and Section 3 that this institutional stance illuminates and supports *The Law of Peoples*' view on duties among societies. Let me repeat that institutions is an empirical stance in an ongoing debate, and that Rawls's view will be implausible if institutions is refuted. Still, institutions is plausible enough a claim, and its importance considerable enough, for philosophers to explore its implications carefully.

The view of our duties to the global poor that has emerged is a complex one. On the one hand, we have argued that what is required is support in building institutions. On the other hand, we have also seen that, due to the nature of such institutions, there are some *prima facie* reasons that will constrain what outsiders *can* and or *ought* to do. Still, I think these considerations together offer a framework within which one can assess what is to be done in specific cases. At any rate, it would be wrong to think that my arguments against further-reaching redistributive duties show that Rawls only requires a minimal duty towards burdened societies. Assistance in institution-building may be extremely taxing, depending on how difficult it is to build them, and depending on how reasoning about the prima facie reasons against assistance works out. So Rawls does formulate a stringent duty (shaming the status quo) in a philosophically sound manner that has a genuine chance of persuading policy-makers, while integrating normative argumentation and empirical claims in a way that does justice to both in a domain in which claims about facts and claims about values are intricately intertwined. Rawls gives us, in his words, a *realistic utopia*. He proposes a normative framework within which the Millennium Declaration finds its place and thus guides the way of global justice in the 21st century.

John F. Kennedy School of Government
Harvard University
79 JFK Street
Cambridge, MA 02138
USA
E-mail: mathias_risse@harvard.edu

SANJAY REDDY

THE ROLE OF APPARENT CONSTRAINTS IN NORMATIVE REASONING: A METHODOLOGICAL STATEMENT AND APPLICATION TO GLOBAL JUSTICE*

(Received 14 May 2004; accepted in revised form 14 June 2004)

ABSTRACT. The assumptions that are made about the features of the world that are relatively changeable by agents and those that are not (constraints) play a central role in determining normative conclusions. In this way, normative reasoning is deeply dependent on accounts of the empirical world. Successful normative reasoning must avoid the naturalization of constraints and seek to attribute correctly to agents what is and is not in their power to change. Recent discourse on global justice has often come to unjustified conclusions about agents' obligations due to a narrow view of what is changeable and by whom.

KEY WORDS: causes, constraints, facts, global justice, institutions, obligations

This essay is concerned with a central feature of normative reasoning and its relevance to problems of global distributive justice; in particular, the role played by judgments concerning constraints in normative reasoning.

The identification of apparent constraints plays a crucial role in our ascription of obligations to different actors and in our understanding of the content of those obligations. The phrase "*apparent* constraints" is a useful one because constraints that are deemed to exist are often in fact not present. The misrecognition of constraints can lead to insufficient attention to feasible revisions in the existing social order (and in particular in institutional arrangements) and a resulting failure to identify the actions that would best advance normative ends (of social justice and individual morality). It can also lead to an inappropriate attribution of responsibilities to different agents. I shall argue that it is crucially necessary in normative reasoning to combat the tendency to misidentify apparent constraints.

The argument is a species of a more general one. It is necessary to identify relevant facts about the situation faced by moral agents if they

* I would like to thank for their helpful comments Christian Barry, Rudiger Bittner, Darrel Moellendorf and Thomas Pogge.

are to form normative judgments that are usable by these agents. What the facts are is of course often a matter of dispute. This is especially true of the facts concerning causal relations, which are deeply relevant to the identification of obligations. Because propositions concerning causal relations are of an inextricably counterfactual character they are often quite reasonably disputed. It is of great importance that we seek to identify relevant facts (despite the difficulties involved) as otherwise we will be unable to give practical application to normative principles. However, it does not follow that we should act on the basis of the single theory we take to be most likely to be true. Rather, moral decision-making and evaluation must be appropriately informed by the fact we are uncertain about the facts.

1. The Nature and Role of Constraints

All normative reasoning takes place against a factual background. An aspect of our accustomed descriptions of such a factual background is the identification of constraints, understood as fixed features of the natural or the social world. I shall argue, however, that our understanding of certain features of the world as constraints is often not ultimately sustainable. Rather, apparent constraints must often be viewed as changeable through the appropriate actions of agents (individuals and collectivities).

We may, of course, reject the concept of constraint in favor of that of costly actions. From such a standpoint, very few constraints would exist. Rather, there would exist many features of the world that may be changed only at a cost to the agent that is high (and perhaps prohibitive). This is a coherent standpoint, which is indeed the one to which I subscribe. However, it is customary to refer to circumstances that are very (and perhaps prohibitively) costly to change as constraints. This accustomed usage is the one that I adopt here. Constraints, understood in this sense, are a feature of any plausible description of a problem of normative evaluation, as in their absence the evaluator's problem would bear no relationship to any real evaluative context encountered in the world.[1]

[1] In other words, I am setting aside here the suggestion of Rudiger Bittner that what I refer to as constraints can be described merely as facts about the world concerning features of the world that are difficult or costly to change, from the standpoint of a particular decision-making actor and for purposes of a particular decision-making problem.

I propose the following definition of a constraint:

A constraint faced by an agent is a feature of the world that can reasonably be judged to have the property that the agent cannot change it without substantial cost or difficulty, if at all.

Pragmatic judgments play a critical role in the identification of constraints as just defined. Constraints are identified through pragmatic judgments concerning what it is that is reasonable to judge that an agent cannot readily change. It is evident that a constraint arises as a consequence of the *relation* between an agent and her context. The features of a context that may be described as constraints vary with the pair {agent, context}. It may be in the power of a particular (individual or collective) agent to change certain features of her environment, and not in her power to change other features of her environment and this judgment is agent-relative. It is also clear from this definition that many features of the world that are constraints from the point of view of individual agents are not constraints from the point of view of those agents when they are considered collectively (or indeed, when considered as members of a coalition sufficient to generate change). A full description of a choice situation must specify constraints, but it must also note that these constraints are potentially changeable. As a consequence, there are always two morally relevant forms of action that are feasible – actions that respect constraints and actions that change them. This idea is given mathematical form in the Kuhn–Tucker theorem, which shows that a maximand can always be achieved to a greater extent if a binding constraint is relaxed.[2]

2. Application to Global Distributive Justice

The identification of certain features of the world as constraints, and others as changeable, is a task that is central to debates on global distributive justice. Such identification plays a critical role in the determination of the content and the distribution of obligations.

---

[2] See for example A. Mas-Colell, M. Whinston and J. Green, *Microeconomic Theory* (Oxford: Oxford University Press, 1995), Theorem M.K.2. The "complementary slackness" condition of the Kuhn-Tucker Theorem ensures that in problems involving constrained maximization the relaxation of a binding constraint (i.e., one that is relevant to the problem) necessarily increases the level of achievement of the maximand.

For example, the innumerable ghoulish debates that have occurred as to where the marginal dollar should flow – to the United States poor or the Kenyan poor, to the handicapped Chinese or to the able-bodied Sudanese – presuppose the existence of a constraint which prevents both of these goals from being fulfilled simultaneously. It is not unreasonable to question this frame work and to ask, why not fulfill both goals? We live in a world of unprecedented plenty. As a result, the presupposition that there exists a constraint requires justification. Moreover, this justification must be itself a moral justification, and cannot take as given merely on the basis of empirical facts.[3]

An important current debate concerns the reasons that poor countries are poor. Did they come to be poor (or do they continue to be poor) because of choices that they have themselves made, or rather because of the features of the world order in which they find themselves, and because of the actions of other agents? The answer to this question will properly influence our judgments concerning the distribution of responsibilities for the alleviation of poverty. For instance, as Mathias Risse points out in this issue of *The Journal of Ethics*, a debate has occurred recently on the question of whether the most important determinant of economic growth in poor countries is their geographical location or the institutions that they possess (including those that influence the degree of their integration with the world economy). What is the correct description of the situation faced by poor countries? Is it that they are constrained from raising their incomes by their poor geographical circumstances or other such factors beyond their control or rather are they constrained from raising their incomes by their poor institutions, which may be modified through actions that they can take? As Risse points out, our judgments and ascriptions of responsibility may depend on which of these empirical characterizations we accept.

It is important to note three points here. First, the determinants of cross-country differences in income (and in economic growth) continue to be controversial. Given that this important empirical issue on which moral judgments crucially depend is not settled, it is necessary to adopt an approach to moral decision-making and judgment that takes note of this uncertainty.

Such an approach must recommend actions after assessing the moral desirability of all possible outcomes that may arise as a result

---

[3] See, for example, the essays in Deen Chatterjee (ed.), *The Ethics of Assistance: Morality and the Distant Needy* (Cambridge: Cambridge University Press, 2004).

of those actions, including those that will arise if the theory of empirical causation on which the choice of action is predicated happens to be false. It may be morally greatly important to avoid having been responsible for worsening the severe disadvantages of others, or allowing them to languish in those disadvantages, if one was bound to assist them as a requirement of justice. Yet it is precisely such an outcome that may arise if an incorrect causal theory leads one to the false conclusion that one has no duty to benefit others. To the extent that our judgments as to whether the present world is just are grounded in fallible empirical judgments, we must exercise caution when acting (or failing to act) on the basis of these judgments.

Second, the assumption that a population is causally responsible for the features of its domestic institutions and the outcomes that result in the presence of these institutions may not be correct. For example, a country's domestic institutions may have been shaped profoundly by events or circumstances for which other countries were, or are, directly responsible. We can consider here the impact (for example) of European colonialism and the cold war on presently poor countries, as well as features of the international order such as the willingness of other countries to recognize a "resource and borrowing privilege" through which corrupt elites benefit from illegitimate rule.[4] Indeed, that institutions are deeply shaped by external forces is the supposition of the economists that Risse quotes in support of the view that "institutions matter."[5] The point is not that institutions are not an important determinant of subsequent development trajectories. On the contrary, we have every reason to think that they are, *inter alia*. The point is rather that a population cannot rigidly be held *morally* responsible for the nature of its institutions, which reflect many historical factors, including external imposition and the accretion of institutional structures and norms over genera-

[4] On this see Thomas Pogge, *World Poverty and Human Rights* (Cambridge: Polity Press, 2002).

[5] See e.g., D. Rodrik, A. Subramanian and F. Trebbi, "Institutions Rule: The Primacy of Institutions over Geography and Integration in Economic Development," 2002 (http://ksghome.harvard.edu/~.drodrik.academic.ksg/institutionsrule, %205.0.pdf) and Daron Acemoglu, James A. Robinson and Simon Johnson, "The Colonial Origins of Comparative Development: An Empirical Investigation," *American Economic Review* 91 (2001), pp. 1369–1401. This work argues that countries that were more thoroughly colonized and had institutions put in place by the colonizing countries are those that now possess ostensibly "superior" institutions.

tions. The current members of the population of a country may have inherited these institutions from their predecessors, and may now find it difficult or impossible to change them.

Another reason that the outcomes that result in the presence of specific domestic institutions may not be ones for which the population of that country may be held responsible is that these outcomes may in fact depend jointly on the nature of the world order in which the country finds itself situated (and which it has not played a significant role in shaping) and its domestic institutions. It is not difficult to think of ways in which this may be so. For example, a country that attempts as an integral part of its development strategy to undertake land reforms, significant taxation of capital, and other policies that are deemed unfriendly to holders of conventional private property rights is more likely to be punished with capital flight in a world in which other countries respect these conventional property rights (and may even actively seek to attract fleeing capital, through measures such as banking secrecy).

Third, there does not exist a one-to-one mapping from retrospective causal responsibility to moral responsibility.[6] Even if institutions are thought of as plastic – radically transformable – it does not follow that a population can be held morally responsible for the outcomes produced by the poor institutions that they do in fact have. Although institutions are transformable, it requires imagination, courage and luck to transform them. What we know about institutions tells us that they contain a significant element of path-dependence. Institutional arrangements can settle into (low- or high- level) strategic equilibria that are difficult or impossible for individual agents, acting in isolation, to change. The collective action problems involved in reforming institutions may be exceedingly difficult to overcome. Nevertheless, foreigners may have the ability to act in ways that decrease the disadvantages realized by the population in a country, either through helping to reform domestic institutions within the developing or developed countries, by helping to reform global institutions, or by undertaking other measures, including resource transfers. The (prospective) causal capacity of foreigners to reduce the disadvantages suffered by the population of a poor country may by itself generate obligations, of justice and not merely of charity – irrespective of retrospective causal responsibility for the

[6] See Joel Feinberg, *Doing and Deserving* (Princeton: Princeton University Press, 1970).

institutions that exist. This would be true, for instance, in a theory of justice that responded in however moderate a way to the moral arbitrariness and consequent unacceptability of massive differences in life chances that have arisen through the accident of birth.

The arguments of Risse are unconvincing because they involve unjustified restrictions of at least three kinds. First, they focus solely on the special case in which moral responsibility is entirely derivative of retrospective causal responsibility. Second, they focus solely on retrospective causal responsibility for domestic institutions, neglecting retrospective causal responsibility for all of the other features of the world that act (conjointly) to produce a particular distributive outcome, within countries and globally. Third, they deny the retrospective causal responsibility of foreigners for the nature of domestic institutions in poor countries.

What is useful in Risse's work is that it reminds us of the parametric dependence of our moral judgments on the constraints that we believe to exist. However, it demonstrates equally that if we change our perception of these constraints our attribution of responsibilities to agents will change accordingly and indeed profoundly.

However, if we give more substantial attention to the potential for the transformation of apparent constraints we are drawn robustly into a territory of realistic utopian moral reasoning. Our attention is drawn to possible actions to transform institutional structures, practices, and rules of the domestic and world system so that they may better promote our normative ends. We are drawn away from problems of how to choose individual action while respecting existing institutional structures and toward problems of institutional design and transformation through collective action. The assessment of whether social institutions are just requires the identification of relevant counterfactuals. Similarly, the requirements of individual morality extend to the support that individuals do or do not extend to alternative institutional arrangements and not merely to the way in which they act within existing institutions.

Department of Economics
Barnard College
Columbia University
3009 Broadway Avenue
New York, NY 10027
USA
E-mail: sr793@columbia.edu

RICHARD J. ARNESON

DO PATRIOTIC TIES LIMIT GLOBAL JUSTICE DUTIES?

(Received 14 May 2004; accepted in revised form 4 June 2004)

ABSTRACT. Some theorists who accept the existence of global justice duties to alleviate the condition of distant needy strangers hold that these duties are significantly constrained by special ties to fellow countrymen. The "patriotic priority thesis" holds that morality requires the members of each nation-state to give priority to helping needy fellow compatriots over more needy distant strangers. Three arguments for constraint and patriotic priority are examined in this essay: an argument from fair play, one from coercion, another from coercion and autonomy. Under scrutiny, none of these arguments qualifies as successful.

KEY WORDS: autonomy, coercion, distributive justice, global justice, Michael Blake, Richard W. Miller

Not everyone embraces egalitarian justice. Libertarians find the idea morally distasteful.[1] For those attracted to the ideal, the question immediately arises, whether or not there are principled limits on the scope of its application. Is the jurisdiction of egalitarian justice local, national, or global? Global egalitarianism strikes many of us as satisfying from the standpoint of principle but counterintuitive in its policy implications. Philosophers have tried to bolster this intuitive sense of unease with principled arguments. This essay examines some promising arguments and finds them lacking.[2] The upshot of this exercise is to cast doubt on the doubters of the claim that the principles of egalitarian justice have wide scope.

Some preliminary clarification of the question at issue is in order. For the purposes of this essay, principles of justice are moral

[1] The locus classicus of libertarian advocacy is still Robert Nozick, *Anarchy, State, and Utopia* (New York: Basic Books, 1974).

[2] My focus here is on two excellent essays: Richard W. Miller, "Cosmopolitan Respect and Patriotic Concern," *Philosophy and Public Affairs* 27 (1998), pp. 202–224; and Michael Blake, "Distributive Justice, State Coercion, and Autonomy," *Philosophy and Public Affairs* 30 (2001), pp. 257–296. For criticism of these writings (and more) very much in the spirit of this essay, see Kok-Chor Tan, "Patriotic Obligations," *The Monist* 86 (2003), pp. 434–453.

The Journal of Ethics (2005) 9: 127–150

principles that assert moral requirements that are presumptively enforceable and the violation of which involves wrongs to individual persons. Egalitarian principles of justice hold that it is either intrinsically or instrumentally morally valuable that everyone has access to the same – or closer to the same – level of benefit or advantage over the life course.[3] (The measure of benefit might be resources, or primary goods, or capabilities, or utility construed as desire satisfaction, happiness, or objective well-being, or the like.) The instrumental egalitarian views equality not as *per se* desirable but as a means to desirable ends such as improvements in the conditions of life of the worse off. In this essay, I shall focus on the instrumental versions of egalitarianism.

The basic idea of instrumental egalitarian justice is that there is a natural enforceable moral duty to help those who are badly off through no fault or choice of their own. The worse off the person is, the greater is the duty to aid. Characterizing the duty as "natural" means that it holds independently of social arrangements, conventional understandings, or subjective opinions. If a duty is enforceable, then it is generally morally permissible, and may be morally required, to use physical force and violence and the threat of these evils to coerce people into compliance with the duty, the magnitude of the permissible evils used for this leverage being proportional to the harm that would be suffered if the duty is not upheld.[4]

Some deny that principles of justice have wide, global scope. These skeptics deny that there are significant moral obligations to aid others just on the ground that they are persons and badly off. For these skeptics, serious obligations to aid others are always local and rooted in particular ties and special relations.

---

[3] Significant formulations of egalitarian justice include John Rawls, *A Theory of Justice*, rev. ed. (Cambridge: Harvard University Press, 1999); Amartya Sen, *Inequality Reconsidered* (Cambridge: Harvard University Press, 1991); and Ronald Dworkin, *Sovereign Virtue: The Theory and Practice of Equality* (Cambridge: Harvard University Press, 2000).

[4] Mention of "proportionality" here just points to a topic that needs to be addressed. What is appropriate proportionality? Act-consequentialism holds that force and violence and the threat of these evils should be deployed just in case doing so produces the best outcome all things considered. Violence is proportionate on this view if and only if it produces a better outcome, even if only by a tiny jot, than would any alternative act that refrains from violence. The defense of act-consequentialism lies beyond the scope of this essay.

The position that is the target of attack for this essay is more limited and moderate than the skepticism just described. The moderate does not deny that there are significant moral requirements under the heading of global egalitarian justice. The issue is the comparative strength of these requirements. The moderate holds that it is morally required to give priority to alleviating poverty and misery that afflict one's fellow countrymen over contributing to the alleviation of poverty and misery wherever they may be found. If we are Canadians, we are morally bound to contribute resources to improve the lives of badly off people in Quebec or Vancouver even though these resources would do more good – produce more moral value – if channeled to the aid of more desperately impoverished people elsewhere in the world.

Call the moderate claim just described, that morality requires that the members of each nation-state give priority to helping needy fellow compatriots over helping needy foreigners, the "*Patriotic Priority Thesis*." Sometimes the thesis is qualified, so that it applies to governments and to individuals acting in the role of citizens to influence the policies of governments, but not to individuals in their private lives.

A related moderate claim holds that morality requires that each person should do her part to ensure that all humans are brought to a minimal acceptable threshold level of access to benefit, but requires additionally that each member of a nation-state should do her part to ensure that fellow compatriots have their needs satisfied to a degree that is far above the minimal threshold level or that the worst off within the nation receive significant special favor beyond this global minimum.

One might try to defend patriotic priority or another form of moderation by appeal to special felt ties of solidarity.[5] The claim would be that we have special duties to those we specially care about, and just as we owe special treatment to family and friends, we owe special consideration to fellow countrymen. A problem with this line of thought is that many people do not experience

[5] See Thomas Hurka, "The Justification of National Partiality," in Robert McKim and Jeff McMahan (eds.), *The Morality of Nationalism* (Oxford: Oxford University Press, 1997), pp. 139–157; Samuel Scheffler, *Boundaries and Allegiances* (Oxford: Oxford University Press, 2001, Chapter 6); and Yael Tamir, *Liberal Nationalism* (Princeton: Princeton University Press, 1993), Chapter 5. For criticism, see Richard Arneson, "Consequentialism vs. Special-Ties Partiality," *The Monist* 86 (2003), pp. 382–401.

special feelings of solidarity with compatriots as such. Nor does such lack of feeling seem deviant or unreasonable. Moreover, the most unproblematic and uncontroversial special obligations to friends and family originate in voluntary undertakings, but membership in a nation state is for the most part not voluntary.

The main argument this essay considers is that the members of a nation-state are bound together by a strong web of governmental coercion and support the imposition of this extensive coercion on one another. Co-nationals are involved in mutual state coercion and are not involved in similar coercion of foreigners. Hence, egalitarian justice requirements single out co-nationals for special favored treatment to compensate, as it were, for the imposition of coercion. A related argument holds that, coercion aside, considerations of fair play require those bound by important public goods provision schemes to give priority to fulfilling the duties imposed by these schemes.

1. The Significance of the Issue

In recent years philosophers have argued about the nature of our putative moral obligations to aid the needy.

In some cases the practical significance of these theoretical disputes is not at all obvious and may in the end be slight. The issue concerning the scope of justice obligations is strikingly different in this regard.

For example, debates about "What should be distributed?" or about whether the currency of justice should be conceived as well-being, primary goods, capabilities, some other notion of resources, and so on are intellectually stimulating, but their practical significance is a subtle matter.[6]

[6] See Amartya Sen, "Equality of What?," in Sterling McMurrin (ed.), *Tanner Lectures on Human Values*, Volume 1 (Salt Lake City: University of Utah Press, 1980); John Rawls, "Social Unity and Primary Goods," in John Rawls, *Collected Papers*, ed. Samuel Freeman (Cambridge: Harvard University Press, 1999), pp. 359–387; G. A. Cohen, "On the Currency of Egalitarian Justice," *Ethics* 89 (1989), pp. 906–944; also the references in footnote 3 of this essay.

In contrast, the scope issue has palpably significant implications.[7] For example, suppose that justice requires Rawlsian maximin.[8] If justice obligations to compatriots take priority, then people in wealthy nations are obliged above all to bring about alleviation of their most disadvantaged members, who are still far, far better off than the globally worst off. If maximin instead applies everywhere across national borders, then people in wealthy nations including their worst off members are required to make sacrifices for the sake of the distant needy, the globally worst off.

2. Fair Play

One promising argument for something close to patriotic priority appeals to the duty of reciprocity or fair play that is triggered by the local networks of cooperating agents who produce benefits for each other that call for reciprocal cooperation. The idea is that the requirements to aid other people that the duty of local fair play imposes standardly take priority over weaker ties of mere beneficence owed to distant strangers.

Consider the principle of fairness formulated by Herbert Hart and John Rawls:

> [W]hen a number of persons engage in a just, mutually advantageous, cooperative venture according to rules and thus restrain their liberty in ways necessary to yield advantages for all, those who have submitted to these restrictions have a right to similar acquiescence on the part of those who have benefited from their submission.[9]

---

[7] To clarify: I suggest that "What should be distributed?" has less practical significance than the issue, whether justice obligations have global or restricted scope. Of course there is also "What form should the distribution take?" – should the principle of distribution be equalize, maximin, prioritize, maximize-the-aggregate, or something else entirely – and this issue sometimes has clear policy implications. I am indebted to Peter Vallentyne for this phrasing of the two questions. The scope issue that is my focus in the text can be seen as an aspect of "What form should the distribution take?"

[8] As characterized in John Rawls, *A Theory of Justice*, pp. 72 and 132–133. See also Amartya Sen, *Collective Choice and Social Welfare* (San Francisco: Holden-Day, 1970), p. 138; Amartya Sen, "Rawls Versus Bentham: An Axiomatic Examination of the Pure Distribution Problem," in Norman Daniels (ed.), *Reading Rawls* (Stanford: Stanford University Press, 1989), pp. 283–292.

[9] Nozick, *Anarchy, State, and Utopia*, p. 90. See also Nozick's references to the relevant work by Hart and Rawls. Nozick of course is quoting the principle of fairness as a preliminary to demolishing it.

The principle of fairness has provoked a considerable skeptical literature.[10] The critics note that it is not in general true that by giving you a benefit I thereby bring it about that you have a duty, much less an enforceable duty, to reciprocate. A gift is different from a contract. This point holds when the recipient of the gift only gets the benefit if she voluntarily accepts it. In other cases, in which one person generates a benefit for another that falls on the other and benefits her independently of whether or not she consents to receive the gift, it is all the more mysterious to the critics that anyone should think that the generation of a benefit in and of itself establishes a duty to repay on the part of the beneficiary.

I am not a skeptic about the principle of fairness. Moreover, I believe that it can establish duties of reciprocity even in cases in which the receipt of benefits is unaccompanied by voluntary acceptance of the benefit on the part of the recipient. To see this, one needs to see that the intended scope of the principle of fairness is limited to cases of public goods provision. With respect to a group of people, a good is *public* to the degree that three conditions obtain: consumption is non-rival (one person's consumption of some of the good leaves no less for others), exclusion is impossible or unfeasible (if some consume the good, others cannot be prevented from consuming), and all must consume the same amount of the good (more weakly: all must consume some if anyone consumes any of the good). A good is *private* to the degree that none of these three conditions obtains. The three conditions do not all rise and fall together, so the analysis becomes complex. Simplifying, I submit that the key feature is non-excludability. When a group of people in an area cooperate to provide important public goods, they do not have the option of providing the good only to those who agree to join in the scheme. The goods to be produced will be available to anyone in the area, and in certain cases the goods are such that they will just fall on people without any mediation of consent to receive the benefit. A classic example is the organization of a defense force that protects the region from external aggression by marauders. If the area defense force is functioning well, deterring invasion, and I am a resident of the territory, I automatically receive a very valuable

[10] See A. John Simmons, *Moral Principles and Political Obligations* (Princeton: Princeton University Press, 1979), pp. 101–142. A recent discussion is in Garrett Cullity, "Moral Free Riding," *Philosophy and Public Affairs* 24 (1995), pp. 3–34. The defense of the principle of fairness in the text draws from Richard J. Arneson, "The Principle of Fairness and Free-Rider Problems, *Ethics* 92 (1982), pp. 616–633.

good of security from harm, whether I consent or not. In this sort of case, the principle of fairness can be restated as a norm against free riding. If one benefits from a fair and reasonable cooperative scheme that supplies one and others with important public goods, one should cooperate by doing one's part in the scheme. As a further claim, I submit that such duties are sometimes enforceable duties. It is permissible to employ coercion to force would-be free riders to contribute their fair share.

Given all this, it might seem plausible to add that the duty to aid distant strangers is simply standardly overridden by stronger duties arising from the principle of fairness. Public goods provision schemes may operate in very small-scale and local contexts, but a very important class of cases involves the mediation of the state. It just turns out to be the case that the most important public goods that we gain in the course of social life that trigger strong duties of fair play are supplied by peoples organized through national governments. Hence, the duties of fair play follow the lines of governmental jurisdictions and especially the lines of national borders. Canadians benefit from the cooperation of fellow Canadians to supply important public goods, not (to anything like the same degree) the cooperation of Mexicans, South Africans, or Romanians.

Although in this essay I adopt an agnostic stance on the question of the exact nature and strength of the moral duties to aid distant needy strangers, assessment of the argument just raised requires some balancing of the strength of the conflicting moral considerations and hence some specification of the strength of the beneficence duties that are the substance of global justice. If duties to aid the distant needy were utterly trivial or entirely optional and discretionary, they would be utterly swamped by the duties generated by local fair play requirements. But to make the case that this swamping does not occur, it suffices to insist that these beneficence duties are nontrivial and non-optional.

Take non-optionality first. Suppose non-localized duties to aid the needy give rise to duties (of some unspecified strength) to aid the distant needy. Whatever the size of the aid the duties demand, let us suppose, as is plausible, that these duties are strict requirements. One does not have the moral discretion to abide by them or pay them no heed. Then one does not have the moral right to engage with others in a scheme of public goods provision that imposes requirements the fulfillment of which reduces one's resources to the point that one cannot fulfill the prior and standing beneficence duties. For concreteness, suppose the global justice duties require that one give one penny per year to the distant needy. Then it is a constraint on the principle of fairness that it cannot be invoked to require someone to give up resources that would leave him unable to pay his required penny contribution per year. The same goes if the global justice duties are more substantial.[11]

Let us suppose that global justice beneficence duties are nontrivial, significant in strength, as well as non-optional. This is an appropriate assumption here – recall that we are not arguing with libertarians and other skeptics about beneficence duties, but rather with egalitarians who say local duties come first. The following analogy then suggests itself: Suppose I owe a $100 debt to Smith, and suppose Smith desperately needs the money. Then some affluent friends of mine organize a local public goods provision scheme, which showers benefits on me. A duty of reciprocity is triggered, but surely it does not cause the duty to Smith to evaporate, and given Smith's assumed greater need, surely the duty of reciprocity stands behind the duty to Smith in the queue that assigns priority rankings among my duties. The same goes for global justice allegedly in conflict with local reciprocity, I say.

The foregoing thought might seem to just beg the question. I have been writing as though the duty of beneficence comes first in time and a public goods provision scheme is established afterward. In that context, it might be plausible to suppose that the initiation of a cooperative scheme must not preclude fulfillment of prior duties (though if the duties were morally of little consequence, even this might be doubted). But one might just as well imagine that one is born into a world in which there are distant needy strangers and also an ongoing scheme that provides one important public goods.

In my view, the issue is not really temporal but moral priority. If my being better off and your being well off triggers a duty to aid, I cannot evade this duty by cooperating with other well off persons in ways that make the initially well off even better off. Imagining the needy already stretching out their arms before the cooperative scheme among the affluent is started just makes the point vivid.

A further clarification should be added. The duty triggered by the principle of fairness is not a duty of a sort that could establish patriotic priority. Patriotic priority says that one should give priority

[11] In this connection, see Samuel Scheffler's discussion of the "distributive objection" in Scheffler, *Boundaries and Allegiances*, pp. 66–81.

to helping local needy fellow citizens as opposed to helping distant more needy strangers who are not co-nationals. Even if the principle of fairness generates a duty to provide goods to one's fellow countrymen, this is a return for services rendered, not any sort of response to the neediness or badly off condition of those to whom the duty is owed. Those to whom I owe a duty of fair play arising from the principle of fairness might all be wealthy individuals who are among the very best off persons on earth. The argument considered here is one that suggests (wrongly, in my judgment) that duties to aid distant needy strangers are overridden by duties to provide benefits to fellow countrymen. The putative upshot of reflection on the principle of fairness was supposed to be a moral relationship that mimics patriotic priority but is not identical with it. But given that my arguments against the priority of the duty of fair play are found convincing, the exact character of that priority is moot.

3. Against Reciprocity

The preceding section affirms the principle of fair play but argues that its proper jurisdiction is constrained by global justice duties. In passing, I want to register a doubt about reciprocity, regarded as a fundamental source of moral obligation. Our pre-reflective view is that reciprocity obligations are powerful, but this view is likely to confound a moral and a purely strategic idea of reciprocity. The motivational pull of strategic rationality is strong, but should not be confused with the pull of moral reasons.

The strategic idea of reciprocity is that one should return good for good and evil for evil. This is a counsel of prudence that if followed will redound to one's long-run advantage if one is interacting with a population of reciprocators acting on this same maxim. (Of course, if the population is diverse, a more sophisticated prudence tailors one's policy to the character of those one is interacting with – reciprocity for the reciprocators, avoidance of interaction with non-cooperators, and exploitation of unconditional cooperators.) We humans are powerfully drawn to reciprocity insofar as it can be rationalized by prudent calculation, and social life is importantly shaped by such reciprocity.

But prudence is not to be confused with morality. If reciprocity is proposed as a moral requirement, the question arises, reciprocity on what terms? Reciprocity needs a standard, a measure. What should trigger reciprocity, and what is the measure of adequate repayment? When the issue is posed, it is clear that the measure has to be set by whatever correct moral principles specify. Moral reciprocity then becomes a formal notion. Its requirement is that one should be disposed to behave toward others according to whatever the principles of morality require. Morality might require the well off to help the badly off forever, with no actual behavioral reciprocity demanded of the recipients of help. What reciprocity formally conceived requires is that each person be disposed to interact with others as correct moral principles dictate – so that if correct moral principles require you to aid me in certain circumstances, I should be disposed to do the same if our positions were reversed (which they may never be). More broadly, I should be disposed to behave toward anybody at any time as morality requires. In a society of moral agents, all would be so disposed, and the mutual knowledge that all of us are so disposed brings about a sense of moral community, in which nobody fears exploitive or immoral treatment at the hands of another.

These sketchy reflections are intended to reduce our inclination to suppose that requirements of reciprocity might be substantive and high-priority requirements of morality that in principle can conflict with and should trump mere requirements of beneficence. Since global justice duties are duties of beneficence, securing that reduced inclination would be good news for the advocate of the position that the duties of global justice are stringent and are not trumped by local ties. Further arguments against that conclusion await a hearing, however.

4. Coercion

The claim to be considered in this section is that what fundamentally separates our relationship to fellow countrymen from our relationship to distant strangers is that fellow members of a nation state benefit from being involved in a dense web of coercion that demands special justification. A government routinely and massively coerces those within its territorial jurisdiction. A government enforces a large set of laws including criminal and civil law by an apparatus of courts, prisons, and police.

On its face there is something deeply puzzling about the claim that being subject to significant coercion automatically triggers a requirement of compensation.[12] If I have no moral right to do *X* and indeed am morally obligated to refrain from doing *X*, why should it be deemed *prima facie* wrongful to coerce me from doing *X*? To be sure, it may be that doing or refraining from *X* is not a big deal, morally speaking, so too little is at stake to warrant coercion that protects people from being harmed ever so slightly by my doing of *X*. So let us confine our attention to wrongful conduct and violations of rights that are not *de minimis*.

Coercion might take the form of physically preventing one from doing a certain act, as when a concrete barrier erected by the state highway department blocks me from swerving the car I am driving into traffic headed in the opposite direction. Coercion might also take the form of a threat that attaches negative consequences to my doing some act and hence gives me disincentive to doing it that suffices to deter me from doing it (or would suffice if I was otherwise attracted to choosing it). But again, if I have no right to do *X* and would significantly wrong someone if I did it, why is it morally problematic to issue a coercive threat "Don't do *X* or else!"? If I am not anyway tempted to do *X*, the threat is idle, and if I am tempted, it hardly seems initially plausible that I am then owed compensation for being coerced not to do what I anyway should not have done.

In special cases coercion intended to block agents from immoral action would be gratuitous and insulting, and perhaps wrong on that ground. In a community of stalwart teetotalers, each of whom abstains entirely from consumption of alcohol on principle, a coercive

---

[12] I deny that coercing someone automatically puts one under special obligations to that person. Coercion is an act to be assessed like any other (according to its consequences, I would hold). But I do not argue in this essay against the claim that it can matter morally whether one does or allows harm to others, as deontologists hold. Nor is it the case that duties of global justice entirely consist of duties to aid distant needy strangers. A deontologist will pay special heed to duties to refrain from harming distant needy strangers (in certain ways that violate rights). Consider in this connection the agricultural subsidies that the United States and European governments lavish on their farmers, which enable them to compete on unfair terms with poor farmers in developing nations. "Reducing these subsidies and removing agricultural trade barriers is [sic] one of the most important things that rich countries can do for millions of people to escape poverty all over the world," said Ian Goldin, the World Bank's Vice President for External Affairs. "It's not an exaggeration to say that rich countries' agricultural policies lead to starvation" (quoted from Elizabeth Becker, "Western Farmers Fear Third-World Challenge to Subsidies," *New York Times*, Tuesday, September 9, 2003, p. A8).

rule forbidding drunken driving might be deemed to carry the implication that there is a substantial possibility that someone might drink and drive drunk. If this insinuation is false, instituting such a rule might constitute an immoral insult.

I myself am not at all sure that a coercive rule need be insulting in these circumstances. The legislature might enact the law against drunken driving and accompany it with an explicit declaration that the passage of this law does not reflect doubts about the virtue of the citizens, but simply expresses the idea that it is morally important that the rights of people to travel about the roads without being molested by drunk drivers be upheld. Be that as it may, this is a special case.

5. Miller's Argument

Richard W. Miller advances an argument from coercion to the moral imperative of patriotic priority that is well worth considering.

He asserts that one would not be morally required to save a person falling from a height if saving his or her life would bring serious injury (less than death) on oneself.

Next consider the position of someone who is asked to agree to be subject to a scheme of political coercion. Miller writes that "until domestic political arrangements have done as much as they can (under the rule of law and while respecting civil and political liberty) to eliminate serious burdens of domestic inequality of life-prospects," one can reasonably reject such political arrangements.[13] On a contractualist view, political arrangements are morally acceptable just in case no one (who is motivated to live in conformity to norms that no one similarly motivated could reasonably reject) could reasonably reject them.[14] I shall interpret Miller as here claiming that political arrangements for a society are reasonably rejectable unless (given priority to principles of basic liberty and equal opportunity) they satisfy domestic maximin: These arrangements must maximize the resources that go to the worst off. In particular, domestic maximin takes strict priority over government-mandated aid to foreigners.

[13] Miller, "Cosmopolitan Respect and Patriotic Concern," p. 210.

[14] T. M. Scanlon, *What We Owe to Each Other* (Cambridge: Harvard University Press, 1998), Chapters 4–5.

The idea is that those who are burdened by domestic inequality have a good excuse not to accept a scheme of political coercion that channels aid to those who are most impoverished anywhere on the globe at cost to arrangements that could lessen the serious burdens of domestic inequality. The good excuse is just like the good excuse that the person has, who could save a person's life in an emergency, but only at the cost of serious injury to oneself. In each case the cost that must be borne by the one who would be in effect giving aid is more than one can reasonably demand.

But if foreign aid to the global needy is not morally required, it would be morally wrong coercively to impose it on people who suffer the greatest loss if aid is given. Miller puts the point this way: "It shows a lack of respect for another to force her to do more than she must to do her fair share in the task of world-improvement."[15] He holds that insistence on global egalitarianism at cost to those who would benefit from patriotic priority would erode the mutual trust and solidarity among members of the nation-state. Those who are burdened by global egalitarianism could not give willing and informed consent to their domestic political arrangements and simultaneously maintain their self-respect. For self-respect involves upholding one's own significant moral rights, and one's significant moral rights include a right to domestic maximin that trumps any putative right of foreign strangers to aid. In this way a Kantian impartial morality of respect is drawn into service to support patriotic priority.

In response, I do not accept Miller's starting point, the thought that it is morally permissible to refrain from rescuing a (healthy, innocent) person if the rescue would impose serious injury on oneself. If a life is at stake, and there is no alternative action one could perform instead of this rescue that would do even more good, the balance of good to harm is so favorable that one morally ought to perform the rescue. So say I. But I do accept that in the circumstances he describes it would be excusable not to perform such a brave rescue. Almost anybody would flinch, and shrink back from incurring broken bones or an equivalent violent injury to oneself, even to save a life. Declining to rescue would strictly speaking be morally wrong, impermissible, but likely not blameworthy.

At any rate, the choice of refraining from engaging in a heroic rescue at great and palpable and immediate cost to oneself is morally

[15] Miller, "Cosmopolitan Respect and Patriotic Concern," p. 215.

very different from the issue, can one reasonably reject a political scheme that takes inequality-alleviating benefits that might have gone to oneself and fellow compatriots and instead channels them to people elsewhere on the globe who are worse off than oneself and in greater need of the benefits. In the one case one is asked to make a psychologically difficult choice to throw oneself in harm's way. In the second case no actual choice is required. The hypothetical question for anybody is, would it be reasonable to reject political arrangements on the ground that they do not maximin the resource share of the worst off of those subject to the arrangements, but instead shift resources to other people not subject to the arrangements who are even worse off. The question here is just what is reasonable, what is justified. The further question whether it might be excusable to reject what it would not be reasonable to reject is not in play.

Of course, the question whether it is excusable to refrain from extreme and immediate self-sacrifice that impartial principle demands is not the same as the question, whether coercion to induce one to make the self-sacrifice would be justified, or whether one could not reasonably reject a moral principle that allows coercion in these circumstances. I suppose it would likely be excusable and not blameworthy at all for a person to refrain from a severely self-sacrificing act that provides greater offsetting benefits to others. But at the same time I think it would not be reasonable to reject a moral principle that allows coercion for the greater good in cases of this sort. If you could credibly threaten me in such a way as to induce me to do the morally justified self-sacrificing act that I would otherwise not do, you would be justified in making such a coercive threat. The questions discussed in this paragraph, which should elicit "Yes" answers, are closer in substance to the question whether a state coercive scheme that deviates from patriotic priority by giving higher priority to getting aid to those who are most in need wherever they might live is justifiable.

The issue, how demanding are the morally reasonable principles that dictate that better off persons are obligated to alleviate the needs of the truly disadvantaged, is distinct from the issue, whether or not the existence of a web of mutually beneficial coercion binding the better off and some of the less needy brings it about that these less needy persons move higher in the queue that reflects who should benefit from morally required efforts of the better off to aid the needy. This essay defends the position that however demanding or undemanding are the principles that require aid to the needy, national borders and the webs of mutually beneficial coercion within them are strictly irrelevant to determining who should be aided. One's place in the queue that reflects the comparative moral urgency of channeling aid to one person rather than another depends only on how badly off one is and to what extent one's condition would improve with an infusion of resources. So patriotic priority should be rejected. However, it should be noted that the practical significance of this result depends on the demandingness and stringency of duties to aid the needy. If such duties require little or if the requirements they impose are easily overridden by other moral considerations, then there is lots of moral slack, which might be taken up by many sorts of moral considerations including patriotic ties. The three preceding paragraphs point toward arguments that reduce this slack if they prove successful.

Miller inserts another thought in the web of argumentative support for patriotic priority. We should hold it to be a morally urgent matter to do what we can to ensure that our relations with fellow participants in the nation-state scheme of cooperation should be marked by willing trust and shared principled commitment to do our assigned part in the scheme. Moreover, this moral concern to sustain willing cooperation among all members of society is inherently agent-relative. We have special reason not just to do whatever produces greater principled commitment to schemes of cooperation wherever and whenever they might be found but specifically to contribute to sustaining the moral quality of our own political community. If political society coerces individuals in a mutual benefit scheme that benefits some far more than others, without doing the most that can be done to minimize the burdens of this domestic inequality, but instead expends resources to alleviate misery and human need across the globe, the self-respecting person burdened by this scheme cannot sustain principled acquiescence to it.

This appeal to what self-respect requires does not advance the argument in support of patriotic priority. A self-respecting person values her own moral rights and does not lightly accept a political scheme that coercively tramples on them. But this does not tell us where the borders of one person's rights are and where the boundaries of other people's rights begin. A moral agent acts toward others with respect, in a way that befits their human dignity. But what way is that? I would say, whatever way is required by moral reasons rightly considered. The appeal to the imperative of respect does not by itself indicate what those reasons are or how to gauge their strength. But then I am puzzled by the position that the advocate of patriotic priority claims to occupy. One might claim there is no case for global egalitarianism. One might develop this skepticism from libertarian premises, for example. But the dispute I am engaged in is an intramural dispute among would-be egalitarians. All sides agree that the sheer fact that there are people in the world whose life prospects are (a) bad and (b) remediable by better off persons (c) at tolerable cost (so that the losses the better off would suffer from aiding the worse off are more than made up by the consequent gains to the worse off) itself constitutes a strong reason to bring it about that aid is forthcoming. But given this moral reason to aid the global needy, why does one forfeit self-respect by accepting a coercive political scheme that gives priority to alleviating global neediness? Why does the respect that each moral agent owes every other moral agent require that one not benefit from or support a coercive political scheme unless it operates to channel benefits to the domestic worse off according to patriotic priority?

6. The Patriotic Priority Position Is Unstable

I want to return to Miller's starting point, the assumption that it is morally acceptable to prefer one's own lesser good to the greater good of others at least when one is choosing among actions none of which would violate the rights of any other person. In another terminology, one always has the morally permissible option to favor oneself (and those near and dear to oneself) in deciding what to do, within the limits of moral constraints that forbid certain actions.

Suppose we accept this starting point, and suppose we accept that the option to favor oneself permits the poor person in a rich society who would be disadvantaged by a national policy that helps the global poor to prefer instead a policy of patriotic priority that favors her. Then my worry is that this line of thought is an unstable support for Miller's position. On the same ground a person with above-average prospects in a rich society can reasonably reject a policy of patriotic priority that insists on egalitarianism at the level of the nation state. The advantaged person in a rich society can reject this domestic egalitarianism on the ground that its implementation would impose costs on him and these costs are greater than it is reasonable to expect him to bear. After all, it is wrong to force anyone to do more than she must to do her fair share of world-improvement, as Miller has reminded us. If the personal prerogative to favor oneself negates that presumption in favor of global egalitarianism when the person with below-average prospects in a rich society insists on the patriotic priority, then I do not see why by parity of reasoning the personal prerogative to favor oneself does not likewise negate the presumption in favor of domestic egalitarianism (the personal prerogative) when the person with above-average prospects in a rich society insists that domestic egalitarianism would impose costs on him that it is reasonable for him to reject.

This argument, so far as I can see, holds across positions that take the egalitarian justice obligation to help the needy and disadvantaged to be more or less demanding. Perhaps egalitarian justice, as it were, imposes a tax rate of one per cent on the incomes of the better off, or a tax rate near 100%, or anywhere in between. This essay leaves this issue to the side. My question concerns the distribution of the resources that egalitarian justice gathers from better off individuals in wealthy societies. My claim is that one's place in the queue for receipt of these benefits is set by how needy and disadvantaged one is, not by national borders. Some egalitarian justice function that pays no attention to borders determines a redistribution of resources across various levels of advantage and disadvantage. Now we are to imagine individuals lodging a moral objection against their treatment by this queue. The objection is that they should be specially favored by egalitarian redistribution because they are compatriots of the better off individuals who are being required to disgorge some of their advantages. After all, a scheme of coercion is being imposed on them, and this scheme operates in such a way that inequalities arise that are burdensome to them. The response is that the scheme of coercion, in other words the rule of law that operates within a nation state, is mutually beneficial. All who are not bent on wrongful criminality are better off with the scheme in place than they would be if the scheme were eliminated or had never been established. Benefiting by being a part of a productive coercive scheme does not give one special claims on others who happen to benefit even more – and especially not special claims that trump the rights that neediness per se establishes to the wherewithal for a better life when the cost of its provision is reasonable, all things considered.

We can pose this issue in contractarian terms. What rules would it be reasonable for people to agree to as norms to govern their interactions with others similarly motivated? Again, we set aside the issue, to exactly what extent it is reasonable that the lucky and advantaged should be required to submit to measures that improve the life prospects of the unlucky and disadvantaged. Let us suppose with Miller that obligations to aid others are limited and that one has the option to favor oneself up to a point.[16] What I still do not see is why any reason so far has been given to suppose that it is reasonable for those who are relatively worse off within a rich nation, though still advantaged when compared to people everywhere, to insist on special favor as against the globally worse off.[17] True, the worse off national compatriots are coerced by the rule of law in place in the nation, and true, they cannot reasonably be said voluntarily to participate in this scheme of coercion. It is simply imposed on all who reside within the territory marked off by the national borders. But, so far as I can see, this subjection to coercion is a lucky unchosen advantage, a windfall from which they benefit. No reason emerges from this quarter that makes it reasonable for poor members of rich nations to insist on patriotic priority or that renders it unreasonable for the global poor to reject it.

On the other hand, if it is reasonable for the relatively disadvantaged in rich nations to insist that resources that would render them significantly better off not be exported to aid people who are far needier, by the same token it would be reasonable for the relatively advantaged in rich nations to insist that resources that would render them significantly better off not be transferred to people who are far needier than they are, whether these people reside within the nation in question or in some other region of the globe. What is sauce for the goose is sauce for the gander.

---

[16] We can also accept that some forms of priority for friends and others to whom one has special ties are morally permissible. What I deny in this essay is that *patriotic* priority is acceptable. Merely being co-residents of the same country does not suffice to establish a special tie that warrants partiality. Nor can individuals acquire such obligations merely by voluntarily asserting them.

[17] One might entertain the thought that the poor who live in proximity to the rich and super rich suffer from relative deprivation that renders them objectively worse off than distant others who are materially more poor. But this sort of consideration, whether correct or incorrect, has no tendency to justify patriotic priority. To the extent that relative deprivation really does make one worse off according to the proper measure of people's condition, the global egalitarian justice function would already properly adjust for this factor.

7. Coercion and Compensation Reconsidered

Consider a simple case of morally unproblematic coercion. Suppose that *A* is well-off, on the way to leading an extremely good, enviable life. *B* lives close to *A*, *C* farther away. Both *B* and *C* are very needy, on the way to leading a bad, unenviable life, but *C* is far worse off than *B*. As it happens, *A* could transfer some of her resources to *B* or to *C*, and could secure a significant welfare gain of the same size for either *B* or *C* at reasonable cost to herself (the same cost, whether she picks *B* or *C* to be the recipient of aid). Now add the further detail that *B* and *C* are equally disposed violently to attack *A* wrongfully if the chance arises. This ill will reduces the entitlement of either *B* or *C* to a share of *A*'s plentiful resources, but for the sake of the example suppose that allowing for reduction, there is still ample moral reason for *A* to transfer resources to some of *B* and *C*. In response to the ill will, *A* credibly threatens harm to *B* if *B* wrongfully inflicts violent attack on her. The threat is effective, so *B* is coerced not to harm *A*. *A* does not threaten and coerce *C*, who is located farther away, and hence poses no threat to *A* that would justify a coercive response by her.

According to many plausible conceptions of global justice, *A* has greater obligation in these circumstances to aid *C* rather than *B*. *C* is needier than *B*, worse off on the whole, and can be aided to the same extent by a given level of sacrifice by *A*. The fact that *B* is closer to *A* than *C* is not per se morally relevant.

In this scenario as described, it would (I submit) be wildly implausible to hold that the sheer fact that *A* justifiably coerces *B* somehow increases *B*'s entitlement to be the beneficiary of *A*'s obligation to aid the needy. True, *A* benefits from imposing a scheme of coercion on *B*, but if this scheme is justified, suffering coercion at the hands of *A* simply does not constitute a *prima facie* wrong of any sort that might demand compensation.

But this simple scenario contains everything that the advocates of patriotic bias hold to be morally necessary to shift an individual's obligation toward favoring compatriots over needier foreigners. *A* helps to sustain a scheme of coercion that constrains *B* but not *C*. The scheme benefits *A*. It is then claimed that the morality of respect requires that *A* give resources to *B* rather than to *C*, even if this means that *C*'s urgent needs go unmet while *B* ends up far better off than *C*. The claim is that *B* could not submit to a set of rules that mandated no priority be assigned to the satisfaction of her needs over the greater needs of *C* without forfeiting self-respect. In contrast, *C* could submit to a set of rules that mandated favoring *B* even at great cost to herself without forfeiting self-respect.

If the coercion that *A* imposes on *B* were morally unjustified, then it is quite plausible that, at the least, *A* should compensate *B* for the damage done by this coercion (if not desist from it altogether). But why suppose this is the case? No reasons have been proposed. The considerations of respect and self-respect that advocates of patriotic bias cite as justifying the bias under examination turn out to be neutral between this policy and straight egalitarian global justice without any bias at all. In other words, the argument begs the question.

Of course there is the possibility that *A* is justified in coercing *B*, but only if *A* compensates *B* for the insult of coercion. The way would then be open to argue that maintenance of egalitarian policies that strongly favor the badly off who are subject to this coercion, but not others, would be appropriate compensation.

However, I see no argument in the vicinity that makes this possibility look anywhere near compelling. Here we return to the discussion of the previous sections, which searched in vain for such arguments.

This point can be restated. One cannot just say that either coercion is justified, in which case no compensation to the coerced is owed, or the coercion is not justified, in which case it should not occur. There is a third alternative: perhaps coercion is morally permissible but only on the condition that adequate compensation is paid to those coerced. Here what should be said is that if I am contemplating coercion of others to benefit myself, a condition on the acceptability of such coercion is that it does not prevent me from fulfilling prior serious moral duties. Given that global justice duties are fulfilled, it might be acceptable for me with others to institute a coercive scheme that benefits us at cost to others, provided those coerced to their disadvantage are adequately compensated.[18]

8. Coercion and Autonomy

Another view of the significance of coercion stresses the value of autonomy. The idea is that coercion requires a justification, that

[18] Recall that this essay does not take a stand as to how demanding such pure beneficence requirements to aid the needy are. My claim is that whatever their size, one cannot whittle them into smaller size by instituting coercion to benefit oneself and then claim one now has a strict duty to compensate the coerced that trumps the beneficence obligation.

shows how the cost to autonomy that coercion involves is here morally offset. States massively coerce the inhabitants of their territory, so they massively infringe their autonomy, which requires a justification. State coercion is morally acceptable only if it could elicit the consent of all affected parties if they were fully reasonable.[19]

Autonomy here is self-rule. This is partly an individual achievement. I fail to rule myself if I succumb through weakness of will to desires that I disavow. Autonomy on this conception is also in part a feature of the environment of the agent. I fail to rule myself if the actions I choose are selected solely to avoid penalties imposed by other people. If the actions I choose throughout my life are dictated by a natural threat that gives me little scope for developing myself in ways I would prefer, my life is ruled by the threat, not by me. In Joseph Raz's example, if I spend my life on a small island moving about to avoid a tiger that continuously seeks to devour me, I am deprived of autonomy.[20]

An autonomous person lives her life in conformity with values and desires that she affirms after critical reflection. This condition could be satisfied by a person who entirely lacks external freedom. She is imprisoned, say, and tied down, so she has no significant scope for choosing what actions to perform. But her will remains steadily oriented to conformity to the values and desires that she affirms. Autonomy requires an environment that cooperates with self-rule by allowing scope for choice of any of a variety of plans of life that would seek different valuable aims. In addition, as often conceived, autonomy is especially averse to coercion. Throughout the course of her life the more an individual's important life choices are constrained or manipulated by coercion, the less autonomous is the person over the course of her life.

Coercion occurs when one person threatens another and the threatened person complies with the threat, choosing the act that complies in order to avoid the threatened penalty for noncompliance. This definition is rough, but good enough for present purposes.[21]

---

[19] Michael Blake develops this line of thought in Blake, "Distributive Justice, State Coercion, and Autonomy."

[20] Joseph Raz, *The Morality of Freedom* (Oxford: Oxford University Press, 1986), p. 374. On the notion of autonomy, see also George Sher, *Beyond Neutrality: Perfectionism and Politics* (Cambridge: Cambridge University Press, 1997), Chapters 3 and 4.

[21] See Robert Nozick, *Socratic Puzzles* (Cambridge: Harvard University Press, 1997), pp. 15–44.

Notice that threats, even those that pose severe penalties, do not coerce an individual who complies if desire to avoid the threatened penalty does not lead the individual to choose the act that happens to comply. Laws forbidding murder threaten very severe penalties, but these laws do not coerce me not to murder my wife if my reasons for refraining from murder that actually cause my refraining do not involve the threat of penalties. Generalizing from this case, a full panoply of criminal and civil laws that are all morally justified might be backed up by the gallows, prison, and fines, but would not in the slightest diminish the autonomy of fully moral and reasonable persons, who are moved to do what is moral because they see that there are good moral reasons for doing it. The laws do not actually coerce fully reasonable and moral persons.

Nonetheless we can concede that if one is wandering about a city surrounded by impassable high walls, even if one never wants to wander outside the city walls (and even if one's desires in this regard are not distorted by adaptive preference formation), one would have greater freedom to live one's life as one chooses if egress from the city were possible. The city's laws enforced by criminal law sanctions might limit one's freedom in much the same way.

But not every limitation of one's freedom significantly reduces one's opportunity to be autonomous. The rule of law blocks one from doing certain things but opens other possible courses of action that would not otherwise be available. A set of laws that reduces one's freedom in order to ensure that everyone's moral rights are respected, including one's own, can leave one enormous freedom to live one's life in any of many significantly different ways, to be a significant part-author of one's life, to live autonomously.

If one is set on a criminal life, or would venture on this path if it were not for the effective deterrence set in place by the system of criminal justice, then one does clearly suffer significant coercion and significant loss of autonomy. But this example shows that autonomy does not have constant value across all of the settings in which people's actions might expand or contract it. If one has morally innocent life aims, and state coercion wrongfully and coercively blocks one from pursuing them, one has suffered grievous loss of autonomy. If the state coercion that blocks one from effective pursuit of one's innocent aims is non-wrongful (because the cost to oneself is outweighed by gains to others as assessed by fair principle), the loss to one's autonomy is morally of less significance. This is especially so if the system of criminal justice law and state coercion leaves one large freedom to pursue a wide array of life plans and if one significantly benefits on the whole from the fact that the scheme is in place (compared to some anarchic alternative in which one is not troubled by state coercion). State coercion and individual autonomy are fully compatible.

Of course, if the imposition of state coercion on less well off members of a wealthy nation would be wrongful unless those imposed on were compensated by special intrastate egalitarian redistribution in line with patriotic priority, then according to the view just set forth, the imposition of this coercion on the less advantaged would constitute a significant injury to their autonomy. But it would be question begging for the advocate of patriotic priority to just assume this is so. Once again the considerations marshaled by the advocate of patriotic priority do no more than pose the issue and do not under scrutiny reveal reasons to favor the patriotic priority resolution of the issue.

My conclusion, then, is that it is not so that the coercive laws that the state enforces must massively infringe the autonomy of those subject to the laws and can only be justified *inter alia* if the system of laws provides adequate compensation for this loss of autonomy. If the laws steer people toward acts that all things considered they morally ought to perform, then either they do not actually infringe on autonomy (if those regulated by the laws are reasonable and moral) or they do infringe on autonomy (if those regulated by the laws are prone to act immorally and coerced by the laws to refrain from doing so), but the autonomy that is thereby lost is not significantly valuable. In neither case does the imposition of state coercion generate an obligation to compensate those who are coerced. The reasonable and moral are not coerced and the unreasonable and immoral are not deserving of compensation to offset the harm coercion imposes on them.

9. Coercion Excluding Would-Be Immigrants

Assume for the sake of the argument that I am wrong to deny that coercion per se seriously dampens autonomy and so coercion is generally justifiable only if those who coerce adequately compensate those who suffer losses of autonomy due to coercion. This concession does not improve the case for patriotic priority in the contemporary world.

Notice that rich nations coerce would-be entrants at the border to refrain from entry. The members of rich nations on the whole and on the average gain advantages, or believe they gain advantages, from coercively denying entry to would-be immigrants. Consider those immigrants who are impoverished and disadvantaged, worse off than the worst off members of the rich nations that exclude them.

If coercion seriously injures autonomy, this coercion at the border seriously injures the autonomy of those who are forcibly excluded. This exclusion is far more negatively consequential for the expectable quality of the lives of the excluded than is the scheme of coercion imposed on everyone within the rich nation via the rule of law, which tends to advantage all those coerced even though the advantages are not spread evenly across the members.

So if coercion injures autonomy and automatically calls for compensation, then I submit that the coercion imposed by the members of rich nations on impoverished would-be immigrants is a far more serious violation of their autonomy and demands far more compensation than the mutually beneficial scheme of coercion the members impose on each other.

Once again the moral scenario conjured up by the advocates of patriotic priority collapses under examination.

Department of Philosophy
University of California at San Diego
9500 Gilman Drive
La Jolla, CA 92093-0119
USA
E-mail: rarneson@ucsd.edu

DALE JAMIESON

DUTIES TO THE DISTANT: AID, ASSISTANCE, AND INTERVENTION IN THE DEVELOPING WORLD

(Received 14 May 2004; accepted in revised form 4 June 2004)

ABSTRACT. In his classic article, "Famine, Affluence, and Morality (*Philosophy and Public Affairs* 1 (1972), pp. 229–243)," Peter Singer claimed that affluent people in the developed world are morally obligated to transfer large amounts of resources to poor people in the developing world. For present purposes I will not call Singer's argument into question. While people can reasonably disagree about exactly how demanding morality is with respect to duties to the desperate, there is little question in my mind that it is much more demanding than common sense morality or our everyday behavior suggests. Even someone who disagrees with this might still find some interest in seeing what a demanding morality would imply for well-off residents of the rich countries of the world. I proceed in the following way. First, I survey humanitarian aid, development assistance, and intervention to protect human rights as ways of discharging duties to the desperate. I claim that we should be more cautious about such policies than is often thought. I go on to suggest two principles that should guide our actions, based on an appreciation of our roles, relationships, and the social and political context in which we find ourselves.

KEY WORDS: development, famine, intervention, poverty, Peter Singer

1. Introduction

In his classic article, "Famine, Affluence, and Morality," Peter Singer claimed that affluent people in the developed world are morally obligated to transfer large amounts of resources to poor people in the developing world.[1] He derived this conclusion from two principles, both of which he believed are backed by the authority of common sense. The first principle is "that suffering and death from lack of food, shelter, and medical care are bad."[2] The second is that "if it is in our power to prevent something bad from happening, without

[1] Peter Singer, "Famine, Affluence, and Morality," *Philosophy and Public Affairs* 1(1972), pp. 229–243.
[2] Singer, "Famine, Affluence and Morality," p. 231.

thereby sacrificing anything of comparable moral importance, we ought morally to do it."[3]

Peter Unger has estimated (conservatively, he thinks) that donating $200 to UNICEF or OXFAM will save the life of a child.[4] $200 does not go very far when it comes to buying new clothes, and some couples spend that much for opera tickets, seats at a Rolling Stones concert, or a fancy dinner in a trendy restaurant. Clearly, these goods are not of comparable moral importance to saving the life of a child. Even a weaker principle, one that requires us to prevent something bad from happening so long as we do not sacrifice "anything morally significant," appears to have similar consequences, since new clothes, fancy dinners, and concerts do not appear to be morally significant goods.[5] It appears that we should be prepared to sacrifice quite a lot by way of such luxury goods in order to save lives.

Singer demonstrates the urgency of our duty with the following analogy. Suppose that "I am walking past a shallow pond and see a child drowning … I ought to wade in and pull the child out. This will mean getting my clothes muddy, but this is insignificant, while the death of the child would presumably be a very bad thing."[6]

For those of us who can afford concert tickets and restaurant meals, donating $200 to OXFAM is equivalent to getting our clothes muddy. The fact that the child who would be saved by our donation is distant or not personally known to us does not relieve us of the obligation to act. What matters is that lives can effectively be saved simply by donating to organizations such as OXFAM. The duty to transfer these resources is not a matter of charity or supererogatory behavior, but of moral obligation.

There are questions, Singer admits, about the conditions under which aid is efficacious, and he grants that if for some reason such aid would not save lives, or paradoxically would produce more suffering, then we have no obligation to engage in such transfers. However, he regards these concerns as "more practical than philosophical"; they do not touch his conclusion about what morality demands.[7]

---

[3] Singer, "Famine, Affluence and Morality," p. 231.

[4] Peter Unger, *Living High and Letting Die* (New York: Oxford University Press, 1996), pp. 136–139.

[5] I would challenge this view in a fuller exposition but, even so, Singer's central claim would emerge unscathed.

[6] Singer, "Famine, Affluence, and Morality," p. 231.

[7] Singer, "Famine, Affluence, and Morality," p. 239.

The present paper is almost wholly "practical." I make no apology for this since, as Singer writes, "[W]hat is the point of relating philosophy to public...affairs if we do not take our conclusions seriously?"[8] We act in the world and not (only) in some conceptual ether. Addressing these "practical" questions is part of taking our conclusions seriously.

For present purposes I will not call Singer's argument into question. While people can reasonably disagree about exactly how demanding morality is with respect to duties to the desperate, there is little question in my mind that it is much more demanding than common sense morality or our everyday behavior suggests. Even someone who disagrees with this might still find some interest in seeing what a demanding morality would imply for well-off residents of the rich countries of the world.

I proceed in the following way. First, I survey humanitarian aid, development assistance, and intervention to protect human rights as ways of discharging duties to the desperate. I claim that we should be more cautious about such policies than is often thought. I go on to suggest two principles that should guide our actions, based on an appreciation of our roles, relationships, and the social and political context in which we find ourselves.

2. Humanitarian Aid

"Famine, Affluence, and Morality" was written in response to an immediate humanitarian crisis. In November 1971, the confluence of war, poverty, and natural disaster had created nine million refugees in East Bengal, and Singer was appealing for immediate life-saving aid.

Such appeals became increasingly common throughout the 1970s and 1980s, and reached their peak in response to the Ethiopian famine of 1983–1985. On 7 October 1984, the British Broadcasting Corporation (BBC) broadcast horrific images from a refugee camp in Korem, Ethiopia, showing dying children and starving women as far as the eye could see. The voiceover by Michael Buerk characterized the scene as "a Biblical famine – now in the twentieth century...the closest thing to hell on earth."[9] The Irish rock musician, Bob Geldof,

[8] Singer, "Famine, Affluence, and Morality," p. 242.

[9] As quoted in Jenny Edkins, *Whose Hunger? Concepts of Famine, Practices of Aid* (Minneapolis: University of Minnesota Press, 2000), p. 108.

immediately rushed into the studio with an all star line-up to record "Do They Know It's Christmas." The record sold nearly 4 million copies in the United Kingdom alone, and was quickly followed by "We Are the World," produced by Quincy Jones, in the United States. Geldof went on to organize the LiveAid concert the following July, which was broadcast simultaneously from London and Philadelphia, and viewed by 1.5 billion people around the world. The records and concert ultimately raised between $100 and $500 million for famine relief in Africa.

These celebrity-driven, media-centered projects were valuable for a number of reasons. They created awareness of suffering in Africa, motivated people to act, and raised large sums of money. However, these events also contributed to creating some important misconceptions about the causes, consequences, and context of the suffering which they highlighted.

We can call the picture of humanitarian aid that emerged from these events the "LiveAid Conception." On this view, humanitarian aid is a response to the immediate needs of innocent people (primarily women and children), whose lives are threatened by hunger as a consequence of an anomalous event (typically a natural disaster such as a drought). This picture invites a strong sympathetic response: "there but for fortune..." However, in many respects the LiveAid Conception is at odds with most recent understandings of such events. This conception decontextualizes, depoliticizes, and dehistoricizes famine, as well as masking the victims' agency.

Famine has a history: it is not simply a series of random occurrences, caused by nature, that happen to strike unfortunate people. Over the last century famine occurred on almost every continent, but within that period there was a dramatic movement towards isolating famine, first to Asia and Africa, then to Africa alone. While in recent years famine has occurred in North Korea, and food insecurity has increased in parts of the Middle East, Central Asia, and perhaps India, Africa remains famine's epicenter.

Increasingly, famine is seen as a dramatic moment in a process that almost always involves war, vulnerability, systematic violations of human rights, and radically unequal power relationships.[10]

[10] There is quite a lot to say about each of these phenomena, perhaps especially vulnerability. Ecological degradation is often overlooked as a dimension of vulnerability. For a convenient way into the literature of vulnerability, see James Lewis, *Development in Disaster-Prone Places: Studies of Vulnerability* (London: Intermediate Technology, 1999).

Extreme natural events such as droughts or cyclones may be the proximate causes, but without these other conditions famine almost never occurs. In addition to taking a terrible toll of its own, war is now seen as almost essential to famine and to complex humanitarian emergencies generally.

From 1990–2000, two million children died in wars, three times the total number of American soldiers killed throughout history. In twentieth century wars it was generally safer to be a soldier than a civilian. Since the Treaty of Westphalia in 1648 established the modern state system, about 150 million people have been killed by their own governments. Indeed, it is civil wars, rather than wars against external enemies, that are most often implicated in famine. The Ethiopian famine of the early 1980s should be seen in this light.

Most scholars now agree that the main cause of the famine was not drought, but the government's policy of forcible resettlement, a policy used as a tactic in its war against secessionist rebels.[11] As part of a commemoration of the tenth anniversary of the famine, a diverse group of officials, activists, and academics gathered in Addis Ababa, and at the end of the meeting issued a communique which began: "[T]he 1984–1985 famine was in fact a political crisis characterized more appropriately by war than by drought."[12]

Other aspects of the LiveAid conception are misleading as well. While many of the victims of famine and other humanitarian emergencies are women and children, statistics suggest that men and adolescents are more at risk.[13] Females may be less vulnerable because they store more body weight than males. Famines also lead to declines in fertility, thus lowering rates of maternal mortality. Perhaps the BBC documentarians saw a sea of women and children at Korem because the men had migrated to seek employment or had already succumbed.

Most famine victims die of disease rather than literally starving to death. Displacement and the breakdown in systems of water supply and waste disposal lead to increased exposure to disease. A compromised nutritional status leads to increased susceptibility. Together they result in epidemics of diarrhea, gastro-enteritis, dysentery, and other infectious diseases.

---

[11] David Rieff, *A Bed for the Night: Humanitarianism in Crisis* (New York: Simon and Schuster, 2002), pp. 39–40.

[12] As quoted in Edkins, *Whose Hunger?*, p. 6.

[13] Stephen Devereux, *Famine in the Twentieth Century*, Working Paper 105, Institute of Development Studies, University of Sussex, Brighton, UK, p. 11.

Nor are those who suffer in famines always passive victims struck down by the fickle finger of fate. They are often agents in highly complex political struggles. Those who suffered most in the Ethiopian famine of 1983–1985 were members of ethnic groups hostile to the government or involved in the civil war. Many of the Hutus dying in the refugee camps in Zaire from 1994–1996 were implicated in the 1994 genocide directed at the Tutsis. Elements of the Kosovar community, forcibly expelled from Serbia in 1998–1999, had been involved in attacks on government officials for more than a decade in deliberate attempts to provoke a Serbian reaction that would lead to international intervention – a tactic that succeeded.

Widespread acceptance of the LiveAid Conception can have important consequences. The quick disillusionment of the US public with the Somalian intervention after the "Blackhawk down" incident in 1991 was related to the way the intervention had been framed: The Somali people were starving in a famine caused by drought, and the US was there to help feed them. No wonder many in the US were angry and bewildered when their well-meaning soldiers were killed and their bodies dragged through the streets.

Singer's analogy of the drowning child in the pond mirrors the LiveAid Conception. We have no idea of the history, context, and politics surrounding the situation that we confront. Whose child is this? How did the child get into the pond? What is likely to happen to the child once she or he is saved? While the answers to these questions are unlikely to alter the fact that we ought to save the child,[14] they affect the meaning and significance of our action.

Moreover, a further question can be asked.

> What if, every day, as Singer walks past the pond, fifty children were close to drowning? Every day, he takes his self-imposed obligation seriously, and spends the day rescuing them, abandoning his lectures. Princeton gets wind of this and does not share his ethical orientation. Now it is one thing to expect someone to save a drowning child and give up one lecture, but it is quite another–if there are tens or thousands drowning (or starving, or ill) everyday–to expect him to devote himself to being a lifeguard instead of a teacher. [15]

Since rich people in affluent countries are only a thin veneer on a global population that largely lives in poverty (about one-sixth

[14] If we were certain that the child would grow up to be an Adolf Hitler or a Charles Manson, that would be a different matter.

[15] This question is raised by Andrew Kuper, "More Than Charity: Cosmopolitan Alternatives to the 'Singer Solution,'" *Ethics and International Affairs* 16 (2002), p. 110.

compared to one-half), this latter scenario which requires repeated acts of life-saving is in fact a more apt analogy than Singer's original "one off" example.

Reflecting the persistent ubiquity of global misery, humanitarian assistance has become an industry rather than a temporary response to isolated disasters in distant lands. $66 billion per year is spent on humanitarian assistance programs, including about 10% of the foreign aid budget of the US. There are sites around the world where humanitarian assistance has been continuously delivered for decades, with no end in sight (e.g., some Palestinian refugee camps). In such cases, rather than providing temporary life-saving aid, humanitarian assistance has become the *de facto* policy of a world that is unwilling to take decisive action to address the underlying causes of global poverty.

In the summer of 2003, millions of Ethiopians were again at risk from famine, and *The New York Times* was once again blaming nature, asserting that "[D]rought is the primary reason Ethiopians go hungry."[16] Yet a report from Save the Children and the Institute for Development Studies claims that:

> Almost 20 years on from the Ethiopian famine that captured the imagination and generosity of the world, millions of people in the historically famine-prone north-eastern highlands of Ethiopia are worse off and more vulnerable than ever...Ethiopia is now chronically dependent on food aid...[I]ncreasing volumes of... international assistance to meet emergency appeals and annual food deficits cannot be a substitute for addressing the underlying causes of chronic food insecurity.[17]

Statistics underline this point. In 1984 the average annual income in Ethiopia was $190; today it is $108. Each year the population increases by 2.7% while the same percentage of topsoil is lost. A recent Christian Aid report blames structural problems such as "the decline in people's assets, collapse of livelihoods and lack of infrastructure...not simply drought, for creating vulnerability to starvation."[18] The report goes on to say that "food aid is not the answer."

It is difficult to believe that our duties to the distant poor are exhausted simply by contributing to programs that keep them alive from one crisis to another. Certainly the opera fans among us would hope that sacrificing our tickets would produce more far-reaching

[16] 28 July 2003; available on the web at http://www.cindybeads.com/famine.htm.

[17] http://www.reliefweb.int/w/rwb.nsf/0/4b99bcc13144b864c1256d660057dee8?OpenDocument (accessed 4 October 2003).

[18] http://www.christian-aid.org.uk/indepth/0302ethio/fallback.htm (accessed 4 October 2003).

benefits. Instead of saving a child everyday at the cost of missing a lecture and dampening our clothes, it would be far better to prevent these children from falling into the pond in the first place. Providing humanitarian aid is at best a small part of what we should do to address the plight of the poor. It is not the solution to global poverty.

3. Development Assistance

The solution, it might be thought, is development assistance. In the words of an old adage, "if you give a man a fish he will eat for a day, but if you teach him how to fish he will never be hungry." Ethiopia is a good example of the world's failure to act on this insight. While it has received more relief aid in the past 20 years than any other country, it has received very little development aid, even compared to other poor countries.

In the postscript to "Famine, Affluence, and Morality," Singer endorses the idea that providing development assistance is one way we might discharge our duties to the poor. He writes that such assistance "is usually the better long-term investment."[19]

The distinction between development assistance and humanitarian aid is not sharp, and any attempt to draw such a distinction can be challenged. For present purposes let us consider humanitarian aid to be resources provided in order to relieve immediate suffering, and development assistance as resources provided in order to reduce poverty over the long-term.

In recent years a body of literature has developed challenging the effectiveness of development aid.[20] What is striking about this literature is that much of it has been produced by people in the development community, who care deeply about poverty reduction. The main charges are that the funds provided are typically spent inefficiently in ways that benefit special interests rather than the poor; that there is little empirical evidence that development assistance actually

[19] Peter Singer, "Famine Affluence and Morality," in W. Aiken and H. La Follette (eds.) *World Hunger and Moral Obligation*, First Edition (Englewood Cliffs: Prentice-Hall, 1977), p. 35.

[20] This literature includes the following: Thomas W. Dichter, *Despite Good Intentions: Why Development Assistance to the Third World Has Failed* (Amherst: University of Massachusetts Press, 2003); M. Maren, *The Road to Hell: The Ravaging Effects of Foreign Aid and International Charity* (New York: Free Press, 1997). An older but very influential work, is P. T. Bauer, *Equality, the Third World, and Economic Delusion* (Cambridge: Harvard University Press, 1981).

contributes significantly to development; and that there are good theoretical reasons for supposing that development is a multi-dimensional, historical process, which cannot be jump-started by development assistance.

The first point can be illustrated by some statistics. The US spent $30.4 billion on foreign aid between 1948 and the mid-1950s, of which 77% went to suppliers in the US.[21] In the late 1990s the United States Agency for International Development (USAID) reaffirmed that about the same percentage of US aid was still being used to purchase U.S. goods and services. In a 2002 report (that subsequently has been removed from its website), USAID stated that

> [T]he principal beneficiary of America's foreign assistance programs has always been the United States. Close to 80 percent of the U.S. Agency for International Development's (USAID's) contracts and grants go directly to American firms. Foreign assistance programs have helped create major markets for agricultural goods, created new markets for American industrial exports and meant hundreds of thousands of jobs for Americans.[22]

This should not be surprising since US federal law specifies more than forty distinct missions for USAID, ranging from disposing of US agricultural surpluses to strengthening US land grant colleges and universities.[23] While the US is extreme in using foreign assistance programs to benefit domestic political constituencies, it is not alone. In 2001 roughly 40% of all international aid flows were tied to providing such benefits to donors.[24] Perhaps the most egregious example is provided by *Guardian* columnist, George Monbiot. He writes that Britain's Department for International Development gives more money to the right-wing Adam Smith Institute in consultancy fees than it does to such countries as Liberia and Somalia.[25] Even NGOs have become part of this self-serving system through their increasing dependency on government funding. From 1973–1986 the USAID share of the budgets of US NGOs went from 5 to 20%.

---

[21] Cited in Dichter, *Despite Good Intentions*, p. 56.

[22] United States Agency for International Development, "Direct Economic Benefits of US Assistance Programs (By State)." As of this writing (May, 2004), a fragment of the report including this quotation, can be found on the web at http://www.professionalserve.com/CovenantBK/usaid-my.htm.

[23] United States Agency for International Development, p. 188.

[24] http://www.cgdev.org/rankingtherich/home.html (accessed 4 October 2003).

[25] George Monbiot, "On the Edge of Lunacy," Tuesday, 6 January 2004; available on the web at http://www.guardian.co.uk/Columnists/Column/0,5673,1116884,00.html.

Development aid has many purposes, but to a great extent, it is intended to help donors rather than the recipients of aid. Thus it is not surprising that such aid is not spent efficiently when viewed from the perspective of poverty reduction. Poverty reduction is only one of its aims, and in some countries, it is the aim with the weakest political constituency.

Those who benefit from the present system, both donors and recipients, have strong incentives to maintain it. Although development assistance is low compared to other capital flows (a tiny fraction of 1% of global GDP), these funds can be extremely important to particular recipients. For example, according to figures from the mid-1990s, Burkino Faso received 98% of its annual government budget in development assistance, Laos about 80%, Nepal about 50%, Ethiopia about 25%, and Kenya about 15%. Haiti received twice its government's annual budget in development assistance.[26]

Moreover, development aid is not primarily distributed on the basis of need. Together, Russia and Israel receive more than 20% of US development aid, and large sums are increasingly being spent in relatively well-off countries such as Bosnia and Iraq, while the needs of Africa continue to be ignored. Taken together, only 19% of all development aid goes to the 43 least developed countries.[27] The incentives run strong and deep for various parties to continue these flows, even if the plight of the poor is not being substantially improved.

Once the complex, mixed purposes of development aid are understood, it is not surprising that there is little empirical evidence that it has substantially improved the welfare of the poor. A recent report from the Commonwealth Secretariat claims that although more than $1.2 trillion was spent on official development assistance between 1950 and 2000, the gap between the incomes of people in developed and developing countries has widened.[28] The 2002 report from the

---

[26] http://www.cgdev.org/rankingtherich/home.html (accessed October 4, 2003). In view of the latter statistic, it is not surprising that the suspension of aid by the US and the European Union in 2000 ultimately brought about the collapse of the government of Jean-Bertrand Aristide.

[27] As cited in Thomas Pogge, *World Poverty and Human Rights* (London: Blackwell Publishers, 2002), p. 8. For documentation and more recent data, see Bob Bauleh, "Aid for the Poorest? The Distribution and Maldistribution of International Development Assistance," Working Paper 35, Chronic Poverty Research Centre, September 2003 (available on the web at http://www.chronicpoverty.org/pdfs/Aid%20for%20the%20Poorest-%20WP35.pdf).

[28] As reported at http://www.id21.org/society/s9bpm1g1.html (accessed 4 October 2003).

United Nations Development Programme shows that more than 60 countries are poorer today than they were a decade ago. Indeed, in the 3 years since the United Nations adopted its eight Millennium Development Goals, the first of which is to eradicate extreme poverty and hunger, the number of people living on less than a dollar per day in sub-Saharan Africa has increased from 315 to 404 million.[29]

At best, such macroeconomic data are only suggestive about the aggregate effects of development aid, and it is certainly true that at least some development projects benefit poor people. It may also be the case that poor people generally would be even worse off without development aid than they are now. Still, it is difficult to be certain, since little has been done by way of meaningful evaluation.[30] Both Singer and Thomas Pogge admit that development aid is often ineffective in reducing poverty, and then go on to argue that we ought to work harder to make it more effective.[31] However, this response fails to address seriously the fact that rather than failing, development aid may well be succeeding in realizing the goals of both donors and recipients. Development assistance may not lift up the poor, but there is little reason to believe that this was ever its primary purpose. If this is correct, then there is little reason to be optimistic about changing the present system, which is succeeding in its own terms, so as to make development assistance more effective in reducing poverty.

Moreover, there is some reason to believe that, even at its best, development aid will largely be irrelevant to development. While it is difficult to name a single country for which development aid has been crucial for stimulating development, there are many countries that have successfully developed without substantial aid.[32] The most

---

[29] id21News Number 121, March 2004.

[30] Leif Wenar, "What We Owe to Distant Others," *Politics, Philosophy, and Economics* 2 (2003), pp. 283–304, makes a lot of this point and recommends that development projects be subject to much more extensive evaluation. I am not enthusiastic about this proposal since such evaluation is intrinsically difficult to do, and attempts at evaluation carry their own costs and can also distort incentives. On this point, see Lisa Bornstein, "Management Standards and Development Practice in the South African Aid Chain," *Public Administration and Development* 23 (2003), pp. 393–404.

[31] Pogge, *World Poverty and Human Rights*; Peter Singer, *One World: The Ethics of Globalization* (New Haven: Yale University Press, 2002).

[32] There is no question that the Marshall Plan was important in helping the countries of Western Europe to restore their economies after World War II, but this challenge was profoundly different from that currently faced by the poor countries of the world which have no history of economic development.

obvious examples are China, and the "Asian tigers." In 1950 these countries were poorer than some African and Latin American countries, yet they took off despite relatively low levels of development assistance. The reasons for this are complex and not well-understood, but there is an emerging view that development is more strongly related to culture and total investment than to aid. At most, development aid provides 30% of investment capital in developing countries. Remittances and private funds provide the remainder. While these private flows can be highly unstable, the "Asian tigers" benefited greatly from overseas workers remitting their earnings and providing investment capital, as well as from maintaining a generally favorable investment climate.

Thus far I have treated development and poverty reduction as interchangeable, yet many would claim that various cultural, non-economic factors are part of the very notion of development. Sustainability, democracy, capabilities, and women's rights have all received a great deal of attention in recent years. Although I cannot discuss these concerns in detail here, it is an interesting question to what extent they can be taken up in an expansive conception of human rights. While there is disagreement about what exactly a full system of human rights consists in – whether, for example, all the rights listed in the Universal Declaration of Human Rights really count as rights – there is substantial agreement about what constitutes the core of human rights.[33] Whether or not implementing such a system is part of development or conducive to development, it is clearly very important indeed. Some groups in the humanitarian community, for example the US branch of Médecins du Monde, have gone so far as to explicitly characterize themselves as human rights groups.[34]

In his recent work Singer has emphasized the importance of promoting a global human rights agenda through international action.[35] He has gone so far as to say that "the last line of defense against genocide and similar crimes must be law enforcement…and where other methods of achieving that fail, the method of last resort will be military intervention."[36]

---

[33] On this point, see James Nickel, *Making Sense of Human Rights* (Berkeley: University of California Press, 1987).

[34] Rieff, *A Bed for the Night,* p. 219.

[35] Singer, *One World.*

[36] Singer, *One World,* p. 12.

4. Humanitarian Intervention

Concern with human rights has been growing since at least the end of World War II, but it was in the fires of Rwanda and Bosnia that this concern became welded to the idea of military intervention. At a news conference at the height of the 1994 Rwandan genocide, Philippe Biberson, president of Médecins sans Frontières – France, called for military intervention, declaring that "[O]ne cannot halt a massacre with medicines."[37] Many in the humanitarian community praised the NATO intervention in Kosovo, even though it did not have UN authorization. For many theorists, both on the right and the left, humanitarian intervention directed towards the promotion of human rights has seemed to be the fullest expression of our duties to the distant.

However, there are serious dangers in supporting military intervention, even for the purpose of promoting human rights. What armies do very well is to kill people and smash things; what they are not is humanitarian organizations. On occasion military intervention may create space in which human rights and development can be pursued, but such intervention does not in itself promote these values. Even Michael Ignatieff, a liberal supporter of humanitarian intervention, has written, "[I]ntervention, rather than reinforcing respect for human rights, is consuming their legitimacy, both because our interventions are unsuccessful and because they are inconsistent."[38]

Second, when humanitarian organizations become complicit in military adventures, this creates conflicts and dilemmas for organizations whose stated goals are to relieve suffering, whomever the victims and whatever the causes. Beginning with the wars in the Balkans and continuing with the wars in Afghanistan and Iraq, the humanitarian community has become increasingly identified with one side or another in military conflicts. This has led to an erosion of credibility on the ground and increasingly acrimonious debate within agencies.[39] Moreover, when humanitarian agencies join forces with governments and militaries, it is difficult to avoid

---

[37] As quoted in Rieff, *A Bed for the Night*, p. 167.

[38] Michael Ignatieff, *Human Rights as Politics and Idolatry* (Princeton: Princeton University Press, 2001), p. 39.

[39] See Rieff, *A Bed for the Night*; and Maren, *The Road to Hell*. Many of these debates are covered on www.alertnet.org.

having their priorities shaped by these vastly more powerful institutions.[40]

A recent report by the International Federation of the Red Cross and Red Crescent Societies focuses on ethics in aid, and raises many important concerns.[41] The authors worry especially that when powerful nations decide to go to war in countries with vulnerable populations, this leads to a massive mobilization of humanitarian resources in an attempt to mitigate the possible consequences, often to the neglect of far more serious and long-standing humanitarian emergencies. They point out that in April, 2003, at the same time that donors were pledging $1.7 billion in relief and reconstruction aid for Iraq, there was a billion dollar shortfall in funds pledged to the World Food Program to avert starvation among 40 million Africans in 22 countries. Such responses appear contrary to the code of conduct subscribed to by the International Federation, along with many of the largest NGOs, that rejects acting as instruments of government foreign policy and setting priorities on any other basis than need. Indeed, some humanitarian organizations have at various times been complicit in denying aid to Afghans, Serbs, and Hutus (for example) as a way of punishing the political leaderships of their communities.

Even more important, in the current climate it is difficult to support humanitarian intervention without signing up for the imperial project emanating from Washington. The US government has made clear its intention to remake the Middle East, and perhaps the world, in an image that is more consonant with what they take to be US values. Two recent news stories indicate the depth of this commitment.

Thomas Friedman, one of the leading liberal supporters of humanitarian intervention, writes that "we are not 'rebuilding' Iraq. We are 'building' a new Iraq." He quotes approvingly Colonel Ralph Baker, who oversees two Baghdad districts.

> First we taught them how to run a meeting. We had to teach them how to have an agenda. So instead of having this sort of group dialogue with no form, which is what they were used to, you now see them in council meetings raising their hands to speak.

---

[40] For discussion of these issues, see *The Future of Humanitarian Action: Implications of Iraq and Other Recent Crises* (Feinstein International Famine Center, Friedman School of Nutrition Science and Policy, Tufts University), available on the web at http://hwproject.tufts.edu/pdf/Humanitarian.mapping.final.report.jan14.pdf

[41] Jonathan Walter (ed.), *World Disaster Report 2003* (Bloomfield: Kumarian Press, 2003).

They get five minutes per member. It's basic PTA stuff. We've taught them how to motion ideas and to vote on them.[42]

Another example of how totalizing the US project can be comes from Bosnia where, to a great extent, the military intervention simply froze an ethnic civil war in place rather than resolving the fundamental conflicts. The status of the town of Brcko was so disputed that in the Dayton Accords of 1995 it was decided that it would be administered directly by a US supervisor. It benefited from a disproportionate amount of US aid, and Brcko now has the highest per capita income in Bosnia. It is considered the shining success story of Bosnian reconstruction. It is the only town in which Muslim, Serb, and Croat children are mandated to go to school together. The history curriculum ends with World War II, and the schools emphasize mathematics and computers. The US supervisor imposed the school integration law, and has annulled other laws, as well as sacking local officials and businessmen who are seen as divisive or troublesome. Local elections have not taken place, so as to not endanger the progress that has been made (though they are now scheduled for October, 2004).

This new imperial project raises two related questions: First, is it just? And second, is it likely to succeed?

With respect to justice, many people would want to contrast this new imperialism with the old imperialism of the British Empire. The new imperialism is undertaken for humanitarian purposes; the old imperialism was about enriching the motherland. But this view paints too benign a picture of the new imperialism, and is too cynical about the old.

The great public justifications for British imperialism were the abolition of the slave trade and the spread of civilization, which was closely identified with Christianity. In 1807 the British abolished the slave trade and by 1816 they were patrolling the West coast of Africa claiming the right to board slave ships, though some might have thought them guilty of arrogance and hypocrisy since slavery was not abolished in the British Empire itself until 1833. The abolition of slavery was the ostensible focus of the Congress of Berlin in 1884–1885, which effectively divided up Africa among the European powers. When in 1896 the British forces were moving up the Niger River and occupying areas of Northern Nigeria, a popular weekly magazine ("The Globe") printed a picture of Islamic princes swearing

---

[42] "Starting from Scratch," *New York Times*, 27 August 2003, p. A21.

on the Koran that they would renounce slavery. The caption said, "Here we see our civilizing mission in action bringing civilization to the less fortunate."[43] Slavery continued to be a justification for British incursions into the Muslim world up to the 1920s.

These days we have a difficult time believing that the promoters of the old imperial project were sincere in their beliefs. But even the great utilitarian philosopher, John Stuart Mill, said that British rule in India was "not only the purest in intention but one of the most beneficent in act ever known to mankind."[44] The more businesslike Cecil Rhodes defined colonialism as "philanthropy plus five percent."[45] If this were really the case it would be a pretty good deal for all concerned.

From the perspective of the twenty-first century, the old imperialism appears to be a moral disaster (though not an unmixed one), whose consequences continue to haunt the world. In a masterful study of the Great Lakes region in central Africa, the French historian Jean Pierre Chretien has shown how the roots of the Rwandan genocide lie not in ancient hatreds, but in destructive animosities stemming from the recent colonial past.[46] While there is a tendency in the US today to dismiss lessons that might be learned from the experience of old Europe, we would have to be very arrogant indeed to believe that our imperial project is necessarily better intentioned or more assured of success.

5. Taking Stock

I am not arguing that aid, assistance, or intervention in the developing world never do any good, are never justified, or should be abolished. What I am claiming is that we should have a great deal more humility than we do about saying when such actions are called for and what shape they should take. This is not only because there are questions about the efficiency of aid, but also because the

[43] Quoted by Lawrence James in an interview accessed at http://www.pbs.org/empires/victoria/text/empirejames.html.

[44] As quoted in Niall Ferguston, "America: An Empire in Denial," *The Chronicle Review*, 28 March 2003, available at http://chronicle.com/free/v49/i29/29b00701.htm.

[45] As quoted in Rieff, *A Bed for the Night*, p. 60.

[46] Jean Pierre Chretien, *The Great Lakes of Africa: Two Thousand Years of History*, trans. Scott Strauss (Cambridge: Zone Books, 2003).

provision of aid creates winners and losers within societies that can lead to worse consequences overall. For example, one of the concerns of the International Federation of Red Cross and Red Crescent Societies is that the arrival of over 350 international aid agencies in Afghanistan since the fall of the Taliban has driven up local rents, inflated salaries, and sucked away skilled, experienced Afghans from the government and vital public services. While a driver at the US Embassy in Kabul can now earn $500 per month, a doctor in a government clinic receives about $45. It is difficult to believe that aid that creates such perverse incentives can in the long run really benefit people.[47] Even more shocking is the claim by one aid worker that development aid strengthened the elements in Hutu society that instigated the genocide, at the expense of moderate Hutus and Tutsis.[48]

Moreover, we should be reminded that the language of beneficence is not the sole property of liberal democracies bent on humanitarian missions. Benito Mussolini too claimed the abolition of slavery as a justification for the invasion of Ethiopia. Japan claimed that it was invading Manchuria to rescue it from Chinese bandits. Even Adolf Hitler claimed that he was putting an end to ethnic strife when he invaded the Sudetenland. Once the principle is accepted that a country may be invaded for the good of its own people, the floodgates are open, especially if there is no requirement that such invasions be sanctioned by a legitimating international authority.[49]

What then, should be the policy of those of us who believe with Singer that we have demanding and rigorous duties to the distant?

First, seek to make things better by trying to do no harm.[50] Rather than advocating ambitious agendas to remake the world, we should

---

[47] *World Disaster Report 2003.*

[48] Tony Vaux, "Aid Workers Still Grappling With Rwanda Demons," available at http://www.alertnet.org/thefacts/reliefresources/108195149548.htm. Amy Chua, *World on Fire: How Exporting Free Market Democracy Breeds Ethnic Hatred and Global Instability* (New York: Doubleday, 2003) has challenged the very idea that free markets and democracy are necessarily progressive forces, arguing instead that in many parts of the world they exacerbate ethnic conflict.

[49] Indeed, it can be questioned whether there is any such legitimating authority in the current international system. The United Nations Security Council claims such authority, but it is quite unrepresentative and undemocratic.

[50] Much of what I say in this paper is meant to be neutral among competing moral theories, but the idea that our duty is to bring about a better world rather than the best one is a view that I call "Progressive Consequentialism" and explore in an unpublished paper of the same title (co-authored with Robert Elliot).

focus first and primarily on challenging those structures that bring about and maintain global poverty. These include trade barriers imposed by the US and the EU, the appropriation of the global commons by the rich nations, and various policies of such international organizations as the World Bank and the International Monetary Fund. I will discuss these in turn.

Trade barriers take different forms including subsidies for domestic industries, tariffs, and quotas. According to the World Bank, developed country trade barriers cost developing countries more than twice what they receive in foreign aid. There are many striking examples of such barriers. Here is one: Government subsidies to the 25,000 US cotton farmers is greater than the entire economic output of Burkina Faso, a country in which two million people depend on cotton for their livelihoods.[51]

The appropriation of the global commons by the rich countries is illustrated by the problem of climate change. In fueling their development with the generous use of cheap fossil fuels, the rich countries have used the atmosphere as a sink for disposing of carbon dioxide. They have gathered most of the benefits of this intensive energy use, while the entire world must cope with the consequences of the climate change that is occurring as a result. Indeed, it is even worse than that. While everyone is at risk from the possibility of a catastrophic collapse of the current climate regime, it is poor people in poor countries who will suffer most even on the most optimistic scenarios. For they are most directly dependent on climate and therefore most vulnerable to the impacts of climatic events. They also have fewer resources for adapting to climate change. For example, rising sea levels will not damage Dutch farmers behind their system of protective dikes, but farmers in Bangladesh and Egypt will be devastated. The current global policy with respect to climate change can be characterized as an instance of the polluted pay principle: polluters benefit from their pollution, while those who suffer from the pollution bear the costs.[52]

---

[51] For more on trade barriers visit http://www.foreignpolicy.com/story/cms.php?story_id=24&page=0, and follow the links to the background papers. Days after I wrote these words the World Trade Organization declared U.S. cotton subsidies illegal. It is not yet clear what will be the final outcome of this case.

[52] This idea is presented in "Climate Change and Global Environmental Justice, P. Edwards and C. Miller (eds.), *Changing the Atmosphere: Expert Knowledge and Global Environmental Governance* (Cambridge: MIT Press, 2001), pp. 287–307, and further developed in my forthcoming paper, "Adaptation, Mitigation, and Justice."

The World Bank and the International Monetary Fund, institutions effectively controlled by the rich countries of the North, have often imposed policies on developing countries that have left them worse off than they otherwise would have been. Again, many examples can be given. Consider Malawi, a country that became heavily indebted during the thirty year rule of the pro-Western dictator, Hasting Banda. Despite receiving debt reduction under the Heavily Indebted Poor Countries (HIPC) initiative, Malawi is still required to spend 29% of its national budget servicing the debt – more than is spent on health, education, and agriculture combined – this in a country in which 60% of the population lives below the poverty line and 20% are HIV positive. In 2001, conditionality imposed by the HIPC initiative swept away the system of subsidies, controlled prices, and state grain stores that had kept famine at bay in this chronically food insecure country. As a result, in 6 months, beginning in October, 2001, the price of maize increased by 400%, and hoarding and corruption became endemic. By March, 2002, Malawi had plunged into famine, yet was continuing to service its external debt.[53]

There are many different kinds of actions that can be taken in attempts to refrain from causing harm, ranging from the very personal, such as buying "fair trade" products, to the political, such as supporting particular candidates. However, taking such actions, while extremely important, does not exempt us from directly transferring resources to the poor when we can be sure that the consequences will be good. It is in connection with this obligation that a second principle comes into play: "follow the money." We need to act through networks and channels that are transparent enough to allow us to assess even the indirect and remote consequences of our actions. This may involve acting at multiple levels of social organization including through friends, colleagues, professional organizations, faith communities, sister city programs, and so on.

Together these two principles bring out an important point. Good intentions are not enough. The goal of our actions should be to improve the world, not to make us feel good about ourselves. Susan Sontag goes so far as to claim, perhaps paradoxically, that sympathizing with the poor can actually inhibit us from the hard work of

[53] Kwesi Owusu and Francis Ng'ambi, "Nature or the North: Who Is to Blame for Famine in Malawi," available at http://www.id21.org/zinter/id21zinter.exe?a=0&i=s5cko1g1&u=40899253. See also http://www.globalpolicy.org/socecon/develop/africa/2002/10wdm.htm.

understanding our role in the production of distant horrors. She writes:

> So far as we feel sympathy, we feel we are not accomplices to what caused the suffering. Our sympathy proclaims our innocence as well as our impotence. To that extent, it can be (for all our good intentions) an impertinent – if not an inappropriate – response. To set aside the sympathy we extend to others beset by war and murderous politics for a reflection on how our privileges are located on the same map as their suffering and may – in ways we might prefer not to imagine – be linked to their suffering, as the wealth of some may imply the destitution of others, is a task for which the painful, stirring images supply only an initial spark.[54]

6. Concluding Remarks

In this paper I have accepted Singer's claim that we have a demanding and rigorous duty to aid the distant poor, but I have gone on to suggest that we should be modest and self-critical about our ability to discharge this duty successfully. However, rather than making us complacent about our duties, these claims should provoke us to recognize additional demands on our knowledge and attention. It is not enough to write checks in the hope that they will do some good; we must at least be sure that in doing so we will do no harm. And this, surprisingly, turns out to be a very demanding requirement.[55]

Environmental Studies and Philosophy
New York University
246 Greene Street
Suite 300
New York NY 10003-6677
USA
E-mail: dwj3@nyu.edu

[54] Susan Sontag, *Regarding the Pain of Others* (New York: Farrar, Straus and Giroux, 2003), pp. 102–103.

[55] This paper is greatly indebted, obviously, to the work of Peter Singer. I have also been influenced by conversations with Leif Wenar. Discussions with audiences at the University of Girona in Catalonia, Spain, and at the American Philosophical Association, Mini-Conference on Global Justice, in Pasadena, California, have helped to shape the final version.

LUIS CABRERA

THE COSMOPOLITAN IMPERATIVE: GLOBAL JUSTICE THROUGH ACCOUNTABLE INTEGRATION*

(Received 14 May 2004; accepted in revised form 14 June 2004)

ABSTRACT. Cosmopolitan political theorists hold that our obligations to distribute resources to others do not halt at state borders, but most do not advocate a restructuring of the global system to achieve their distributive aims. This article argues that promoting democratically accountable economic and political integration between states would be the most effective way to enable cosmopolitan, or routine, tax-financed, trans-state distributions. Movement toward a more integrated global system should encourage the view that larger sets of persons have interests in common that should be protected and promoted in common. Democratically accountable integration also should enable those within less-affluent states to more vigorously press trans-state distributive claims. The still-evolving E.U. is examined as a partial model for the integrated alternative in other geographic regions, as well as, in the much longer term, for some form of democratic global government capable of ensuring that any person born anywhere would have access to adequate resources and life opportunities.

KEY WORDS: cosmopolitan, global poverty, human rights, sovereignty, world government

Cosmopolitan theorists of distributive justice hold that there is nothing morally special about political boundaries, and that our obligation to redistribute wealth to those overseas is generally as strong as to those who share our citizenship.[1] However, while

---

*A version of this paper was presented at the global justice "mini-conference" at the American Philosophical Association (Pacific Division) annual meeting, Pasadena, California, 26–29 March 2004. Some of the arguments in this article were introduced in Luis Cabrera, *Political Theory of Global Justice: A Cosmopolitan Case for the World State* (London: Routledge, 2004), Chapter 4. They have been revised and further developed for this article. I would like to thank for their generous comments Jamie Mayerfeld, James A. Caporaso and Mika LaVaque-Manty.

[1] For surveys of recent cosmopolitan thought, see Daniele Archibugi and Mathias Koenig-Archibugi, "Globalization, Democracy and Cosmopolis: A Bibliographical Essay," in Daniele Archibugi (ed.), *Debating Cosmopolitics* (London: Verso, 2003), pp. 273–291; Fred Dallmayr, "Cosmopolitanism: Moral and Political," *Political Theory* 31 (2003), pp. 421–442; Simon Caney, "International Distributive Justice," *Political Studies* 49 (2001), pp. 974–997; Charles Beitz, "International Liberalism and

cosmopolitans argue that the scope of our moral concern should be global, most do not advocate global institutional change. In other words, they attempt to draw a clear distinction between a *moral* cosmopolitanism that would apply principles of distributive justice globally, and an *institutional* cosmopolitanism that would seek to facilitate actual distributions through a transformation of the sovereign states system.[2] Moral cosmopolitans tend to focus on the duties of individuals to make charitable donations, or on the obligations of states to make larger voluntary transfers within the existing system.[3] Some explicitly reject a strong institutional approach, arguing that it is not necessary, and perhaps not feasible, to transform the global institutional framework wholesale.[4] Others, whom I will call the "limited institutional cosmopolitans," support a partial restructuring. They reject a full world state but do call for movement toward some strong supranational institutions, meaning those above the state that could obtain compliance from states in

---

Distributive Justice: A Survey of Recent Thought," *World Politics* 51 (1999), pp. 269–296; For individual cosmopolitan arguments, see Peter Singer, "Famine, Affluence and Morality," *Philosophy and Public Affairs* 1 (1972), pp. 230–243; Charles Beitz, *Political Theory and International Relations* (Princeton: Princeton University Press, 1979); Thomas Pogge, *Realizing Rawls* (Ithaca: Cornell University Press, 1989); Martha Nussbaum, "Patriotism and Cosmopolitanism," in Joshua Cohen (ed.), *For Love of Country: Debating the Limits of Patriotism* (Boston: Beacon Press, 1996), pp. 2–17; Brian Barry, "International Society from a Cosmopolitan Perspective," in David Mapel and Terry Nardin (eds.), *International Society: Diverse Ethical Perspectives* (Princeton: Princeton University Press, 1998), pp. 144–163; Charles Jones, *Global Justice: Defending Cosmopolitanism* (Oxford: Oxford University Press, 1999); Darrel Moellendorf, *Cosmopolitan Justice* (Boulder: Westview Press, 2002).

[2] For the distinction, see especially Charles Beitz, "Social and Cosmopolitan Liberalism," *International Affairs* 75 (1999), pp. 125–140.

[3] For a nuanced proposal seeking to increase international development aid through existing intergovernmental institutions, see George Soros, *On Globalization* (New York: Public Affairs, 2002).

[4] See Beitz, "Social and Cosmopolitan Liberalism"; Martha Nussbaum, "Duties of Justice, Duties of Material Aid," *Journal of Political Philosophy* 8 (2000), pp. 176–206; Jason D. Hill, *Becoming a Cosmopolitan: What It Means to Be a Human Being in the New Millennium* (Lanham: Rowman and Littlefield Publishers, 2000). Most cosmopolitans do support the creation of some limited supranational institutions. Those described as moral cosmopolitans, especially Nussbaum, give emphasis to individual moral duties and relatively little attention to institutional design.

some legal or distributive areas.[5] A final group, the cosmopolitan democrats, demands somewhat deeper near-term institutional changes, but for reasons primarily of democratic accountability in a globalizing system where polities are viewed as rapidly losing their power to set domestic policy.[6]

I argue here that the moral cosmopolitan should be committed to strong institutional cosmopolitanism. Specifically, the moral cosmopolitan should advocate democratically accountable economic and political integration between states in order to promote broader distributions of resources and opportunities. The current system of competitive, "separate but equal" states discourages cosmopolitan distributions, and it does so at the deepest level. Observed norms of internal and external sovereignty give rise in each state to powerful, mutually reinforcing biases against full acknowledgment of the moral claims of non-compatriots. Exhortation to charity in such a system is highly unlikely to generate distributions sufficient to satisfy the demands of moral cosmopolitanism. Likewise, the changes sought in the relatively near term by the limited institutional cosmopolitans and cosmopolitan democrats are unlikely to be realized, as state leaders and their constituencies will be resistant to ceding aspects of sovereignty outright. The gradual creation of a more integrated global system should help to encourage the view that much larger sets of persons have interests in common that should be protected and promoted in common. It should work to transform the perceived zero-sum character of trans-state distributions, and it should help to discourage defection from distributive schemes by

[5] See Thomas Pogge, "Cosmopolitanism and Sovereignty," *Ethics* 103 (1992), pp. 51–73; Thomas Pogge, "Economic Justice and National Borders," *ReVision* 22 (1999), pp. 27–43; Brian Barry, "Statism and Nationalism: A Cosmopolitan Critique," in Ian Shapiro and Lea Brilmayer (eds.), *Nomos XLI: Global Justice* (New York: New York University Press, 1999), p. 40; Jones, *Global Justice*, pp. 227–232; Moellendorf, *Cosmopolitan Justice*, pp. 171–176; Commission on Global Governance, *Our Global Neighborhood* (Oxford: Oxford University Press, 1995). An example of a supranational institution is the World Trade Organization, which is able to achieve compliance from states with its trade rules in part through the threat of trade penalties.

[6] See David Held, *Democracy and the Global Order: From the Modern State to Cosmopolitan Governance* (Cambridge: Polity Press, 1995); David Held, "From Executive to Cosmopolitan Multilateralism," in David Held and Mathias Koenig-Archibugi (eds.), *Taming Globalization: Frontiers of Governance* (Cambridge: Polity Press, 2003).

individual states, whose citizens would have strong incentive to maintain privileged access to markets, low tariffs and the other benefits of economic integration. Ultimately, we should want to see all states embedded in networks of regional organizations broadly similar to – though more democratically accountable than – the EU, where routine, tax-financed distributions are made to less-affluent states or sub-state regions, and where individuals are able to move across political boundaries in pursuit of life opportunities. We also should want to see, in the longer term, such regional organizations embedded in larger networks of similar institutions, up to the global level, in service of extending distributions over ever-broader geographic areas.

The structure of the argument is as follows: to show more clearly what is at stake in the distinction between moral and institutional cosmopolitanism, I begin with more precise definitions of both. I then discuss the foundational principles of the current global system and some tensions between its norms of sovereignty and the moral cosmopolitan approach. I detail three biases against trans-state distributions that are reinforced by the sovereign states system, and I examine how a more integrated alternative system could lessen the force of those biases. I close by considering some trans-state integration already underway and the possibilities it creates for realizing the kind of just, democratically accountable integration that could effectively promote more cosmopolitan distributions.

1. Moral and Institutional Cosmopolitanism

The work of Charles Beitz represents perhaps the most sustained and rigorous exploration of cosmopolitan distributive justice, as well as the most straightforward challenge to the advocacy of strong institutional cosmopolitanism. Beitz's definitions of "moral cosmopolitanism" and "institutional cosmopolitanism" have been influential, and in the interest of simplicity and remaining close to recent debates, I will follow them here.

Moral cosmopolitanism, according to Beitz, is that approach to distributive justice that is fully inclusive and non-perspectival. It is impartial, universal and accords the interests of all individuals equal weight. It "aims to identify principles that are acceptable when each person's prospects, rather than the prospects of each society or people, are taken fairly into account."[7] Thus, it is to be used to assess the justice of political practices, arrangements and institutions according to how well individuals fare within them. By contrast, Beitz says, *institutional cosmopolitanism* advocates the restructuring of the global system to bring states under the authority of just supranational institutions, including possibly the institutions of a global government, to ensure that cosmopolitan distributional obligations will be fulfilled. Beitz is explicit that there is no *necessary* link between moral and institutional cosmopolitanism. He asserts that the cosmopolitan should remain agnostic about the shape the global system should take. The following passage of Beitz's will help demonstrate what is at stake in the distinction and the broader argument.

> The doctrine of universal human rights is cosmopolitan in its foundations without being cosmopolitan in its institutional requirements ... Instead, it specifies minimum conditions that any institutions should satisfy. Accordingly, human rights doctrine does not rule out the possibility – indeed it trades on the hope – that its institutional requirements can be satisfied within a political structure containing nation-states more or less as we know them today.[8]

I will suggest that such a hope is misplaced where the rights in question are economic rights corresponding to cosmopolitan distributions. Now, it should be noted that there is some disagreement among cosmopolitans about the defensible minimum level of distributions. Some, including Beitz, Thomas Pogge and David Richards,[9] have considered a full global application of the Rawlsian difference principle. Others argue that the most extensive scheme of transfers that can be justified is one that satisfies the basic wants or needs of individuals in less-affluent states.[10] I believe that a plausible moral cosmopolitanism would require more than the minimum, but the argument here does not depend on such a claim. Even if distributive demands were limited to the amount needed to provide minimum food, shelter, education and medical care for all of those in less-affluent states, that would represent a substantial increase over what is currently distributed, as discussed below. Such

---

[7] Beitz, "Social and Cosmopolitan Liberalism," p. 129.

[8] Beitz, "Social and Cosmopolitan Liberalism," p. 127.

[9] Beitz, *Political Theory and International Relations*; Pogge, *Realizing Rawls*; David Richards, *A Theory of Reasons for Action* (Oxford: Oxford University Press, 1971).

[10] Jones, *Global Justice*, p. 27.

transfers would be inhibited by the nature and structure of the sovereign states system.

2. The Westphalian System

In order to demonstrate more clearly how the current Westphalian global system discourages cosmopolitan distributions, I will briefly sketch the formal principles of sovereignty expressed or observed within it. I do not presume that state sovereignty is or ever has been indivisible or absolute.[11] I do presume, however, that states generally observe and especially claim sovereign rights, and that states' leaders retain considerable latitude to act domestically. "Westphalia" refers to the 1648 Treaty of Westphalia, which ended the 30 Years' War and marked the transition to a system in which state borders were viewed as impermeable and individual rulers as the final arbiters on matters within their own borders. Most commentators on the Westphalian system note two key features: internal and external sovereignty. To say a state is internally sovereign is to say its executive, judicial and legislative institutions have final authority over its own people. A Native American reservation in the US would be an example of a political entity that does not exercise supreme jurisdiction in its own territory, as would be the remaining colonies and overseas territories of the colonial states, and increasingly the member states of the EU in certain aspects. "External sovereignty" refers to the independence of the state itself in the global system. Sovereign states are considered equal in the system, and they are the direct subjects of international law. An externally sovereign state can enter a treaty as an equal with other state signatories. It can press claims in the International Court of Justice or join an international organization such as the UN Embedded in sovereign equality are principles holding that each state's territorial integrity and political independence are inviolable, and that each state has a duty to respect the legal personalities of other states. That leads to a strongly worded

[11] See Stephen D. Krasner, "Compromising Westphalia (Nuclear Issues in Asia)," *International Security* 20 (1995), pp. 115–152; Daniel Philpott, *Revolutions in Sovereignty: How Ideas Shaped Modern International Relations* (Princeton: Princeton University Press, 2001), Chapters 1–2.

prohibition on intervention in a state's domestic affairs.[12] Observance of the norm has loosened recently in cases of large-scale human rights violations,[13] but direct intervention by other states remains very much the exception, and states, or state leaders, retain considerable latitude to independently order their internal affairs. It is within this general system that the moral cosmopolitan, or any advocate of universal human rights, is obliged to work.

3. Sovereignty and Universal Rights

"Sovereignty," Harold Laski famously proclaimed, "is incompatible with the interests of humanity."[14] My claim is more that sovereignty is in significant tension with humanity, or moral cosmopolitanism. In this section, I offer examples of instances where rights fulfillment has been or could be frustrated because norms of sovereignty enable domestic elites to block outside scrutiny or action. The examples are not meant to be construed as decisive in themselves but are intended to highlight some specific ways in which prerogatives of sovereignty are used or have been misused. The discussion will lead us toward an "ideal states system" that aims to correct abuses. Even in the ideal, however, deep tensions remain between norms of sovereignty and a moral cosmopolitan approach to distributions.

It will be appropriate to begin with the International Criminal Court. The ICC does not deal directly with questions of global

[12] See UN, "Declaration on Principles of International Law Concerning Friendly Relations and Co-operation among States in Accordance with the Charter of the United Nations," *Resolution 2625* (24 October 1970); The UN Charter also includes a firm statement of the principle of nonintervention. Article 2, paragraph 7 states: "Nothing contained in the present Charter shall authorize the United Nations to intervene in matters which are essentially within the domestic jurisdiction of any state or shall require the Members to submit such matters to settlement under the present Charter" (http://www.un.org/aboutun/charter/).

[13] See Francis Kofi Abiew, *The Evolution of the Doctrine and Practice of Humanitarian Intervention* (The Hague: Kluwer Law International, 1999), pp. 137–138. Abiew, like many commentators, notes the increasing frequency in the post-Cold War era of UN-sanctioned, multilateral humanitarian interventions: those in Northern Iraq, Somalia, Haiti, Rwanda and Bosnia; See also Martha Finnemore, "Constructing Norms of Humanitarian Intervention," in Peter Katzenstein (ed.), *The Culture of National Security, Norms and Identity in World Politics* (New York: Columbia University Press, 1996), pp. 153–185.

[14] Harold Laski, *A Grammar of Politics* (New Haven: Yale University Press, 1925), p. 64.

distributive justice, but in structure and aims it is similar to the narrowly mandated supranational legal institutions proposed by limited institutional cosmopolitans such as Thomas Pogge, who calls for "more world government," but not a fully realized world state.[15] The ICC "aims to prevent a set of crimes that, potentially and in fact, encompass the violation of fundamental human rights of large numbers of individuals. It thus forms one piece of the effort to achieve the global protection of human rights."[16] It attempts to achieve such protection in a global system containing more than 200 sovereign nation-states. Examining the specific limitations of the ICC, including the leeway states' leaders retain to avoid prosecution, will point us toward more general difficulties with attempting to achieve moral cosmopolitan aims in a sovereign states system.

Backers of the ICC have enjoyed notable success in securing the participation of states, including briefly the US, which more recently has been the court's most vocal opponent.[17] More than 90 states have ratified the 1998 treaty establishing the court, and its principals were in place by late 2003, when newly installed chief Prosecutor Luis Moreno Ocampo of Argentina was studying the more than 600 complaints already filed to determine which to prosecute. More than 100 of those complaints were filed against US forces in Iraq, but they were discarded without examination of their merits.[18] Because neither Iraq nor the US were party to the ICC treaty, they could not be prosecuted under its terms. The treaty, by

[15] Pogge, "A Global Resources Dividend," p. 536; See also Brian Barry, "Statism and Nationalism," pp. 39–40. Barry calls for the creation of an international legal system with some power over state systems.

[16] Jamie Mayerfeld, "Who Shall Be Judge? The US, the International Criminal Court, and the Global Enforcement of Human Rights," *Human Rights Quarterly* 25 (2003), p. 98.

[17] The US became a signatory to the treaty on 31 December 2000, under the Bill Clinton administration, but did not ratify. In 2002, the George Bush administration formally withdrew, and the US has pursued bilateral agreements with numerous states exempting US citizens from possible ICC prosecution for acts committed in those states. In July 2003, the Bush administration suspended $48 million in aid to 35 countries that had failed to sign such agreements [Bert Wilkinson, "Guyana Signs Agreement Not to Hand over U.S. Troops for Prosecution Before International Court," *The Associated Press* (13 December 2003); See also Jean Galbraith, "Humanitarian Law: The Bush Administration's Response to the International Criminal Court," *Berkeley Journal of International Law* 21 (2003), pp. 683–702].

[18] Norma Greenway, "Judging Cases Trumps Politics at World Court," *The Ottawa Citizen* (12 October 2003), p. A-5.

such provision, observes the Westphalian principle of external sovereignty that prescribes respect for the independent legal personalities of states.

In addition to the ability of non-signatories to remain out of court jurisdiction, the ICC treaty allows signatory states to declare themselves exempt for seven years from war crimes prosecution. And, the UN Security Council is empowered by the treaty to demand postponement of ICC prosecutions for renewable one-year periods.[19] The ICC also must rely in significant ways on the cooperation of states in which individuals would be sought for prosecution. Prosecutors will have to depend in most cases on local law enforcement to arrest and detain those charged. They also will need the cooperation of local authorities to protect witnesses both before and after they give testimony against compatriots charged with genocide or war crimes.[20] That is not to say that the ICC will not be able to achieve compliance in many cases from compatriots of those prosecuted. Pressure may be brought to bear through concerted force of international opinion, selective inducements or progressive sanctions, and weak states may turn to the court for help in pursuing powerful internal aggressors. However, the points raised here should highlight sources of tension. The court is mandated to help protect the rights of all individuals, but states' leaders have considerable power, grounded in norms of sovereignty, to see that their citizens are not under the court's jurisdiction, or to otherwise impede prosecution.

Let us turn to more narrowly distributive issues. As is often noted, the leeway states' leaders have to order internal affairs in the Westphalian system can lead to the redirection of international aid away from those most in need.[21] This is an important concern for the moral cosmopolitan, who would exhort individuals within affluent states, or their governments, to significantly increase transfers. Because of the

[19] Mayerfeld, "Who Shall Be Judge?," p. 123.

[20] Stefanie Grant, "Matching Rhetoric with Action: The Challenge of an International Criminal Court," *Criminal Justice Ethics* 16 (1997), pp. 2–9.

[21] See World Bank, *Assessing Aid, What Works, What Doesn't and Why* (Oxford: Oxford University Press, 1998), p. 1. The full report is available at http://www.worldbank.org/research/aid/aidtoc.htm. The report notes some states where billions in aid has made little noticeable difference, in large part because of corrupt leadership, as in Zaire (Democratic Republic of Congo) under Mobutu Sese Seko, 1965–1997. But see Pogge, *World Poverty and Human Rights*, p. 111-113, where Pogge reserves his harshest criticism for an international system that continues to formally recognize corrupt leaders.

principles of sovereignty that generally are observed within the states system, the most basic subsistence rights of the worst-off within states in crisis may go unfulfilled, even when the international community makes significant transfers. That was the case in Bangladesh in the mid-1970s. Though the international community responded to calls for famine assistance in amounts exceeding $1 billion per year, much of the aid failed to reach those most in need. Funds were diverted by the Bangladeshi regime to powerful urban interests and rural elites, while large numbers of the rural poor starved to death. Aid agencies did set increasingly stringent implementation requirements, but their means of ensuring compliance with the requirements were quite limited, or so blunt as to be considered too harmful, as in the case of withholding aid.[22]

Another, more recent, example may illustrate the tensions more starkly. In the Sudanese civil war during the late 1980s and early 1990s, both the regime and opposition forces denied international food aid to a large portion of the population for strategic military reasons. "In 1988 alone, more than 250,000 southern Sudanese died from starvation as the military leaders on both sides refused to allow food to reach civilian populations believed to be loyal to one side or the other. The greatest numbers of the dead were women, children and the elderly."[23] The regime, under strong pressure from the US and other states, did agree in 1989 to allow food aid to reach its intended recipients. However, starvation tactics resumed the following year, as both sides prevented food aid from reaching hungry persons and actually attacked relief planes and trains. In addition, regime leaders adopted the stance that there was no food crisis and refused to formally request aid from international agencies, effectively denying it to individual citizens.

Defenders of Westphalia, of course, could argue that such cases are outliers, gross subversions of the principles that give the

[22] Betsy Hartmann, and James Boyce, *Needless Hunger: Voices from a Bangladeshi Village* (Oakland: Institute for Food and Development Policy, 1982), p. 45; For an edifying discussion of the causes of the Bangladeshi famine of 1974, see Amartya Sen, *Poverty and Famines: An Essay on Entitlement and Deprivation* (Oxford: Oxford University Press, 1982), pp. 131–153.

[23] Judy Mayotte, "Civil War in Sudan: The Paradox of Human Rights and National Sovereignty," *Journal of International Affairs* 47 (1994), p. 505.

sovereign states system its foundational moral significance. Especially in the Sudan case, they could say, the regime is not entitled to the protection offered by the observance of the norms of sovereignty, because it has subverted the moral purpose of a sovereign states system. That purpose, broadly, is for a state to protect and promote the interests of its citizens. In fact, Michael Walzer, a staunch proponent of the view that states have intrinsic moral significance, would argue in favor of international intervention in cases "when the violations of human rights within a set of boundaries is so terrible that it makes talk of community or self-determination or 'arduous struggle' seem cynical and irrelevant…."[24] It is important, then, to consider an ideal sovereign states system. If cases of aid diversion are merely unacceptable subversions of the Westphalian system, then sovereignty may not be in essential tension with humanity, and the case for advocating strong institutional cosmopolitanism will be weakened.

We can consider the UN Charter here, viewing it as a set of guidelines for constructing an ideal states system. Such a system would be comprised of separate but formally equal and sovereign nation states, each attempting to ensure the fulfillment of a robust package of economic and social rights for its citizens. The foundation of such an ideal system would be the understanding, in the words of the Commission on Global Governance, that "Sovereignty ultimately derives from the people. It is a power to be exercised by, for, and on behalf of the people of a state."[25] In such a system, states, or the leaders of states, are assiduous stewards of their citizens' interests. They are concerned with protecting and promoting

[24] Michael Walzer, *Just and Unjust Wars: A Moral Argument with Historical Allusions* (New York: Basic Books, 1977), p. 90. Walzer cites in particular cases of enslavement or massacre, but the allowing of preventable starvation can plausibly be included.

[25] Commission on Global Governance, *Our Global Neighborhood*, p. 69. The commission, initiated by former West German Chancellor Willy Brandt, received some funding for its report from UN sources, among a range of other sources (pp. 376–377). The Commission's work also was endorsed by former UN Secretary General Boutros Boutros-Ghali (p. xv). For a separate, neorealist take on the duty of leaders to be "public regarding" in keeping foremost the interests of their own citizens, see Lea Brilmayer, "Realism Revisited: The Moral Priority of Means and Ends in Anarchy," in Ian Shapiro and Lea Brilmayer (eds.), *Nomos XLI: Global Justice*, p. 212; For a nonrealist approach, see Gerard Elfstrom, *Ethics for a Shrinking World* (London: MacMillan, 1990), pp. 7–8.

the welfare of all of their citizens, and they are limited only by the level of resources at their command, as well as by their states' overall levels of economic and institutional development. Where, in such a model, would tensions arise between humanity and sovereignty, between the norms of Westphalia and the demands of moral cosmopolitanism?

4. Westphalian Biases Against Cosmopolitan Distributions

My answer focuses on three mutually reinforcing biases against cosmopolitan distributions that naturally arise within the Westphalian system. Even in the idealized version, these biases will be powerful inhibitors to achieving cosmopolitan distributions. The first bias arises from the normative foundations of Westphalia. Nonintervention, formal legal equality and other norms of sovereignty are grounded in a presumption that the state's primary role is to promote the interests of its own citizens. States, or state leaders, would be subverting their mandates if they distributed resources overseas at a level consistent with a plausible moral cosmopolitanism. Thus, there is a strong "foundational" bias toward tending primarily to the needs and interests of the citizen set. A second "electoral" bias is concerned with the ways in which states' leaders themselves have strong incentives to distribute resources to powerful internal constituents, rather than sending resources overseas. This bias is present in democratic and, with some modification, in hierarchical states. Finally, and more specific to sets of ordinary citizens, a kind of Lockean "own-case" bias is reinforced by the structure of the sovereign states system. Those in affluent states essentially are judges in their own cases about the appropriate levels of transfers they should make, and their perceptions of their own obligations may be skewed.

The most effective way to approach a fuller discussion of the biases will be to first explain what sort of argument I am not attempting to make. That is, I do not contend that global distributive justice is a collective-action problem, or that states or state leaders *should* find it in their own interests or system mandates to make cosmopolitan distributions. Political thinkers dating back hundreds of years actually have argued that leaders should find it in their interest to integrate in order to eliminate the scourge of war.[26] Proponents of this "collective-action warfare" approach say that the need for integration, most often for a fully global sovereign, has become especially evident since the development of nuclear weapons. States are said to need a Hobbesian "power to keep them all in awe,"[27] i.e., a suprastate governing body capable of transforming a dangerous, anarchic system into a stable, highly ordered one. Even in an ideal sovereign states system, proponents likely would say, leaders' interests in promoting the welfare of their own citizens could lead them into conflict over resources, territory or other issues. Therefore, states should find it in their interest to cede their war-making powers to some larger body capable of effectively policing them all and enforcing a genuine international law. In Jean-Jacques Rousseau's words, "The only thing we assume on their behalf is enough intelligence to see what is useful to themselves, and enough courage to achieve their own happiness."[28]

Collective-action warfare is vulnerable as an independent argument for integration between states. If it is plausible to think that state leaders should find it in their self-interest to try to prevent the common threat of warfare, it also should be plausible to think that they can cooperate to achieve some sort of intergovernmental solution to reducing stockpiles of nuclear weapons, etc., that would make

[26] Jean-Jacques Rousseau, "A Project of Perpetual Peace," in Howard Kainz (ed.), *Philosophical Perspectives on Peace* (Athens: Ohio University Press, 1987); Immanuel Kant, "Perpetual Peace," in Ted Humphrey (ed.), *Perpetual Peace and Other Essays on Politics, History and Morals* (Indianapolis: Hackett Publishing Company, 1993), pp. 107–143. Kant, of course, argues for a "pacific federation" of states rather than a unified global government; Albert Einstein, "The Way Out," in Dexter Masters and Katharine Way (eds.), *One World or None* (New York: Whittlesey House-McGraw Hill, 1946); Betty Reardon and Saul Mendlovitz, "World Law and Models of World Order," in Charles Beitz and Theodore Herman (eds.), *Peace and War* (San Francisco: W.H. Freeman and Co., 1973); Sidney Axinn, "Loyalty and the Limits of Patriotism," in Kenneth Kipnis and Diana T. Meyers (eds.), *Political Realism and International Morality: Ethics in the Nuclear Age* (Boulder: Westview Press, 1987), pp. 239–250. For a thorough survey of world government proposals, see Derek Heater, *World Citizenship and Government: Cosmopolitan Ideas in the History of Western Political Thought* (New York: St. Martin's Press, 1996).

[27] Thomas Hobbes, *Leviathan*, in Michael L. Morgan (ed.), *Classics of Moral and Political Theory*, 3rd edition (Indianapolis: Hackett Publishing Company, 2001), pp. 488–621, 546.

[28] Rousseau, "A Project of Perpetual Peace," p. 63.

the ostensible need for a world government far less pressing.[29] This is not to say that the states of the world have negotiated a peaceful end to their differences, that such an end is in sight, or that the warfare argument offers a fully accurate characterization of the global system and interactions between principal actors. Rather the claim is that, in the same way states are motivated to address global environmental and other joint concerns cooperatively, they should be motivated to try to overcome their collective-action warfare problem through bilateral negotiations, the creation of specific multilateral institutions, or by a host of other means short of immediately ceding sovereignty to a world state.[30]

Again, however, the self-interest argument is not so readily available to those who wish to extend distributions beyond state borders. There lies the core tension between sovereignty and universal rights, or cosmopolitan distributive claims. Those in affluent states will not generally find it in their self-interest, and likely not in their considered moral duties, to make the distributions required by moral cosmopolitanism. Let us consider more fully the first, foundational bias. In the Westphalian system, the interests of states are presumed to be bound to the interests of their own citizens. The interests of those citizens give states their moral standing and justify recognition by other states of norms of territorial integrity, nonintervention and internal sovereignty. The moral imperative on states' leaders in such a system is to promote the interests of their citizens. Thus, if leaders were to adopt a moral cosmopolitan approach to distributions and attempted to extend routine, relatively high-level distributions to

[29] For example, under the Strategic Offensive Reduction Treaty, or "Moscow Treaty" of May 2002, the US and Russia agreed to reduce their nuclear warhead deployments by the year 2012: from 6144 to 2200 for the US, and from 5814 to 1806 for Russia. "A Farewell to Armaments," *Economist* (May 18, 2002), pp. 29–30; For figures on the reductions of nuclear weapons arsenals that states have achieved through negotiation, see Carnegie Commission on Preventing Deadly Conflict, *Preventing Deadly Conflict: Final Report* (New York: Carnegie Corporation of New York, 1997), p. 72; See also Ralph M. Goldman, and Willard M. Hardman, *Building Trust: An Introduction to Peacekeeping and Arms Control* (Aldershot: Ashgate, 1997).

[30] The literature on why states cooperate, including why they form multilateral institutions, is extensive. For a cogent overview, see Robert O. Keohane, *Power and Governance in a Partially Globalized World* (London: Routledge, 2002); See also Jon Hovi, *Games, Threats & Treaties: Understanding Commitments in International Relations* (London: Pinter, 1998), Chapter 5; for an exemplar rationalist argument, see Kenneth W. Abbot and Duncan Snidal, "Why States Act through Formal International Organizations, *Journal of Conflict Resolution* 42 (1998), pp. 3–32.

non-compatriots, they would be subverting their individual mandates. They would be neglecting the interests of their own citizens in order to tend to the perhaps more pressing needs or interests of the citizens of other states.[31] They also could be weakening the very foundations of their sovereign prerogatives. Recall Walzer's claim that leaders who subvert their mandates by tyrannizing their own people are not entitled to the nonintervention and other protections of a sovereign states' system. It could reasonably be asked whether leaders who decide to divert significantly more resources to those in other states, thereby neglecting some of the interests or concerns of their own citizens, are likewise jeopardizing their entitlements to some prerogatives of sovereignty.

The second, electoral, bias focuses more directly on the personal incentives that state-level policy makers have to give more weight to the concerns of their own constituencies. Leaders in both democracies and more hierarchical regimes can be presumed to have an interest in staying in power, and more broadly in being able to implement their policy agendas. That interest reinforces the tendency for leaders to give more relative weight to the interests of those who determine whether they will achieve their aims. In democracies, a vital set of interests to be considered is that of the electorate, which determines at regular intervals whether leaders will be rewarded with continued incumbency, or with continued success for their party and broad policy interests.[32] And, of course, the influence of powerful economic and other interest groups must also be considered. In more hierarchical regimes, the primary interests taken into account are those of powerful elites in government, industry, the military, and religious institutions. In either case, resistance can be expected to proposals that would shrink the pool of resources available domestically

[31] Hedley Bull makes a broadly similar point in Hedley Bull, *The Anarchical Society: A Study of Order in World Politics* (New York: Columbia University Press, 1977), pp. 261–264; See also Andrew Linklater, "Cosmopolitan Citizenship," in Kimberly Hutchings and Roland Dannreuther (eds.), *Cosmopolitan Citizenship* (New York: St. Martin's Press, 1999), pp. 35–59; Menno Kamminga, *On Global Justice*, CDS Research Report Series, No. 17, March 2003, University of Groningen (http://www.eco.rug.nl/cds/pubs.htm). Kamminga essentially argues that it is inconsistent to advocate moral cosmopolitanism without also advocating institutional cosmopolitanism. However, the conclusion he draws, working within an explicitly neo-realist frame and citing the stewardship responsibilities of states' leaders in the Westphalian system, is that institutional cosmopolitanism is not feasible. The analysis fails to consider the ways in which stewardship may evolve and be broadened within an integration project.

[32] See Barbara Geddes, *Politician's Dilemma: Building State Capacity in Latin America* (Berkeley: University of California Press, 1994).

through large-scale transfers overseas. Leaders of sovereign states, especially those outside of the EU who have no formal obligation to transfer resources in a supranational arrangement, have powerful personal incentives to reject cosmopolitan distributive claims.

Finally, and I think most importantly, we can identify a tendency for ordinary persons to reject the claims of moral cosmopolitanism, even if they acknowledge some obligations to transfer internationally. The tendency can be traced in large part to a Lockean own-case bias reinforced by the sovereign states system.[33] Individuals are encouraged by the formally observed norms of Westphalia to view themselves as members of discrete, independent citizen sets. This separateness or isolation from other citizen sets naturally promotes a bias toward tending to the needs or interests of compatriots, a bias that is reinforced by mostly inward-looking systems of national public education, and of course systems of rule that halt at the state level.[34] John Locke argued that one of the great difficulties of the state of nature was the tendency for even well-meaning individuals to take their own sides in a dispute, regardless of what the evidence might suggest to an impartial observer. The need for an impartial third party, or judge, was offered as a significant reason why individuals should eventually decide to leave the state of nature and form a civil union. Locke's insight actually becomes more telling when applied to states, in which questions concerning the justice of cosmopolitan distributions may not even be raised or debated because those whose interests would be served are unlikely to be at the table.

In this context, we can consider the continuing failure of all but a few developed states to meet the UN target of transferring as development aid 0.7%, or seven cents of every ten dollars, in gross national income. In fact, official development aid, as opposed to military aid, from developed states has fallen in percentage terms, from 0.33% of combined GNP in 1985 to 0.23% in 2002.[35] Some

---

[33] For Immanuel Kant's treatment of a similar bias, see Jeremy Waldron, "What Is Cosmopolitan?" *The Journal of Political Philosophy* 8 (2000), p. 238; See also Jamie Mayerfeld, "The Myth of Benign Group Identity: A Critique of Liberal Nationalism," *Polity* XXX (1998), pp. 555–578. Mayerfeld critiques liberal nationalism by demonstrating how Lockean own-case bias can fuel virulent nationalism.

[34] Martha Nussbaum, *Cultivating Humanity* (Cambridge: Harvard University Press, 1998); see also the exchange between Gertrude Himmelfarb, Walter Berns, Todd Gitlin and William Galston, "Symposium: Is Patriotism Compatible with Higher Education?," *Academic Questions* 15 (2002), pp. 21–36.

[35] Singer, *One World*, p. 180.

specificity here will help underscore the point about just how much states may be willing to give in the current system. The US transferred 0.13% of GNP for development aid in 2002, lowest among the 22 highly developed states tracked by the Organization for Economic Cooperation and Development. The amount delivered by the US actually was first, at nearly $13.3 billion, representing some 23 percent of the $58.27 billion total for the affluent states. In descending order of contribution percentage, Denmark, Norway, Sweden, The Netherlands and Luxembourg were the only states to meet the 0.7% goal, with Denmark first at 0.96. Among states with gross domestic products of at least $1.4 trillion, none registered higher than France's 0.38% or $5.49 billion. The UK gave 0.31% or $4.92 billion; Germany 0.27% or $5.32 billion; Japan 0.23% or $9.28 billion; and Italy 0.20% or $2.33 billion.[36]

The amounts still may seem impressive, but not all of the aid is targeted at states or regions with the greatest need. In fact, in the case of the US, less than half of development aid goes to low-income states, as opposed to strategically important middle-income states such as Egypt.[37] The aid that does reach low-income states is far below what would be sufficient to help many secure even minimal subsistence standards for all of their people, as UN Secretary General Kofi Annan and other non-state advocates for the global poor have emphasized.[38] The structure of the Westphalian system helps to ensure that there is no impartial judge to settle questions of appropriate transfers, at least not one that can obtain firm compliance with decisions made. In most cases, debates over transfer levels are held exclusively among the potential donors, giving rise to a powerful form of own-case bias and significantly inhibiting movement toward more cosmopolitan distributions.

Some do argue that states should find it in their self-interest to make significant transfers. Pogge, for example, cites increasing threats of terrorism, epidemics, illegal drugs and unauthorized immigration from lesser-developed states as evidence that developed states should have compelling interests in aiding them.[39] Poverty and

[36] Organization for Economic Cooperation and Development, "Table 1: Net Official Development Assistance in 2002" (http://www.oecd.org/dataoecd/3/2/22460411.pdf, available at the OECD Web site http://www.oecd.org).

[37] Singer, *One World*, p. 181.

[38] Kofi Annan, "Make 2004 the Year of Kept Promises," *The Toronto Star* (30 December 2003), p. A-26.

[39] Pogge, "A Global Resources Dividend."

related ills in less-affluent states do indeed have impact on richer states. A plausible argument can be made that affluent states make some of their contributions from an enlightened self-interest in achieving a more stable and just international order. However, transfers at the level required by a moral cosmopolitan approach likely would far outweigh the benefits derived for citizens of the states making the transfers. In fact, affluent states typically have responded to the threats from less-affluent states with increased enforcement and interdiction measures aimed at the specific threats, including through intergovernmental cooperation, rather than by primarily addressing the root causes.[40] Leaders of sovereign states are tasked with finding the most effective means of promoting and protecting their citizens' interests. Programs targeting specific threats to those interests are more cost effective, and therefore more clearly presentable as in the interest of the polity, than making the larger transfers and probably considerable sacrifices that would be necessary to address the threats at their roots. If targeted enforcement generally is adequate to protect the citizens of an affluent state, then there will be little reason to make large-scale transfers.

The same general self-interest critique may be applied to the approach of the cosmopolitan democrats, who cite increasing pressures on domestic democratic rule from the processes of economic globalization as reasons why governing capabilities should be ceded upward in the near term. Such cosmopolitan democrats as David Held do not advocate creating a highly centralized global government, but Held is clear that some institutions must be created or existing ones endowed with strong supranational capabilities to promote democratic accountability to individuals within states.[41] In the near term, that would include the creation of a new International Human Rights Court, compulsory state submission to the jurisdiction of the International Court of Justice, and the creation of an additional UN chamber where the interests of individuals within states, rather than the interests of their governments, would be represented.[42] In the

[40] Roy Godson, and Phil Williams, "Strengthening Cooperation against Transsovereign Crime," in Maryann K. Cusimano (ed.), *Beyond Sovereignty: Issues for a Global Agenda* (New York: Bedford-St. Martin's, 2000), pp. 111–146.

[41] Held, "Democracy and Globalization," p. 25.

[42] For a similar proposal, see Richard Falk and Andrew Strauss, "Toward Global Parliament (Citizen Input on Globalization)," *Foreign Affairs* 80 (2001), pp. 212–218.

longer term, Held's prescriptions would include a global parliament connected to a network of regions, nations and localities and possessing some independent power to raise revenue, an interconnected global legal system, and a progressive transfer of states' coercive capabilities to regional and global institutions.

Many of Held's institutional prescriptions would be those of a plausible institutional cosmopolitanism. The approach offered here differs in that I do not presume that the pressures from the globalizing economy are sufficient to cause state leaders to submit in the near term to the compulsory jurisdiction of the International Court of Justice, or to cede some of their internal sovereignty to a UN chamber that would include their own citizens. Such broad changes may be possible in the longer term, if states have become increasingly embedded in supranational regional and global organizations and gradually have come to address a broader range of interests and issues in common.

In sum, ethical particularism is foundational in the Westphalian system. The norms of internal and external sovereignty observed by states are justified by reference to their roles in protecting and promoting the interests of states' own citizens. The perceived separateness of citizen sets helps to create and reinforce electoral and own-case biases against cosmopolitan distributions. Some significant transfers of food and other aid are made by states, but the transfers are much smaller than the extension of routine distributions prescribed by moral cosmopolitanism. Hopes for broader distributions and improved life chances for the least affluent are frustrated at many turns in the current system.

5. An Integrated Alternative

If the Westphalian system impedes cosmopolitan distributions because it encourages an inward-looking stance, then a more integrated system should promote cosmopolitan ends. It should promote the view that much larger sets of persons have interests in common that should be protected and promoted in common. In a more integrated system, mechanisms for obtaining compliance with state distributive obligations also should be more varied and more effective. And, democratically accountable integration should allow individuals within states to have more significant input on the policies that have impact on their lives at the state and supranational levels. Amartya

Sen, among others, has made a compelling case that political rights, when their full exercise is allowed, are vital to securing economic rights.[43]

We can turn to the EU as a partial model for the integrated alternative. I say "partial" because union-wide democracy remains underdeveloped in many respects,[44] and because it should not be presumed that the European template should or easily could be laid over the rest of the world. That said, the union is extremely significant as an example of a system in which the dynamics of regional economic and political integration have opened spaces for the promotion of more cosmopolitan distributive outcomes, as well as for the securing of a narrow but robust package of individual rights recognized above the state. In the EU, trans-state distributions have been formalized through "structural-fund" initiatives aimed at stimulating development and easing the pressures of integration, mainly within less affluent states.[45] Since 1993, additional "cohesion-fund" distributions have been made to aid development in the historically least affluent EU states: Spain, Portugal, Greece and Ireland.[46] Accompanying this growth in distributions of resources has been an increasing distribution of opportunities in the form of free movement, granted first to workers and gradually to all citizens of participating member states. Citizens have gained the right to live and work across the union, and to stand and vote in local and EU elections.[47] Citizens of member states also have gained independent legal standing and the right to

---

[43] Amartya Sen, "Freedom and Needs: An Argument for the Primacy of Political Rights," *The New Republic* (10 January 1994), pp. 31–36; see also Sen, *Development as Freedom,* pp. 147–149; Andrew Kuper, "Rawlsian Global Justice, beyond the Law of Peoples to a Cosmopolitan Law of Persons," *Political Theory* 28 (2000), pp. 663–664.

[44] The EU organizations long have been criticized as elitist and technocratic, rather than democratic. See Thomas Pogge, "Creating Supra-National Institutions Democratically: Reflections on the European Union's 'Democratic Deficit,'" *Journal of Political Philosophy* 5 (1997), pp. 177–178; Amaryllis Verhoeven, *The European Union in Search of a Democratic and Constitutional Theory* (The Hague: Kluwer Law International, 2002), pp. 57–74.

[45] John McCormick, *The European Union: Politics and Policies* (Boulder: Westview Press, 1999), p. 68.

[46] Steven P. McGiffen, *The European Union: A Critical Guide* (London: Pluto Press, 2001), p. 122.

[47] See Andrew Geddes, *The Politics of Migration and Immigration in Europe* (London: Sage, 2003), Chapter 6. Full free movement – no passports must be shown at borders – is permitted within the Schengen region, which excluded only Britain and Ireland in the 15-member EU.

challenge some actions of their states in the European Court of Justice. For example, a 1982 ruling found British workplace gender-equality laws discriminatory and ordered them modified to comply with supranational law, despite the vigorous legal defense and protests of the British government. A later ruling resulted in the UK being forced to compensate women discharged from military service because of pregnancy, and the court has ruled a number of other times against the express wishes of member states.[48] That is not to say that the ECJ does not consider the impact on member states of its rulings, or that the court, which has focused on cases related to trans-state economic activity, is designed to be a model defender of human rights or a cosmopolitan distributive scheme.[49] However, the legal standing of individuals above their states, itself secured over time in the ECJ, has enabled individuals to contest and occasionally defeat unreasonable rejections of rights claims by their own states.

It could be objected that, though individuals have achieved the right to challenge the rejection of some rights claims at the state level in the EU system, they also have become vulnerable to unreasonable actions at the supranational level. This is an important concern. However, there are two considerations that can mitigate or importantly illuminate it. First, we need not presume that all laws and regulations must be issued as edicts from above in a supranational system. The observance of a principle of subsidiarity, where policy is set at the lowest appropriate level, can help to check tendencies toward excessive interference from supranational policy makers. Subsidiarity, which has been integral in the development of the EU, "seems to reflect the same normative ideals as democracy: policies must be controlled by those affected, to ensure that institutions and laws reflect the interests of individuals under conditions where all count as equals. Only when these considerations counsel joint action is central authority warranted."[50] A number of theorists, including

[48] See Heide Ingeborg, "Supranational Action against Sex Discrimination: Equal Pay and Equal Treatment in the European Union," *International Labour Review* 138 (1999), pp. 381–420.

[49] See Philip Alston, "An 'Ever Closer Union' in Need of a Human Rights Policy: The European Union and Human Rights," in Philip Alston (ed.), *The EU and Human Rights* (Oxford: Oxford University Press, 1999), pp. 3–66.

[50] Andreas Follesdal, "Subsidiarity and Democratic Deliberation," in Erik Oddvar Eriksen and John Erik Fossum (eds.), *Democracy in the European Union: Integration Through Deliberation?* (London: Routledge, 2000), p. 86.

some who are not explicit advocates of integration, have made the related point that the separation of powers common in constitutional democracies would be able to play the same kinds of checks and balances role in a supranational democracy, even one so large as a global government. "This functional approach is in fact the way we deal with the potential for tyranny at the nation-state level: we do not protect against government tyranny by requiring states to split up into smaller units."[51] The operation of a strong principle of subsidiarity, where the higher bodies would be required to demonstrate that a specific issue should be decided at their level rather than at lower levels, could create many more checks on power and balances of power than is currently the case in many constitutional democracies.

Second, it is actually more likely that individual rights protection will be greater the more avenues of appeal individuals have, especially if they are members of an ethnic, national or other minority within a state or sub-state region. An oft-cited example is the civil-rights struggle of African-Americans in the US South during the early and middle parts of the 20th century. A courageous and dynamic social and legal movement gradually led to the recognition of core rights for African-Americans at the federal level, and it was higher-level authorities who finally ensured that those rights would be guaranteed, over the resistance of many authorities and stakeholders in the segregated society at lower levels.[52] Of course, there can be no ultimate guarantee that a supranational judicial or other institution will not overstep its bounds or make an egregious mistake in the case of an individual or group, any more than there is such a guarantee against abuses within a state. However, the expansion of democratic rule above the state can provide significant pressures for the maintenance of democratic rule within states, as well as providing more formal avenues for individuals to challenge policies and actions by the agents of government.

Overall, a more integrated Europe has helped expand the set of persons whose interests are viewed as appropriately consulted in distributive matters. It has resulted in some significant transfers of material resources to poorer member states, as well as in transfers of opportunities to persons in those states in the form of free movement and a broader, European, form of citizenship. EU distributions still

---

[51] Jones, *Global Justice*, p. 229.

[52] For a comprehensive overview, see Peter Levy, *The Civil Rights Movement* (Westport: Greenwood Press, 1998).

may not be at a level sufficient to fully satisfy moral cosmopolitanism. However, the person born into a historically very poor region of a state such as Ireland or Portugal, Spain or Greece, is less handicapped by that starting point than in the past. As integration deepens, that person's children and grandchildren can expect to be more nearly equal to those in the more affluent regions of Europe in the resources and opportunities immediately available to them.[53] And, similar distributions will be available over time to the citizens of the 10 additional states that were approved for accession to full EU membership in 2004.[54]

6. Moving toward the Integrated Alternative

The above is necessarily an extreme simplification of the complex evolution of the EU over the past five decades. However, the process of European integration has been driven by the same general forces that can be seen at work in other regions, and I want to show here why it is plausible to think that achieving a similar program of economic and ultimately political integration is possible elsewhere. The forces I mean are those linked to increases in regional trans-state exchange. Such increases generally follow the creation of regional free trade areas, and they can help to promote the "constitutionalization" of a supranational system, where the rules and policies set at the supra-state level gradually become binding on states.[55] In simplest

[53] A "convergence" has been documented among EU member-state economies, where per capita gross domestic product in less affluent member states has been moving toward the EU average. From 1986 to 1999, for example, per capita GDP rose from 65% to 78% of the EU average in the four poorest states: Greece, Ireland, Portugal and Spain. Robert A. Pastor, *Toward a North American Community: Lessons from the Old World for the New* (Washington: Institute for International Economics, 2001), p. 51.

[54] See the EU web site: http://www.europa.int.

[55] See Alec Stone Sweet, "The New GATT: Dispute Resolution and the Judicialization of the Trade Regime," in Mary L. Volcansek (ed.), *Law above Nations: Supranational Courts and the Legalization of Politics* (Gainesville: University Press of Florida, 1997), pp. 118–141; "Constitutional Dialogues in the European Community," in Alec Stone Sweet, Anne-Marie Slaughter and Joseph H.H. Weiler (eds.), *The European Court and National Courts – Doctrine and Jurisprudence: Legal Change in Its Social Context* (Oxford: Hart Publishing, 1998); Alec Stone Sweet, and Thomas L. Brunell, "Constructing a Supranational Constitution: Dispute Resolution and Governance in the European Community," *American Political Science Review* 92 (1998), pp. 63–82; Alec Stone Sweet, Wayne Sandholtz and Neil Fligstein (eds.), *The Institutionalization of Europe* (Oxford: Oxford University Press, 2001).

terms, this trans-state-exchange approach to the study of economic and political integration suggests that the constitutionalization of the EU occurred in a predictable pattern spurred by increasing trade and other trans-state activities, and by states' increasing need to manage those activities. It holds that

> ...as transnational exchange rises in any specific domain (or cluster of related domains), so do the costs, for governments, of maintaining disparate national rules. As these costs rise, so do incentives for governments to adjust their policy positions in ways that favor the expansion of supranational governance. Once fixed in a given domain, European rules – such as relevant treaty provisions, secondary legislation, and the ECJ's case law – generate a self-sustaining dynamic that leads to the gradual deepening of integration in that sector, and, not uncommonly, to spillovers into other sectors.[56]

The heavy lifting in the constitutionalization model is done by supranational legal bodies such as the European Court of Justice. As such bodies are called on to settle disputes among economic actors and states, important supranational precedents are set. For example, some fundamental workers' rights were recognized by the ECJ as a concession to state courts in the ECJ's battle to establish the doctrine of supremacy, which holds that policy formulated at the European supranational level should be viewed as supreme over member states' laws.[57] That doctrine has been fundamental in promoting political integration and helping to ensure the viability of the EU project. However, the accompanying principle of subsidiarity, again meant to ensure that policy is set at the lowest appropriate level, helps serve as a check on centralized power in the EU.[58]

Economic integration similar to that seen in the early days of the European project, specifically the creation of regional trade bodies designed to ease cross-border flows of capital, goods and services, already is underway in various regions. The most advanced economic integration project outside Europe probably is

---

[56] Alec Stone Sweet and Wayne Sandholtz, "Integration, Supranational Governance, and the Institutionalization of the European Polity," in Alec Stone Sweet and Wayne Sandholtz (eds.), *European Integration and Supranational Governance* (New York: Oxford University Press, 1998), pp. 4–5.

[57] Stone Sweet, "Constitutional Dialogues in the European Community," p. 317.

[58] Andreas Follesdal, "Subsidiarity and Democratic Deliberation," p. 86.

the North American Free Trade Agreement region of Canada, Mexico and the US Trade between NAFTA's three members grew from $306 billion to more than $620 billion in the first decade of operation,[59] and NAFTA's dispute panels have been called on to make some significant rulings. In addition, there has been some elite interest in deepening North American integration. Mexican President Vicente Fox Quesada has pressed over several years for EU-style structural funds to aid his country's development, as well as for freer cross-border movement of workers.[60] I note Fox's proposals as evidence that some prominent leaders of less affluent states support something like the integrated alternative. The argument offered here for the plausibility of achieving that alternative does not depend primarily on negotiation among states' leaders, who must consider first the interests of their national constituencies. However, in an increasingly economically integrated North American system, where states engage in increasing trans-state exchange, where supranational legal precedents gradually are set, and where more policy is coordinated regionally over time, the chances would improve for such far-ranging regional development initiatives.

Nothing here is meant to suggest that there is anything automatic about achieving the integrated alternative. Rather, economic integration, and the process of constitutionalization, can create significant opportunities for individuals and groups within states to press for movement toward the alternative. As supranational bodies, especially adjudicative ones, grow in importance or ability to take autonomous action, they can provide channels of access or influence to disparate groups, including international non-

[59] Office of the United States Trade Representative, "NAFTA: A Decade of Strengthening a Dynamic Trade Relationship" (October 2003), pp. 1–2 (http://www.ustr.gov).

[60] Pastor, *Toward a North American Community*, p. 98; see also "Mexico Leader Pushes Change," *The Boston Globe* [published in *The Seattle Times*, p. A-1 (6 September 2001)]; By early 2004, the George W. Bush administration had proposed a broad guest worker plan that also would allow many undocumented workers to obtain legal-resident status, though the plan was criticized for failing to include any citizenship option and for giving guest workers relatively brief work eligibility. Ricardo Alonso-Zaldivar, "Bush Would Open U.S. to Guest Workers," *Los Angeles Times* (8 January 2004) p. A-1.

governmental organizations.[61] Joint action by trans-state organizations and affinity groups not only raises the prospect of securing important region-wide labor and other protections, but in itself can promote cross-border understanding and cohesion. If groups of workers, environmentalists, or activists on specific issues are to join with like-minded persons across borders and jointly press interests at the supranational level, then that can help promote the view that the set of persons who count is larger than the nation-state.[62] It can promote a recognition that many groups' interests already are in harmony, and a rejection of the Westphalian fixation on the immediate citizen set.

In general terms, if movement toward integration can help to promote the view that the interests of broader sets of persons should be promoted and protected in common, then the moral imperative on the moral cosmopolitan becomes advocacy of deep integration among states and active rejection of the Westphalian status quo. In

---

[61] For example, some NAFTA panels have agreed to admit amicus, or friend-of-the-court, briefs from NGOs. See Duncan B. Hollis, "Private Actors in Public International Law: Amicus Curiae and the Case for the Retention of State Sovereignty," *Boston College International and Comparative Law R*eview 35 (2002), pp. 241–242. Notable among such decisions to admit amici include one in January 2001 in *Methanex Corp. v. United States*, and one in October 2001 in *United Parcel Services of America, Inc. v. Canada.* The NAFTA Free Trade Commission, at its October 2003 meeting in Montreal, Canada, affirmed that dispute panels have the authority to accept such briefs. The US and Canadian representatives, though not the Mexican representative, also announced an intention to open some dispute hearings to the public – if the parties to the dispute agreed. "NAFTA Commission Meets, Announces New Transparency Measures," Office of the United States Trade Representative, 7 October 2003 (http://www.ustr.gov).

[62] For example, the AFL-CIO in 2000 created a Campaign for Global Fairness that aimed, in part, at building "international solidarity with our brothers and sisters in [economically] emerging nations as well as developed nations to create equitable, democratic and sustainable growth" (AFL-CIO, "Campaign for Global Fairness," 16 February 2000, available at http://www.aflcio.org/aboutaflcio/ecouncil). The union also has supported the International Labor Organization's global labor standards. Such public positions may be seen merely as disguised affluent-state protectionism intended to make developing-state labor less competitive globally. Even if that is the case, however, it represents significant pressure that, coupled with pressures for adjustment assistance from developing states themselves, could result in concrete positive change for workers in those states. On trans-state labor and other coalitions, see Jeremy Brecher and Tim Costello, *Global Village or Global Pillage: Economic Restructuring from the Bottom up* (Boston: South End Press, 1994).

the near term, the cosmopolitan should advocate regional economic and political integration, as well as the democratic transformation of existing supranational organizations. Thus, the cosmopolitan should join those calling for an EU that looks more like a fully democratic governing body, where policies that affect individuals in member states are crafted not primarily through a process of consultation among states' leaders and powerful interests within states, but in a more open, more democratic process in the European Parliament. The moral cosmopolitan likewise should support in broad terms Fox's call for deeper North American integration, as well as supporting the expansion of NAFTA to Central and South America in the incipient Free Trade Agreement of the Americas, while demanding that civil society groups be allowed access to negotiations, and that more robust provisions for protection of labor and human rights be included. For the longer term, the cosmopolitan should consistently advocate the creation of "more world government," or genuinely democratic institutions above the state, including and especially those that extend beyond local geographic regions. Regions such as Southern Africa, which are attempting to reap benefits from localized economic integration, likely will find it difficult to realize robust economic development in a global system of "separate but equal" economic areas. Thus, further constitutionalization coupled with increasing openness and democratization of the global economic system regulated by the World Trade Organization should be emphasized. The cosmopolitan should support the transformation of the WTO into a more transparent, more accountable, supranational body,[63] while opposing those activists and political thinkers who call for states to immediately withdraw from the WTO, or who demand that the organization be disbanded in the name of protecting state sovereignty.[64] For the much longer term, we should want to see the transformation of the WTO, or the creation of a new organization with more prominent legislative and adjudicative functions, into a supranational body that could facilitate cosmopolitan distributions of resources and opportunities globally. The ultimate aim would be the creation of a global body, or global network of sub-state, state,

---

[63] See, for example, Robert Howse, "Membership and its Privileges: The WTO, Civil Society and the Amicus Brief Controversy," *European Law Journal* 9 (2003), pp. 496–510. Howse argues that, despite the resistance of some member states, there is sound basis in WTO jurisprudence for admitting amicus briefs.

[64] See Adam Lynn, "Presidential Candidate Kucinich Vows to Leave WTO," *The News Tribune* (Tacoma, Washington), 6 October 2003, p. B-1.

regional and global institutions, that would be able to ensure that all persons, regardless of birthplace, would have access to adequate distributions of life resources and opportunities.

Of course, the mention of any entity resembling a world state will provoke a host of objections. I have discussed at length elsewhere the feasibility and desirability of realizing integration at the global level in the long term.[65] Space constraints prevent a detailed discussion here. Briefly, however, the standard objections concerning armed tyranny in a world state may be addressed through an emphasis on the dispersal of coercive forces. The developing EU rapid reaction force offers an example of how such an armed body might be constructed and controlled at the supranational regional level.[66] Likewise, recent proposals for a UN force capable of rapidly responding to armed crises within states give some idea of the kinds of forces that the highest level governing bodies might control. Common objections about the untenability of democratic rule on a global scale also may be addressed, through emphasis on a principle of subsidiarity. Under such a principle, intermediary governing bodies at the sub-state, state and regional supra-state levels could be expected to decide most policy questions, leaving to the higher level those issues such as global environmental threats that are most appropriately addressed on a global scale.

Those and other objections are significant and do deserve much fuller treatment. However, the argument here has not been primarily concerned with global government, but with the initial case for strong institutional cosmopolitanism as a means to help ensure that the distributions demanded by moral cosmopolitanism actually are made. If it does not seem feasible or desirable to create a full global government, even in the very long term of hundreds of years, accountable integration on a regional scale promises significant,

---

[65] Luis Cabrera, *Political Theory of Global Justice: A Cosmopolitan Case for the World State* (London: Routledge, 2004). Chapter 5 addresses the objection that a supranational system, at the global level or well below, cannot be ruled democratically. Chapter 6 addresses the potential for tyranny by supranational bodies, including at the global level, in such a system.

[66] In 1999, member states formally agreed to create a force of up to 60,000 troops, deployable within 60 days and capable of sustaining a deployment for at least one year. Neill Nugent, *The Government and Politics of the European Union*, 5th edition (New York: Palgrave, 2003), pp. 418–420; In June 2003, members agreed to send a 1400-troop peacekeeping force to the Congo, replacing a smaller UN force there [Thomas Fuller "European Peacekeepers Go to Congo on Non-NATO Mission," *International Herald Tribune* (4 June 2003)].

relatively near-term improvements in the life chances of hundreds of millions of persons.

Department of Social and Behavioral Sciences
Arizona State University West
PO Box 37100,
Phoenix, AZ 85069-7100
USA
E-mail: luis.cabrera@asu.edu

OMAR DAHBOUR

THREE MODELS OF GLOBAL COMMUNITY

(Received 14 May 2004; accepted in revised form 7 June 2004)

ABSTRACT. Debates about global justice tend to assume normative models of global community without justifying them explicitly. These models are divided between those that advocate a borderless world and those that emphasize the self-sufficiency of smaller political communities. In the first case, there are conceptions of a community of trade and a community of law. In the second case, there are ideas of a community of nation-states and of a community of autonomous communities. The nation-state model, however, is not easily justified and is one that has been criticized extensively elsewhere. The model of a community of trade underlies both advocates of market-oriented development and exponents of global schemes of redistribution of resources and incomes. I analyze the work of Charles Beitz, Peter Singer, and Thomas Pogge to show that the assumption that global interdependence is beneficial is poorly justified. The model of a community of law, as seen in the work of Henry Shue and others, is the basis for arguments against state sovereignty and in favor of international human rights regimes. I argue that this model suffers either from a problem of practicability or of hegemony. Finally, the model of a community of autonomous communities uses notions of patriotism and sovereignty to maintain that disengagement and independence are the best routes to global peace and justice.

KEY WORDS: global justice, international law, patriotism, peace, sovereignty, sustainability

1. JUSTICE, PEACE, AND GLOBAL COMMUNITY

There has been considerable recent discussion about what kind of a global community can provide the proper context for the achievement of justice and peace on a world scale. Current debates about global justice abound with the jargon of "one world," "global governance," and the like. Yet, though much attention has been given, on the one hand, to the moral foundations of claims to global justice, and, on the other hand, to the institutional design of schemes of international cooperation, less thought has been devoted to the ethical justification of particular end-states of world society – what John Rawls has referred to as "realizable utopias."[1] This paper is

[1] John Rawls, *The Law of Peoples* (Cambridge: Harvard University Press, 1999), pp. 7, 11–12. For an earlier, and still relevant, statement of a similar idea, see Herbert Marcuse, *An Essay on Liberation* (Boston: Beacon Press, 1969), pp. 3–5.

concerned to evaluate a number of such mid-range conceptions of a global political community – first, by identifying such conceptions within current views about global justice and peace, and second, by assessing their capacity for moving us closer to those goals.

In identifying different models of global community, a basic dichotomy can be made between two visions of world order. One such vision is that of a "world without borders." From this perspective, the goal is to break down barriers between peoples in order to achieve mutual understanding and perhaps some modicum of substantive equality in global living standards. There are actually two rather different versions of this conception of global community that will be distinguished below. One emphasizes the terms of a fair global redistribution of wealth, while the other focuses on the rules of a global system of legal regulation.

But there is a second, and very different, sort of vision – that of a "world of self-sufficient communities." This view is often conflated with that of "nationalism" – that is, the advocacy of "nation-states" as a universal form of political community. But this is a mistake. While a world of nation-states *could* be an instantiation of a world of self-sufficient communities, it is not the only version of such an idea. Moreover, understood properly, a world of nation-states differs quite markedly from a world of sovereign, or self-determining, states, since nation-states are not just any sovereign political communities, but only those congruent with national communities, in the sense of ethnic nations. I, as well as some others, have written on the deficiencies of this nationalist ideal – and it has few unapologetic exponents today.[2] Nevertheless, the ideal of the nation-state persists in various forms and, more loosely construed as not based on ethnic identities, continues to have adherents.[3] But if sovereign states are not understood to be nation-states and yet are not considered legitimate simply because they already exist, some other justification is required to regard them as the basis of a world order.[4] This, I will argue, can

[2] See, most recently, Omar Dahbour, *Illusion of the Peoples: A Critique of National Self-Determination* (Lanham: Lexington Books, 2003), as well as Omar Dahbour, "National Identity: An Argument for the Strict Definition," *Public Affairs Quarterly* 16 (2002), pp. 17–37.

[3] See various writings by Michael Walzer and Charles Taylor and, more programmatically, Yael Tamir, *Liberal Nationalism* (Princeton: Princeton University Press, 1993).

[4] On this point, see Omar Dahbour, "Self-Determination without Nationalism," in Fred Dallmayr and José M. Rosales (eds.), *Beyond Nationalism?: Sovereignty and Citizenship* (Lanham: Lexington Books, 2001), pp. 57–71.

be given by the idea of a world of ecologically sustainable communities – an idea that has been influential in the radical wing of the global justice movement for the last ten years or so.[5] So we have two concepts of a "world without borders" and two concepts of a "world of self-sufficient communities."

In the first case, a world without borders can be thought of as either a "community of trade" or as a "community of law." The idea of a community of trade is based on the notion that increasing global interconnections are conducive to a peaceful, and ultimately just, world. The best way to do this is through encouragement of economic interactions, suitably adjusted to ensure that the conditions for *fair* trade are present. This view is cosmopolitan in the sense that the creation of commonalities, identities, and ultimately loyalties across borders is regarded as a way to obtain peace and justice internationally. The best means of ensuring that this happens is to increase transborder and global interconnections – that is, globalization, in contemporary parlance.

A community of law focuses on the creation of a borderless world through the establishment of laws, rules, procedures, and institutions that will gradually supercede particular sovereignties and political loyalties. Transnational organizations of all kinds, whether governmental or nongovernmental, have a role to play in this process. But the goal is a world in which global standards of justice are eventually applied universally, without restriction by particular states or local laws.

In the second case – that of a world of autonomous or self-sustaining communities – the two possible models are those of a community of nation-states and that of a community of ecological communities. I will set aside here the first model, as having been thoroughly criticized elsewhere, and concentrate on the second. This model of ecological communities, which I will equate with the general notion of autonomous communities, assumes the norm of self-determination as a primary component of global justice (and its maintenance through some conception of sovereignty). But sovereignty is now given a "green" justification – it provides the means of protecting self-sustaining communities in the face of the globalizing tendencies of dominant corporations and states.

---

[5] See Herman Daly and John Cobb, *For the Common Good: Redirecting the Economy Toward Community, the Environment, and a Sustainable Future*, 2nd edition (Boston: Beacon Press, 1994), especially Chapter 9.

So in considering these three remaining models of global community each can be seen to appeal to those espousing particular conceptions of political justice. A global trading community appeals most often to those internationalists who seek global redistributions of income and wealth. Economic interconnections must obtain in order to make an argument for the injustice of particular distributions of goods. Second, it is those most concerned with the establishment and enforcement of human rights of various sorts that find a global legal community most compelling. Such a community would provide a set of norms concerning rights to which appeal could be made – as well as institutions that would make the enforcement of such norms a possibility.

Third, conceiving of the world as a community of autonomous communities is most attractive to those seeking protection for regions, countries, and localities faced with subsumption by aggressive states and corporations within a global market or political empire. As already mentioned, such protection often seems particularly important to those who view environmental sustainability as a necessary component of global justice. Undoubtedly, all these models of global community can seem compelling; a temptation will be to regard them as compatible in some way. But the arguments to be made for them are quite different in nature. It is in the justification of these different models of a global community that their incompatibility becomes clear.

2. A Community of Trade

The first model, a community of trade, assumes the value or benefit of the economic growth that supposedly results from opening domestic markets and economies generally to free trade and foreign investments. World peace will be a result of states' recognition that international trade produces global economic benefits. This recognition should over time yield international trade agreements to ensure the uninterrupted flow of capital, goods, and labor across borders. Military conflict would come to be regarded as an irrational interference with the increasing global interconnections that occur naturally in a relatively unregulated world market.

An early formulation of this idea of a community of trade can be found in Immanuel Kant, who maintained that as long as states recognize the benefits of the global integration resulting from international trade relations, they will have reasons not to act belligerently toward one another.[6] History has not been kind to this view. It now seems clear that the differential results of global trade may just as easily act as incentives for war. J. A. Hobson, V. I. Lenin and other early 20th-century theorists of economic imperialism made this point tellingly.[7] From the colonial wars to enforce "free" trade on China, Japan, and other recalcitrant countries, to the "great game" of controlling Eurasian trade routes, to the "resource wars" of the 21st century, war has frequently been used as a form of trade "by other means." There is a larger truth here: the state has always been instrumental to the process of capital accumulation (though of course it also has had its own goals). But even if trade were to reduce the occasions for conflict – an extremely unlikely scenario – there is still the question of how an international trading system that inevitably enables some countries to accumulate greater wealth than others could result in a just global distribution of income and resources.

The response generally given by advocates of a trade- (or market-) based model of global community is that it is possible to endorse the extension of a global market as the basis of a just and peaceful world, provided that the resulting interdependence is a fair one. The argument is that global economic interdependence is itself the precondition for a just distribution of wealth. Otherwise, countries must rely on arbitrarily distributed natural resources that may result in great disparities globally. The advantage of a global community premised on trade and commerce is that it provides a rationale for redistributing resources fairly to the world's people.

One example of this argument is Charles Beitz's application of a contractualist theory of distributive justice to the global scale. His view is premised on the idea that international relations is characterized by substantial interdependence between different states and societies. While Beitz acknowledges that global economic interdependence has negative consequences for many peoples – and this is where a concept of distributive justice becomes essential – he maintains that a claim to justice need assume no more than that there are benefits *and* burdens distributed differentially on a global scale by the

[6] Immanuel Kant, "Perpetual Peace: A Philosophical Sketch," in Hans Reiss (ed.), *Kant's Political Writings*, trans. H. B. Nisbet (Cambridge: Cambridge University Press, 1970), p. 114.

[7] For a still useful summary and evaluation of these theories, see Wolfgang J. Mommsen, *Theories of Imperialism*, trans. P. S. Falla (Chicago: University of Chicago Press, 1982).

processes of economic integration.[8] This interdependence supposedly justifies the redistribution of benefits and burdens in order to achieve a just international order.

But a crucial step in the theory is the assumption that furthering this economic interdependence can in the end benefit everyone. As Beitz writes, "It is clear that interdependence in trade and investment produces substantial aggregate economic benefits in the form of a higher global rate of growth as well as greater productive efficiency."[9] While Rawls, whose theory Beitz relies on for his conception of justice, formulated a principle of fair distribution based on an abstracted model of one society, Beitz extends this idea to the world as a whole. There is, however, a problem with doing so. Whether or not social cooperation applies internationally – that is, whether or not particular societies become interdependent with others, depends on what sort of society they are. Not all societies – indeed, very few historically – have been globally interdependent to the degree that Beitz sees as fundamental to making claims for a global redistribution of wealth.

The reason this is an issue is that, as Eric Mack has pointed out in a critique of Beitz's theory of international redistribution,[10] such a redistributive scheme only applies to the "cooperative shares" of a country's income or wealth – that part of it that is the result of international economic cooperation. The "precooperative shares" – that part of a country's wealth produced internally and for internal use or consumption – are not, on Beitz's account, rightfully subject to redistribution. So the greater the degree of international cooperation or interdependence, the more wealth is available for a purportedly just global redistribution.

But such interdependence must itself first be normatively justified. Contrary to what advocates of globalization contend, economic interdependence is neither a natural or inevitable tendency in world history. As John Gray has argued, the historical development of virtually all market economies has been marked by a high degree of state intervention to protect internal markets and limit the effects of trade with wealthier countries.[11] It is only the political intervention of wealthier and more powerful states to break down these trade

[8] Beitz, *Political Theory and International Relations*, p. 152.

[9] Beitz, *Political Theory and International Relations*, p. 145.

[10] Eric Mack, "The Uneasy Case for Global Redistribution," in Steven Luper-Foy (ed.), *Problems of International Justice* (Boulder: Westview Press, 1988), pp. 55–66.

[11] John Gray, *False Dawn: The Delusions of Global Capitalism* (New York: New Press, 1998).

barriers and limit the internal development of weaker countries that provides the preconditions for the global economic interdependence advocated by proponents of globalization. The last fifteen years have been marked by just such interventions on the part of the United States in the political economies of countries around the globe.[12] That this intervention has taken place through the venue of international organizations – such as, most recently, the World Trade Organization – that promote the destruction of trade barriers does not change the fact that interdependence is a political project that requires justification.

Beitz thinks he has justified interdependence by showing that global trade yields *aggregate* benefits. This result of international economic interdependence, Beitz asserts, is "beyond dispute."[13] But all that is actually beyond dispute is that global interdependence generates aggregate benefits *and* costs. The aggregate benefits need not be a consideration for a particular country – either because they may choose to forgo such benefits for other goods or because they do not rationally expect to accrue these benefits – that is, short of a global redistribution of wealth.

Beitz's reasoning is therefore disingenuous for two reasons. First, if interdependence is to be preferable to economic autarky for particular countries, such interdependence must yield net gains for those countries – aggregate benefits are not enough. Beitz's reply would probably be that if a country has a just claim, it will benefit, though only *after* a global redistribution has taken place. So, second, if in fact there are benefits for most participants in a globalizing economy, they will only come *after* a global redistribution, not before. Beitz must admit this point or there would be no reason to engage in global redistribution – which is what he wants to justify in the first place. But Beitz gives no reason as to why a country would choose interdependence over independence, given the fact that, absent such a global redistribution, most *cannot* be expected to gain from such interdependence. In other words, economic *independence*, as one aspect of self-determination, itself has value and may even yield greater benefits, relative to any *probable* outcomes of integration into a world capitalist economy. What are the reasons as to why such self-deter-

[12] See Peter Gowan, *The Global Gamble: Washington's Faustian Bid for World Dominance* (London: Verso, 1999); James Petras and Henry Veltmeyer, *Globalization Unmasked: Imperialism in the Twenty-First Century* (London: Zed Books, 2001).

[13] Beitz, *Political Theory and International Relations*, p. 152.

mination ought to be given up? It is instructive that Rawls himself does not endorse the more extreme version of his theory advocated by Beitz, perhaps in part because Rawls gives more weight to a principle of self-determination.[14]

Another approach to trying to argue that a community of trade can lead to a more just world is to maintain that such a community implies a moral obligation to aid the hungry and poor populations of the world. Such aid is not obligatory, however, unless those who help share a moral community with those to be helped. Some, such as Peter Singer, have claimed that just such a moral community exists; this is the significance, in Singer's view of regarding the world as a "global village" in which the suffering of some (anywhere) is the concern of others (everywhere).[15] Others, such as Thomas Pogge, insist that there is a "value overlap" between different societies today that, much as in the case of the wide acceptance of a category of "war crimes," can yield a moral consensus about obligations to aid the global poor. This moral consensus exists (or perhaps could exist?) through the establishment of "firm value-based institutional fixed points" – or, in less tortured language, of an "international ethical dialogue."[16] This view is certainly criticizable on various grounds, not least in terms of its lack of realism concerning the prospects for the achievement of such schemes, given the scale and apparent intractability of the institutions perpetuating global inequalities. While Singer genuinely seems to believe that we do in fact live in some version of a global village, he does concede that the institutions needed to make this a genuine political community are nowhere in evidence.[17] Similarly, Pogge rather abashedly ends a recent argument for his version of global redistribution by maintaining that such a global community is an ongoing concern if it can be shown that it is not impossible (as opposed to merely very improbable)![18]

But the point here is that nowhere do Singer, Pogge, and others argue that global justice – including, e.g., the alleviation of hunger – can only be served by accepting *and furthering* the economic and

[14] Rawls, *The Law of Peoples*, pp. 61–62, and 111–112.

[15] See Peter Singer, "Famine, Affluence, and Morality," *Philosophy and Public Affairs* 1 (1972), pp. 229–243.

[16] Thomas Pogge, "Moral Progress," in Luper-Foy (ed.), *Problems of International Justice* (Boulder: Westview Press, 1988), pp. 290–291 and 300–301.

[17] Peter Singer, *One World: The Ethics of Globalization* (New Haven: Yale University Press, 2002), pp. 196–99.

[18] Thomas Pogge, "The Moral Demands of Global Justice," *Dissent* (2000), p. 42.

commercial interdependence of the wealthy and the poor countries of the world. It must be said that the utilitarian and Kantian moral principles espoused by Singer and Pogge respectively do not provide many intellectual resources for justifying particular conceptions of political community, since they embody rigorously individualistic moral commitments. But since such philosophers have turned to consider – and indeed to assume – the existence of grandiose global communities, they ought to supply some rationale for why the construction of such communities is desirable – and moreover necessary for the achievement of social justice. This is particularly so given their rejection of the traditional idea of a world government. If a conception of a purely moral community is now supposed to provide a sufficient counterweight to the preponderance of political power in the hands of the privileged globally, then we need a theory of moral sentiments that would give us some reason to believe in the efficacy of such appeals to the idea of a global moral community. But we do not get this either. Should we, then, accept globalization as the precondition of a more just world order – on the mere hope that such an order is not impossible? Or should we, to use Walden Bello's phrase, attempt a "deglobalization" that seeks to limit the political sway of the wealthy – by, for instance, destroying or at least neutralizing the power of globalizing institutions such as the W.T.O.?[19] As with Beitz, so with the global moralists – what is needed is a reason for why interdependence is more desirable than independence, a reason that they do not provide.

3. A Community of Law

Turning to the second model of global community, that of a community of law, this model might be considered to be simply an idealization of the current regime of international law. But there are two problems with seeing the current international legal regime as in any substantial way a "community." First, there is the fact that international law actually embodies concessions to the sovereignty of the states that are the primary legitimate actors recognized in international legal documents. Second, the enactment and enforcement of

[19] Walden Bello, *Deglobalization: Ideas for a New World Economy* (London: Zed Books, 2002).

international legal provisions lacks any effective institutional embodiment.

To view a community of law as a goal of global justice is therefore to extrapolate in a utopian vein from the current legal regime to one that realizes certain implicit tendencies within it. On the one hand, the limitation of state sovereignty on the basis of human rights or other considerations suggests that a true community of law ought to be one in which sovereignty was either not recognized at all or only as a principle strictly subordinate to other considerations (such as those of human rights). On the other hand, doing so – overcoming the sovereignty of states in service to universal norms – will require a much more effective mechanism of enforcement of these norms than presently exists.

What reasons can be given to override state sovereignty and create a community of law in a more universal sense? Two reasons are often given today: first, that certain problems are global in nature and cannot be dealt with other than by "eroding" the sovereignty of particular states, and second, that human rights are more important considerations than sovereignty, since they apply to persons directly rather than as members of states that may or may not recognize such rights. But both reasons raise troubling issues – on the one hand, of the value of the sovereignty principle in international law, and on the other hand, of the available means for enforcing norms globally.

One argument for the downgrading of state sovereignty as a consideration, made, for instance, by Henry Shue, focuses on the supposed scale of global problems such as hunger and malnutrition, climate change, financial speculation, environmental pollution, and so forth; these all seem to be global phenomena, without respect for borders.[20] But it is not clear that a global legal community is the best context for solving such problems. Certainly, there is a role for international law in the regulation of states and corporations and their environmental and social impacts on particular societies. But the question is whether a new sort of global community will be able to do this independently of other agents, such as sovereign states or social movements.

Obviously skeptical doubts can be raised concerning the creation of a real international community of law. Why is this necessarily a

[20] For a discussion of this, see Henry Shue, "Eroding Sovereignty: The Advance of Principle," in Robert McKim and Jeff McMahan (eds.), *The Morality of Nationalism* (Oxford: Oxford University Press, 1997), pp. 340–359.

better means to achieve, say, restrictions on global climate change than by way of the actions of states? First, many would argue that this is a matter of principle versus expediency – that no principle is at stake in considering sovereignty, as it is in formulating a global rule of law. Yet, the principle at stake in making respect for state sovereignty a desideratum is that of peace – it is the prevention of war and conflict that is the goal underlying the development of the sovereignty doctrine over the last three hundred years. So the proper question to ask about eroding sovereignty is: why is world peace a less important goal than global justice? Perhaps, both considerations need to be taken into account.

Furthermore, economic and environmental degradation can be viewed as an attack on the security of countries, just as much as aggressive military actions.[21] The real problem here is not the continued existence of states, but the inordinate power and influence of some of them – particularly the imperial US state. The sovereignty doctrine does not protect such a state – indeed, its actions regularly traduce the sovereignty of other states – and eroding the doctrine may actually contribute to making the problem of domination by hegemonic states worse.

A second argument for a community of law is that it is the best means of enshrining and protecting human rights – partly because particular states are often the chief culprits in violating these rights. On this account, human rights are by definition "universal" – applicable to human beings generally – and their realization will entail a similarly universal regime, under which such rights are duly recognized.[22] The question here is whether respecting human rights is a sufficient justification for a global community of law in which states no longer have any separate legitimacy.

Perhaps the models of the International Criminal Court or the European Court of Human Rights might serve to suggest the outlines of such a community. But these raise the problem of enforcement: What would give such institutions dedicated to the pursuit of human rights enough weight to counter opposition from hegemonic or "outlaw" states that refused to recognize their jurisdiction (as the US did with the World Court in the 1980s and the ICC now)?

---

[21] Shue, "Eroding Sovereignty," p. 350.

[22] For a recent account of the philosophy of human rights, see Jack Donnelly, *Universal Human Rights in Theory and Practice*, 2nd edition (Ithaca: Cornell University Press, 2003).

One possibility is that some hegemonic state with a liberal democratic constitution would take it upon itself to aid in the building of regimes compatible with a community of law – though we might well ask: where will we find such a state? Subsequently, the hegemon would keep the peace by threatening war in retaliation for violations of international norms. Lea Brilmayer has argued a qualified case for the US playing this role. She writes that hegemony "creates the *opportunity* for political morality," as well as for oppression or domination of weaker states.[23] The argument is that, without major threats from other powers, the US could afford to act in accordance with the needs of the world community as a whole – and only under its imprimatur; she cites the Gulf War as an example of this.

The claim that Brilmayer makes here is not that a hegemonic power could be non-self-interested in its contribution to the establishment of a global legal community, but that it would benefit from such a community sufficiently to contribute to its creation. Yet, historical evidence suggests that a truly impartial global legal system could not get the assent of a hegemonic power, which would then be subject to its strictures – the US objections to the ICC being the latest example of this. If the construction of a new world government is ruled out – as thinkers otherwise sympathetic to the idea of a community of law have done since Kant – it is hard to see what mechanism other than a hegemonic state could create such a community. But such a state would not itself have the requisite impartiality to do so.

A second possibility is that the establishment of a system of global or cosmopolitan democracy could ensure a minimal respect for human rights, since such a system would enshrine on the global scale such rights – as has been done, for instance, in the European Community. There is considerable debate as to how the desideratum of democratic government could be instituted globally in such a way as to systematize respect for human rights or other entitlements.[24] The fundamental claim made by advocates of cosmopolitan democracy such as David Held and Daniele Archibugi is that today the world

---

[23] Lea Brilmayer, *American Hegemony: Political Morality in a One-Superpower World* (New Haven: Yale University Press, 1994), p. 224 (italics provided).

[24] For a survey of different conceptions of cosmopolitan democracy, see Daniele Archibugi, "Principles of Cosmopolitan Democracy," in Daniele Archibugi, David Held, and Martin Köhler (eds.), *Re-Imagining Political Community: Studies in Cosmopolitan Democracy* (Stanford: Stanford University Press, 1998), pp. 198–228.

consists of "overlapping communities of fate" in which the needs and interests of different countries are involved with one another.[25] Faced with this reality, any desirable form of political community – for instance, democracy – must be realized in such a way that this overlap is recognized and not thwarted. Above all, the traditional principle of the external sovereignty of states cannot any longer be viewed as a countervailing principle of equal weight, since it can be used to legitimate regimes that are undemocratic and lack respect for human rights. It is unnecessary to regard states as completely devoid of legitimacy – only that they are but one of several levels of governance and that the global is also a proper venue for the realization of democracy.[26]

There are at least three serious problems with this cosmopolitan-democracy view of global community. First, there is the logical point that the existence of interconnections between countries does not entail the desirability of these interconnections. The idea of an overlapping community of fate must still be justified normatively. As in the discussion above concerning the assumption that economic interdependence was a good thing, so here the fact of global connections does not make such a state of affairs desirable – and therefore something necessarily to be furthered. Of course, as with economic globalization, so with political: It must be shown that a global system of government will actually benefit the peoples of the world. It cannot simply be assumed that such a system will be beneficial – nor can it be regarded as an inevitability. This is particularly the case since the main form of political interconnection has historically been imperialistic. If there is any reason to imagine that this will not be true in the twenty-first century – that global interconnections will not come primarily from the domination of weaker countries by stronger ones – it should be given. But hierarchies and asymmetries of power that have always existed in international relations are largely abstracted out of cosmopolitan democratic theory. Second, the idea of cosmopolitan democracy is particularly susceptible to the problem of scale that has plagued democratic theory since the eighteenth century. If large states are only problematically democratic because of the elitist character of most forms of political representation and because of the monopoly of power held by party systems in such

[25] David Held, "Democracy and Globalization," in Archibugi et al., *Re-Imagining Political Community*, p. 24.

[26] Archibugi, "Principles of Cosmopolitan Democracy," pp. 216–217.

states, how much more will this be the case for global democratic institutions – especially if they are stable and effective forms of governance?[27] If democracy has any hope of realization, it is in the small countries that are most at the mercy of grand schemes of global governance dedicated to breaking down the sovereignty of such states. Finally, if global democracy is to be realized through the solidification of a global "civil society," this can only occur if the new organizations of civil society achieve some recognition on the part of states.[28] Delegitimating the sovereignty of states in the name of cosmopolitan principles of human rights and democracy may paradoxically make it *harder* to realize these very principles, since the only remaining political organizations with power on a global scale will be precisely the hegemonic states and corporations that are often the perpetrators of undemocratic and anti-humanitarian actions.

It has proved difficult to enforce legal norms that restrict the actions of states and corporations globally, since such entities are not easily held accountable. Without such accountability, a community of law will resemble the current regime of international law – it will be largely a codification of certain moral norms for the behavior of states and individuals – but it will fall short of being a global community. This is perhaps not such a bad thing, given the dangers and uncertainties of entrusting global rule to hegemonic or transnational states or organizations.

4. A Community of Autonomous Communities

If a community of trade can do little to mitigate the injustices resulting from the spread of global capitalism, and a community of law is inevitably too weak to effectively control powerful states and corporations, there may be a third possibility – a world of autonomous communities, coexisting more as a result of mutual indifference than of common concern. The twentieth century contained important attempts at constructing a peaceful and just world on the basis of the greater global interdependence and communication resultant from the advance of global markets and the establishment of international organizations. But these have been shown to be compatible with, and

[27] See Archibugi, "Principles of Cosmopolitan Democracy," p. 207, for some recognition of this problem.

[28] Martin Köhler, "From the National to the Cosmopolitan Public Sphere," in Archibugi et al., *Re-Imagining Political Community*, p. 246.

in some ways contributory to, the perpetration of global injustice and conflict. The models of a world community outlined above – and partly based on the consequences of increasing world trade or elaborating international law – assumed that more involvement and interdependence would yield a better world. But there is little evidence for this. In fact, the opposite seems more likely to be the case.

An alternative vision of world order must therefore seek to limit the degree and intensity of global interdependence through the design and support of truly autonomous communities. A just global community would be a world in which all communities had attained a measure of autonomy. This model is suggested historically both by the Rousseauian vision of autonomous city-states and the Hegelian idea of the rational state. Both have contemporary manifestations–in the case of the Hegelian idea, in the concept of "constitutional patriotism" espoused by Jürgen Habermas and others, and partially realized in the developing constitution of the European Union, and in the case of the Rousseauian notion, in the ideas of environmental sustainability and deglobalization utilized by the contemporary environmental and global justice movements.

The idea of constitutional patriotism provides a justification for allegiance to a state to the extent that it embodies just institutions. G. W. F. Hegel's view of the international community was that those states embodying the most rational ethical principles in their constitutions had rights over those states that did not. Today, Habermas interprets this to mean that only those states embodying procedural justice have a right to command loyalty from their citizens.[29] In both cases, a global community is a place in which rational principles gradually spread from country to country, with the assumption that states become less antagonistic to the extent that they embody these principles.

While this idea of constitutional patriotism is quite suggestive for a way in which solidarity within a community may be combined with adherence to principles of justice, it must be understood in a certain way in order to avoid problems that have arisen with earlier versions. Specifically, two problems could arise that pose something of a dilemma for the implementation of such a concept: Either constitutional patriotism becomes too strong a version of community,

---

[29] Jürgen Habermas, "Citizenship and National Identity: Some Reflections on the Future of Europe," *Praxis International* 12 (1992), pp. 1–18; reprinted in Omar Dahbour and Micheline R. Ishay (eds.), *The Nationalism Reader* (Atlantic Highlands: Humanities Press, 1995), pp. 333–343.

justifying the domestic conformity and international aggression that are often characteristic of hegemonic states, or it remains too weak, existing as an abstract idea that does not take root in the specific political cultures of different countries.

In the first case, the idea of constitutional patriotism could be used to justify the pursuit of power by supposedly more rational states – as Hegel notoriously advocated.[30] A contemporary version of this idea is expressed by John Gray, who argues that only strong states can maintain the coherence of their societies and cultures in the face of the pressures of globalization. Global justice, from Gray's point of view, "begins with the rehabilitation of the modern state."[31] Yet, such rehabilitated states may be better able to justify foreign aggressions, though supposedly in defense of legitimate constitutional principles.

The other side of this dilemma, however, is that constitutional regimes may be too weak to support a society that can be autonomous in the face of a globalizing regime, since espousal of principle does not provide a sufficient means of ensuring solidarity. So providing some countries with constitutions which guarantee democratic participation, civil rights, and perhaps a social welfare minimum – as has been done, for instance, in some Eastern European and Southern African countries recently – does not mean that these countries will be able to withstand the effects of penetration by global capital and the social impoverishment and political instability that frequently result.

Some additional specification of what makes a community autonomous is required. Here, it is important to recall Hegel's point that a constitution is not simply a written document enumerating political rights, but a form of "ethical life" which gives meaning and sustenance to the written constitution. While Hegel saw the political constitution of an autonomous state requiring particular institutions of civil society, he did not see that it would also require a particular political ecology – that is, a certain relationship of society to the natural resources of its locale. We now know that it is not sufficient for communities to have political rights and welfare provisions in order to maintain themselves autonomously, since it is possible for

[30] G. W. F. Hegel, *Elements of the Philosophy of Right*, trans. H. B. Nisbet (Cambridge: Cambridge University Press, 1991), Sections 324 and 331, pp. 360–363, 366–367.

[31] Gray, *False Dawn*, p. 201

international capital to destabilize these institutions if the country is well enough integrated into global commodity and capital markets. The ability to sustain a way of life based on local or regional ecologies is necessary in order for countries to achieve some measure of autonomy.

Jean-Jacques Rousseau's vision of autonomous city-states as the proper context for social justice is important here. While commonly thought to embody an archaic notion of political community, it has been given renewed relevance by the rise of "global cities" such as Singapore and Hong Kong. But beyond the limited significance of the city-state model lies a basic contrast that Rousseau makes between two conceptions of what is required for a just and peaceful world. I refer to Rousseau's distinction in the "Discourse on the Origins of Inequality" between a maxim of "reasoned justice" – basically, the "golden rule" ("do unto others as you would have them do unto you") – and a maxim of "natural goodness" – "do what is good for you with as little harm as possible to others."[32] This is the distinction that I made above between a world of common concern and one of mutual indifference. Both are normatively equivalent in some sense, but the latter is more realizable, given the problems with instituting a form of "common concern" on the global level. Of course, Rousseau made the distinction just mentioned between the two maxims to indicate that natural goodness was operative only in a state of nature, a lost and perhaps fictitious condition; "reasoned justice" must now serve in its place.

International relations, however, has been famously characterized from Hobbes forward as a *perpetual* state of nature. This special character of international relations was recognized even by Hegel, who had contempt for the general idea of a state of nature. Yet, when Hegel considers international relations, he states that, "since the sovereignty of states is the principle governing their mutual relations, they exist to that extent in a state of nature in relation to one another, and their rights are *actualized* not in a universal will with constitutional powers over them, but in their own particular wills."[33] It turns out that *only* on the global scale do peoples and communities exist in a state of nature in relation to one another.

---

[32] Jean-Jacques Rousseau, "Discourse on the Origin and Foundations of Inequality, in *The First and Second Discourses*, trans. Roger D. Masters and Judith R. Masters (New York: Saint Martin's Press, 1964), p. 133.

[33] Hegel, *Elements of the Philosophy of Right*, Section. 333, p. 368.

Even within a state of nature, however, as Rousseau pointed out, contrary to Thomas Hobbes, there are values that limit the self-interest of persons and peoples – in Rousseau's terms, the natural goodness inherent in us. But it is important to note that this maxim of natural goodness manifests itself in the form of self-absorption and disengagement, rather than as a commitment to standards of justice held in common with all others.

The notion of disengagement may find a contemporary manifestation in the idea of environmental sustainability, which implies that autonomous communities would be ones that have found the means for producing and reproducing the basic social goods necessary for survival and flourishing within specific local environments. Having done this, a community would have the autonomy necessary to disengage from at least primary reliance on global markets – in other words, to follow a path of "deglobalization."

Of course, such communities would also be much more self-absorbed than at present. Consequences of this turn inward on the part of autonomous communities would be the strengthening of borders, less capital and labor mobility, restrictions on trade, a weakening of global communication networks, reductions in travel and tourism, and so forth. These changes, among others, should mean a more peaceful and, in some sense of the term, more just world than any globalizing scenario could provide.

It is the sense of justice embodied in a community of autonomous communities that is probably most in question here. If justice is understood on the contractual model used by many liberal philosophers, the value of communal autonomy becomes a strictly secondary consideration. Once a proper distribution of resources and/or incomes is determined according to the strictures of a global social contract, the redistribution of such resources or incomes is in order; the autonomy of those countries subject to redistribution is not a relevant matter.

One problem with this contractual view is that it misses a singular fact about the injustice apparent in underdeveloped societies – it is not the result of too little global interdependence, but of *too much.* It is the *interference* in the affairs of poorer, weaker, and smaller countries around the world by hegemonic states and global financial institutions that is the problem – not any *lack* of engagement. It is this interference – in violation of a principle of the self-determination of peoples – that is responsible for much of the oppression to which the global South is subject today.

While stated so bluntly, this claim may seem highly contestable, it is primarily an extrapolation from the more non-controversial claim that the global South is today much worse off than it was a generation ago and that this is largely a result of the increasing power of multinational corporations, in alliance primarily with the U.S. and its agencies of so-called international development, such as the World Bank. The imposition of a neo-liberal conception of development on much of the underdeveloped world has had two widely reported results – the increasing integration of local economies in the world market and the impoverishment of many of the societies so integrated.[34] Of course, advocates of global integration may contend that this is historically exceptional – that the long-term tendency of global interdependence is an increase in wealth as a result of economic growth. Furthermore, they may point to some exceptions even within the recent period as indicating the compatibility of integration with growth. But the real issue here concerns the role of the state in limiting the unregulated effects of global market intervention into developing societies. Those cases in which real development have occurred have been ones where, almost without exception, the state played a strong role in protecting fledgling local economies from global competition by other countries.[35]

Of course, focusing on self-determination as a primary desideratum will mean toleration of greater differences in global incomes and resources than might be considered just according to a contractual view. Certainly, the global equalization of incomes and resources would be out of the question. But this equalization is, practically speaking, out of the question anyway. Even advocates are content to maintain it as a viable goal not because they foresee the political means of actually achieving it, but simply because it is first, *morally mandated*, and, second, *not impossible*.

But if self-determination is considered to include the ecological conditions for sustainability, then comparisons across quite different societies become less relevant. Only from a point of view that insists upon a unitary global model of economic development and the definition of wealth can a comparison of say, Angola and Switzerland in terms of resources and income be relevant. What is more important

[34] Petras and Veltmeyer, *Globalization Unmasked*, pp. 20–22; Bello, *Deglobalization*, pp. 115–116; Joseph Stiglitz, *Globalization and Its Discontents* (New York: W. W. Norton & Co., 2002).

[35] Gray, *False Dawn*, pp. 7–8

to determine is whether countries can sustain their populations given control of the resources at hand.[36]

Is this vision of autonomous, self-sustaining communities itself a chimera? While it is surely, as all proposals in political philosophy must be, a normative extrapolation from the present – it is clearly a more realizable utopia, to use Rawls' term again, than the idea of a fully integrated, interdependent, and egalitarian world order. Here there are two contrasting historical explanations for how such integration – unquestionably a feature of twentieth-century world history – has come about. One explanation insists on the historical inevitability of a scenario of globalization – itself the product of a long-term trend of capital accumulation. This explanation is thus similar to Karl Marx's vision of the capitalist overthrow of precapitalist societies in the *Communist Manifesto.*

A second explanation, however, rejects the historical inevitability of such a scenario, for two reasons. First, this explanation focuses on the breakdowns of and retreats from globalization that are also evident in nineteenth- and twentieth-century history, largely as a result of recurrent economic crises. There is no reason to think that twenty-first century capitalism will be immune to such crises. Second, even the periods of successful globalization involved massive interventions by powerful states to facilitate such global economic integration. These interventions have met with resistance both internally, by so-called isolationists, and externally, by self-determination movements. Today, parts of the global justice movement are again beginning to constitute such a resistance. Recent historical research on 20th-century imperial states, in particular, the informal empire of the US continues to uncover many ways in which the purportedly natural tendencies of capitalist markets have only worked as a result of overt and covert interventions by states committed to such a globalizing agenda.[37] Philosophically, these divergent historical explanations

[36] For two different versions of such a conception of global justice, one using the concept of subsistence, the other the concept of capabilities, see Maria Mies and Vandana Shiva, *Ecofeminism* (London: Zed Books, 1993), and Amartya Sen, *Development as Freedom* (New York: Alfred A. Knopf, 1999).

[37] See Emily Rosenberg, *Financial Missionaries to the World: The Politics and Culture of Dollar Diplomacy, 1900–1930* (Cambridge: Harvard University Press, 1999); Andrew Bacevich, *American Empire: The Realities and Consequences of U.S. Diplomacy* (Cambridge: Harvard University Press, 2002); Neil Smith, *American Empire: Roosevelt's Geographer and the Prelude to Globalization* (Berkeley: University of California Press, 2003); and David Harvey, *The New Imperialism* (Oxford: Oxford University Press, 2003).

suggest that we continue to be faced with the fundamental choice I outlined at the beginning of this essay – a choice to conceive of political community either as one of an open world without borders, come what may, or as one of relatively more disengaged, yet self-sustaining, communities.

It might also be wondered whether conceiving of the world as a community of autonomous communities gives up too easily on the possibility of a just global order that attempts to control and regulate – rather than avoiding or protecting against – globalizing forces. This is the view, it seems, of Michael Walzer, one of the most important advocates of the value and importance of communal autonomy, albeit of a more nationalist variety.[38] He writes recently of viewing the proper amount of "global governance" as that which allows a substantial pluralism, while still insisting on standards and rules of political behavior for all regimes.[39] Rawls seems to have come to a similar conclusion in arguing that his "law of peoples" is one that establishes legal regulation of regimes, while still embodying a principle of "toleration" for differences among them.[40]

But the real issue here is whether "global governance" takes the form of "regulative (moral) ideals" or of actual political institutions. The concept of governance obviously implies the existence of governing institutions and therefore immediately runs up against the problem of practicability. As Walzer notes, "the kinds of governmental agencies that are needed in an age of globalization haven't yet been developed; the level of participation in international civil society is much too low; regional federations are still in their beginning stages."[41] What reasonable expectation is there that such institutions would ever be developed, especially in the face of intransigent opposition by the world's chief hegemonic power, the US? On the other hand, it is not clear such global governing institutions would be desirable, even if they could be developed. Perhaps a regulative ideal is what a conception of global community *ought* to remain.

---

[38] See Michael Walzer, *Just and Unjust Wars: A Moral Argument with Historical Illustrations* (New York: Basic Books, 1977), especially Chapter. 4, and Michael Walzer, *Spheres of Justice: A Defense of Pluralism and Equality* (New York: Basic Books, 1983), Chapter 2.

[39] Michael Walzer, "Governing the Globe: What Is the Best We Can Do?," *Dissent* (2000), p. 50.

[40] Rawls, *The Law of Peoples*, pp. 60, 84.

[41] Walzer, "Governing the Globe: What Is the Best We Can Do?," p. 52.

5. The Politics of Moral Cosmopolitanism

It should now be clear that the view of the world as a community of autonomous communities constitutes a rejection of the notion – which has been one of the constants of a modernistic world-view from Kant to Marx and beyond – that at the end of the gigantic disruptions and displacements occasioned by the institutions of the global market and the modern state lies a just and peaceful world. The idea that the path to constructing this world lies in *intensifying* the development of markets or the power of states should, I would argue, now strike us as a tremendous gamble not worth taking. A true alternative to the depredations of the market and the state – of globalization and imperialism – lies in preserving what we can of older, more sustainable, forms of life, shorn of their oppressive aspects. Global justice is more probable in a world in which individual societies are for the most part economically self-sufficient and ecologically sustainable rather than in a world in which societies are subject to increasing dependence upon, and involvement with, others.

Is this third model of global community, then, an anti-cosmopolitan view – that is, one opposed not only to greater global integration, but also to any moral equivalence between persons globally? I think this is *not* a necessary corollary of the autonomous communities model. If moral cosmopolitanism is equivalent to a view of all human beings as having equal dignity and worthiness, this sort of cosmopolitanism is *not* inconsistent with a particularistic political philosophy – indeed, it is presupposed by it, since the notion of the self-determination of peoples that underlies the ideal of communal autonomy is based on just such a cosmopolitan outlook.

But what is important to note is that such a view draws a distinction between such a moral outlook and a political cosmopolitanism that seeks to design global governing institutions that will supercede, preempt, or dominate smaller, autonomous communities. This political cosmopolitanism is one of the worst inheritances of the Kantian view that no meaningful distinction ought to be drawn between morals and politics.[42] For Kant, a moral claim – for instance to global justice – could not, by the nature of being a moral claim, be overridden or otherwise limited by any other consideration, including those of practical politics. Politics was morality in practice – why limit the pursuit of a morally perfectible world to persons' individual consciences?

[42] See Kant, "Perpetual Peace: A Philosophical Sketch," pp. 116–125.

This view, despite Kant's modesty concerning the construction of global institutions, has given credence to the view that cosmopolitanism could find concrete political and institutional embodiments. Yet, such embodiments have never been and probably could never be genuinely cosmopolitan; rather they have been defined by the hegemonic states and powers able to create them in the first place – or they have been ineffective as counterweights to such hegemonic forces. If we are to countenance a moral cosmopolitanism, we must find its embodiment in *particular* political communities – not in global arrangements or institutions.

While the idea of an autonomous community, and of a world of such communities, implies significant differences in organization and way of life between communities, the underlying principles that define this autonomy – including those of sustainability and self-sufficiency – are universalist and rooted in an ecological perspective that rejects the disruptive effects of global markets and commodity production. Global justice will result more from adherence to such principles by autonomous communities acting independently than from vain attempts at redistributing resources and incomes globally or at developing global institutions that can coerce states into adherence to supposedly rational ends.

Such attempts at redistribution and regulation will ultimately be undercut or overwhelmed by the gigantism of markets and states that set their own goals of economic growth or military superiority. For much of this century, the illusion that freedom would be the result of a global order based on the dominance of one superior scheme – imposed if necessary by war or revolution – has dominated political discourse to its detriment. Global justice, if it is to have any chance of realization in the near future, must be based on a conception of autonomy that allows communities to find their own path to a more just society. These paths, which will diverge in response to local conditions, if not to underlying principles, cannot wait for or depend upon ever greater global economic or political integration. This is something that has already occurred to many movements of indigenous peoples and ecological resistance in India, Nigeria, Mexico, Brazil, and elsewhere.[43] Such a concept of the self-determination of autonomous communities that not only rejects the ideal of the

---

[43] See, e.g., Wolfgang Sachs (ed.), *Global Ecology: A New Arena of Political Conflict* (London: Zed Books, 1993); and Al Gedicks, *The New Resource Wars: Native and Environmental Struggles against Multinational Corporations* (Boston: South End Press, 1993).

nation-state, but that also refuses the false hopes of global redistribution or international regulation, remains to be adequately theorized. But I hope to have suggested the rudiments of such a conception in arguing for a model of global community that can provide a guideline for local actions toward the achievement of a more just world.

Department of Philosophy
Hunter College of the City University of New York
695 Park Avenue
New York, NY 10021
USA
E-mail: odahbour@hunter.cuny.edu

ROBERT E. GOODIN

TOWARD AN INTERNATIONAL RULE OF LAW: DISTINGUISHING INTERNATIONAL LAW-BREAKERS FROM WOULD-BE LAW-MAKERS

(Received 14 May 2004; accepted in revised form 7 June 2004)

ABSTRACT. An interesting fact about customary international law is that the only way you can propose an amendment to it is by breaking it. How can that be differentiated from plain law-breaking? What moral standards might apply to that sort of international conduct? I propose we use ones analogous to the ordinary standards for distinguishing civil disobedients from ordinary law-breakers: would-be law-makers, like civil disobedients, must break the law openly; they must accept the legal consequences of doing so; and they must be prepared to have the same rules applied to them as everyone else.

KEY WORDS: civil disobedience, customary international law, fairness, hegemony, rule of law

The boldest ambition of moral universalists might be a world government, federal in form, with its sovereign legislature apportioned fairly according to population. That is noble ambition, perhaps – but one without the remotest prospect of realization in this or any remotely proximate possible world. Aspirations, to be of any practical use, have as those to be action-guiding. Impossible dreams are not.

A more minimal aspiration along similar lines might be that, at the very least, the international system ought operate according to a "rule of law."[1] Even that more modest aspiration is not universally shared, often out of realist resignation.[2] One distinguished interna-

[1] For a compelling illustration of such "moral minimalism," see Larry May, *Crimes against Humanity* (Cambridge: Cambridge University Press, 2004), Chapters 3, 11.

[2] The idealism of the League of Nations contrasts sharply with the statism of the United Nations in this respect [Josef L. Kunz, "The United Nations and the Rule of Law," *American Journal of International Law* 46 (1952), pp. 504–508]. The realist position is aptly expressed by Eric Posner as follows:

> behavior that apparently complies with international law can be understood as merely prudential behavior... Because states have no intrinsic desire to comply with international law, all international law is limited by the rational choice of self-interested actors. Efforts to improve international cooperation must bow to this logic, and ... states cannot bootstrap cooperation by creating rules and calling them 'law'. [See Eric A. Posner, "Do States Have a Moral Obligation to Obey International Law?," *Stanford Law Review* 55 (2003), p. 1919, and similarly

tional lawyer urges us, accordingly, not "to weary further that tired phrase 'the rule of law.'"[3] But at least as a matter of morality, international as well as domestic, I take it that the basic principle of "fairness" has wide appeal, and part and parcel of that is yourself being bound by the same rules to which you would have others held.[4]

An international rule of law is not the same thing as a world government. There can be law without any central law-giver. Domestically, the common law is a case in point. No one legislated it; instead, it just grew up "organically" through the disparate judgments of disparate courts over the years. Customary international law, it is standardly said, is another case in point. It too just represents the long-established practices of states in their dealings with one another.

That is not the only sort of international law there is.[5] Treaties represent another. There may also be certain principles of *jus cogens* (like prohibitions on the use of force or respect for human rights, perhaps) that ought be enforced internationally even in the absence of

---

Jack L. Goldsmith and Eric A. Posner, "A Theory of Customary International Law," *University of Chicago Law Review* 66 (1999), pp. 1113–1177].

[3] Louis Henkin, "International Organization and the Rule of Law," *International Organization* 23 (1969), p. 656.

[4] Neither the "rule of law" nor "fairness" more generally is the only moral value in play, of course. We ought, however, be hesitant to trade such values off lightly [see Jeremy Waldron, "Security and Liberty: The Image of Balance," *Journal of Political Philosophy* 11 (2003), pp. 191–210].

[5] In what "is generally recognized as a complete statement of the sources of international law," Article 38.1 of the Statute of the International Court of Justice specifies:

(a) international conventions [i.e., treaties]...;
(b) international custom, as evidence of a general practice accepted as law;
(c) the general principles of law recognized by civilized nations;
(d) ... judicial decisions and teachings of the most highly
qualified pubicists of various nations...

[Ian Brownlie, *The Principles of Public International Law*, 4th edition (Oxford: Clarendon Press, 1990), p. 3]. Died-in-the-wool positivists might prefer to regard only the first as "international law, strictly speaking," regarding the rest as merely "international morality" [see e.g., Henry Sidgwick, *The Elements of Politics* (London: Macmillan, 1891), Chapter 17, pp. 272–284]. I stand here on the plain fact of the matter that international law and courts do recognize all those other sources.

any treaties or customs or indeed in contravention to them.[6] But it is customary international law that concerns me here. In discussing a minimalist sort of "international rule of law," it is respect for principles of customary international law to which I shall be referring.

1. What Is the Rule of Law?

In domestic contexts, we talk about a "rule of law, *not men*." There, the "rule of law" is contrasted with the arbitrary rule of a willful prince or his contemporary counterpart, a public official with unfettered discretion to treat subjects any way s/he pleases.[7]

Even in a well-institutionalized legal system like the US, there remain areas where that is a genuine concern. The Immigration and Naturalization Service used to be the prime example, although state security services operating under the USA Patriot Act might come to assume pride of place. We may well worry that officials there enjoy too much scope for arbitrary discretion in the exercise of their legal powers, and that the "rule of law" suffers in consequence.

The international analogue to a "rule of law, not men" would be a "rule of law, not states." An "international rule of law" would contrast, first, with "international lawlessness" – each state doing just as it pleases, or dares, without restraint from any internalized normative constraints.[8] Rule there would be the rule of "will backed by power."

There may be some regularities in that, of course. But although law-*like*, they are not really laws in the relevant sense. The moment there is a change in will or the balance of power, those regularities disappear or are replaced by some others.[9]

---

[6] Article 53 of the 1969 Vienna Convention on the Law of Treaties holds that, A treaty is void if, at the time of its conclusion, it conflicts with a peremptory norm of general international law. For the purposes of the present Convention, a peremptory norm of general international law is a norm accepted and recognized by the international community of states as a whole as a norm from which no derogation is permitted and which can be modified only by a subsequent norm of general international law having the same characters [*International Legal Materials* 8 (1969), pp. 679–713].

[7] A. V. Dicey, *The Law of the Constitution*, 7th edition (London: Macmillan, 1908), Part 2. Jeremy Waldron, *The Law* (London: Routledge, 1990), Chapter 3.

[8] This is the model of "realist" theorists of international relations such as Hans J. Morgenthau, *Politics among Nations*, 3rd edition (New York: Knopf, 1961); see Headley Bull, *The Anarchical Society* (London: Macmillan, 1977).

[9] As emphasized by Goldsmith and Posner, "A Theory of Customary International Law."

An "international rule of law" might contrast, second, with something internationally akin to arbitrary rule by an all-powerful prince. The international analogue would be one state having power sufficient to impose its will on all others in the world, and that state doing so without any internalized normative constraint.

Of course, no state is ever so all-powerful that it can force all other states to do literally whatever it wants, any more than any prince is so powerful that he can force all his subjects to do absolutely anything he wants. But in both cases, the "rule of law" is lacking just insofar as substantial power is exercised in whatever way its possessor pleases.

Here too, there might be considerable regularity in the patterns we observe. But the regularities are merely law-*like* rather than law-governed. The moment the powerholder's preferences change, so too would the pattern.

There are two logically distinct ways of instituting an international "rule of law," corresponding to those two contrasting cases. A "rule of law" might emerge, externally, as a response to a situation of lawlessness and anarchy, where the power of each would otherwise be countered by the power of others, much to the detriment of all. Then for purely Hobbesian reasons, states would rationally accede to a system of rules limiting their prerogatives in exchange for the prerogatives of others being limited likewise. Alternatively, a "rule of law" might emerge, internally, as those with power to internalize the duties and responsibilities that are seen to be morally attendant upon holding great power.[10]

A "one superpower world" is, of course, what we now inhabit.[11] In purely *realpolitik* terms, that creates a temptation toward lawlessness on the part of the solitary superpower. There is little by way of external check on the exercise of its power; there is nothing much, externally, to stop the one remaining superpower from working its arbitrary will on the world. If the sole superpower succumbs to that

---

[10] Or – for completeness – a "rule of law" might emerge through any practically feasible combination of those two processes. The evidence of experimental game theory, however, suggests the motivational precariousness of mixed cases [see Robert E. Goodin, "How Amoral *Is* Hegemon?," *Perspectives on Politics* 1 (2003), pp. 123–126].

[11] See Lea Brilmayer, *American Hegemony: Political Morality in a One-Superpower World* (New Haven: Yale University Press, 1995) and Joseph S. Nye, Jr., *The Paradox of American Power: Why the World's Only Superpower Can't Go It Alone* (New York: Oxford University Press, 2002).

temptation, it would not be respecting any "rule of law," internationally. That would then just be a case of the "rule of the stronger."

But even if there is no external way of forcing it to respect the "rule of law," the sole remaining superpower might nonetheless internalize those standards itself. Law always has an "internal aspect," whereby agents take a "critical reflective attitude" toward their own conduct, assessing it according to the settled rules that constitute the law.[12] Insofar as a sovereign internalizes such normative standards in that way, it *would* be said to be respecting the "rule of law," however all-powerful that sovereign might be. That is as true of a sovereign state as it would be of a princely sovereign.[13]

The crucial question for the "international rule of law" in the contemporary world, therefore, is whether or not the sole remaining superpower really internalizes the settled rules governing relations between "civilized nations." If it does, then it would be respecting the rule of law, internationally. If on the contrary the hegemon succumbs to the temptation simply to work its will on the world, without reference to or constraint by those settled rules, then it would not be respecting the rule of law, internationally.

2. Law-Making by Law-Breaking[14]

There are of course a great many sites at which the global hegemon might work its arbitrary will on the rest of the world, in plain defiance of an "international rule of law." Some cases will be clear. Others will be less so, with a state's actions admitting of different interpretations. In those more ambiguous cases there is an urgent need for defensible

---

[12] H. L. A. Hart, *The Concept of Law* (Oxford: Clarendon Press, 1961), p. 56.

[13] We might have republican-style worries about the "resilience" of the rule of law, in those circumstances; see Philip Pettit, *Republicanism* (Oxford: Oxford University Press, 1997), Part 1. But the sovereign who internalizes the rule of law, and takes a critical reflective attitude toward its own conduct in light of that rule, is at least far different from one who merely "makes it a rule" (as a behavioral regularity) to do something similar. This is the key distinction in Hart, *The Concept of Law*, pp. 55–56.

[14] My interest in this set of problems was piqued discussing a conference paper with Allen Buchanan, subsequently published as "From Nuremburg to Kosovo: The Morality of Illegal International Legal Reform," *Ethics* 111 (2001), pp. 673–705, and now reprinted in Allen Buchanan, *Justice, Legitimacy and Self-determination* (Oxford: Oxford University Press, 2004), Chapter 11. Although our analyses veered off in different directions, I remain grateful to him for that original inspiration.

criteria for deciding which interpretation is the correct one. That is where philosophers' contributions might be greatest. "Making distinctions," after all, is the philosopher's stock-in-trade.

2.1. *Amending Customary Law*

Within domestic law, jurists tend to draw a sharp distinction between "customary law" and the "common law." For present purposes, however, I shall treat "common law" as a subspecies of "customary law:" *viz.*, the "customary law of judges."[15] Seen in that light, both customary international law and domestic common law can be regarded as forms of customary law.

The great problem with customary law in general is its lack of any amendment procedures. Just as there is no formal mechanism for making customary law, so too is there no formal mechanism for remaking it.[16] In a society governed by customary law alone, Hart observes disapprovingly,

> "There will be no means... of deliberately adapting the rules to changing circumstances, either by eliminating old rules or introducing new ones: ... doing this presupposes the existence of rules of a different type from the primary rules of obligation by which, alone, that society lives."[17]

In Hart's terminology, the problem is that customary law has no "secondary rules" – rules about rules, how to make rules and how to change them.

In domestic applications, common law changes as judges begin to rule differently on cases that come before them. In international applications, customary international law changes as states and tribunals begin to accept practices that previously they did not (Or as

---

[15] A. W. B. Simpson, "The Common Law and Legal Theory" in A. W. B. Simpson (ed.), *Oxford Essays in Jurisprudence*, 2nd series (Oxford: Clarendon Press, 1973), pp. 77–99.

[16] Informally, of course, Ludwig Wittgenstein's point always applies: You are forever remaking rules in the course of acting on them. In customary international law, too, law-applying is law-making [see Philip Allott, *Eunomia: New Order for a New World* (Oxford: Oxford University Press, 1990)].

[17] Hart, *The Concept of Law*, p. 90. Later, Hart worries that international law "not only lacks the secondary rules of change and adjudication..., but also a unifying rule of recognition specifying 'sources' of law and providing general criteria for identification if its rules" (Hart, *The Concept of Law*, p. 209).

they begin not to accept practices that previously they accepted: but it is the first case upon which I shall here be concentrating).[18]

The crucial fact for present purposes is just this: In both common law and in customary international law, change in the law presupposes a case coming before the bar of justice. That is to say, legal change of the sort here in view presupposes someone having done something that was, by the existing standards, a *breach* of the law.

In the absence of any formal amendment procedure, the only way in the situations here in view for states to "propose an amendment" to customary law is by *breaking* that customary law.[19] That is just a plain fact about customary law.

Thus arises the central puzzle that here concerns me, as to whether or not states are respecting the "international rule of law." How can we differentiate actors who genuinely respect the rule of customary law, and who are merely proposing an amendment in good faith to it, from actors who are just plain breaking the law?

2.2. *A Breach Is a Breach?*

One response might be to deny that there is actually any difference between them. The thought here is that if a body of law contains no provision for its own amendment, then that body of law is simply unamendable. Any attempt at amending law that is unamendable is just plain breaking the law.

Take, for example, John Locke's 1669 constitution for the Carolina colony. Its final clause declares, "These Fundamental Constitutions ... shall be and remain the sacred and unalterable form and rule of government of Carolina for ever."[20] Thus, anyone trying to alter Locke's Fundamental Constitutions for Carolina would be acting purely illegally, in flat-out contravention of that clause.

---

[18] International standard-setting is a prime example of the other; for a raft of examples, see John Braithwaite and Peter Drahos, *Global Business Regulation* (Cambridge: Cambridge University Press, 2000).

[19] Alternatively, of course, they may make proposals at the UN or various international meetings, they may file briefs to the International Court of Justice, and so on. But breaching existing law and forcing the issue into some international tribunal "brings the matter to a head" in a way those other methods do not, and can be regarded as the "principal" way for states to propose an amendment to customary international law in consequence.

[20] "The Fundamental Constitutions of Carolina," Section 120, in David Wootton (ed.), *Political Writings of John Locke* (New York: Penguin/Mentor, 1983), p. 232.

Customary law presents a softer case, perhaps. It contains no explicit prohibition on amendment; it merely makes no internal provision for amendment. Of course, customary law changes, as customs change. But it changes only through slow accretions, not through discrete intentional interventions.[21] Someone breaking customary law with a view to ultimately changing it might ultimately be vindicated. But for the moment, and for some time to come, anyone engaging in such an act will be just plain breaking the law.

On that account, where the law makes no provision for its own amendment, respecting the "rule of law" would require us to respect those rules as they are, and not try to amend them. There is no way "respectfully" to propose changes.

That may well be a formally correct analysis, from a narrowly legal point of view.[22] According to the strict (albeit unwritten) letter of customary law, there may well be no difference between the law-breaker and the would-be law-maker.

Morally, however, we surely would want to draw a distinction. And even from a larger legal point of view, I think we should want to do likewise.

Think of it as an issue about the rule of law. The law-breaker wants to operate outside the law. The would-be law-maker wants to install some new provision, within the rule of law. S/he wants conduct to be law-governed; s/he just wants it to be governed according to some slightly different laws. In short: the would-be law-maker wants to perpetuate the rule of law, whilst changing the particular laws within it. The law-breaker, in contrast, wants to undermine the rule of law, or at least its application to his own conduct.

That is an important distinction, certainly morally and perhaps even in some larger legal sense as well: The distinction between those who attempt to exempt themselves from general rules of conduct, and those who attempt merely to alter the general rules of conduct.

---

[21] In Hart's description, "The only mode of change in the rules ... will be the slow process of growth, whereby courses of conduct once thought optional become first habitual or usual, and then obligatory, and the converse process of decay, when deviations, once severely dealt with, are first tolerated and then pass unnoticed" (Hart, *The Concept of Law*, p. 90).

[22] Just as may be Dean Griswold's response to the civil disobedient: "It is the essence of law that it is equally applied to all, that it bind all alike, irrespective of personal motive. For this reason, one who contemplates civil disobedience out of moral conviction should not be surprised and must not be bitter if a criminal conviction ensues" [quoted and critiqued in Ronald Dworkin, *Taking Rights Seriously* (London: Butterworth, 1977), p. 206].

3. STANDARDS FOR WOULD-BE LAW-MAKERS

That is the key feature differentiating would-be law-makers from sheer law-breakers: The former "respect the rule of law," in a way the latter do not. One way of distinguishing them would therefore be this: Would-be law-makers ought be expected to acknowledge and accept the consequences of their breach of the existing law;[23] sheer law-breakers, in contrast, would naturally be expected to try to evade responsibility for any breach of the law.[24]

In operationalizing that distinction, we might apply a set of criteria akin to those used, domestically, to differentiate "civil disobedients" from "ordinary law-breakers." The key difference there, too, is supposed to be that civil disobedients respect the law in general, even whilst breaching some particular law in protest.[25]

To count as "civil disobedients," people must behave in ways that provide external evidence that they do indeed respect the law in general.[26] First, they must openly admit that they are breaking the law: They must break the law publicly, rather than surreptitiously. Second, they must accept the consequences of having broken the law,

---

[23] That is not to say that authorities would be justified in inflicting the same punishments on conscientious law-breakers breaking the law for good reasons [Daniel M. Farrell, "Paying the Penalty: Justifiable Civil Disobedience and the Problem of Punishment," *Philosophy and Public Affairs,* 6 (1977), pp. 165–184]. I merely mean to say that if authorities do choose to impose such punishments genuine civil disobedients ought be willing to take the punishments allocated to them.

[24] As I say, this is "one way" – a broadly procedural one – for distinguishing law-breakers from would-be law-makers. But some agents who pass this procedural test would still count as law-breakers. That would be the case if, for example, the amendment to customary international law that they are conscientiously proposing in this way would itself violate the unamendable (*jus cogens*) core of customary international law. I am grateful to Dora Kostakopoulou for this observation.

[25] These are external indicators of an operational sort, by which we assess (however imperfectly) the actual intentions and motivations of actors breaking the law. Whether a state really is a "would-be law-maker" or simply a "law-breaker," when breaching customary international law, is definitionally determined by its intentions and motivations alone (note that civil disobedients, in contrast, might sometimes be defined in terms of these external indicators alone).

[26] See, e.g.: Richard Wasserstrom, "Disobeying the Law," *The Journal of Philosophy* 58 (1961), pp. 641–653; Hugo Adam Bedau, "On Civil Disobedience," *The Journal of Philosophy* 58 (1961), 653–665, respectively; Hugo Adam Bedau (ed.), *Civil Disobedience: Theory and Practice* (New York: Pegasus, 1969); and Carl Cohen, *Civil Disobedience* (New York: Columbia University Press, 1971); and John Rawls, *A Theory of Justice* (Cambridge, Harvard University Press, 1971), pp. 363–390.

rather than somehow evading those consequences. Were they to do otherwise, they would not really be "civil disobedients," publicly pressing for a change to a law by breaking it. Instead, they would just be ordinary law-breakers.

Some equivalent standards might reasonably be applied when differentiating international law-breakers from would-be international law-changers. Let us consider each requirement in turn.

3.1. *Breaching Publicly*

Consider first the condition that, to properly count as a "civil disobedient," one must break the law openly. The same should be true of states breaking customary international law in a genuine attempt to amend it: They too must break the law openly.

After all, an intervention can directly alter customary law only insofar as it is *seen* to be an act in conspicuous violation of the old law, which is subsequently changed in response to that intervention. Breaking the law *surreptitiously* would be flatly contrary to the project of changing the law. An ordinary law-breaker might want to do that. But such behavior makes no sense for those who are genuinely breaking a rule of customary law purely with a view to instigating a change in that rule.[27] To do that, they need to get their case to court.

Of course, legal change can come about through reinterpretation as well as through repeal. And in practice that is much the most common way for it to occur.[28] That fact gives rise to a second, intermediate strategy for a would-be law-maker.

The would-be law-maker might be "bringing a test case." As part and parcel of that, s/he would insist that what s/he is doing is not contrary to the law but is instead perfectly consistent with what is "really" the law. That is the proposition that the would-be law-re-interpreters would be inviting the relevant authorities to accept.

---

[27] Similarly for a civil disobedient: "It is essential that the government know of his act if it is intended that the government shall change its policy because of the act" (Bedau, "On Civil Disobedience," p. 656; see similarly Rawls, *A Theory of Justice*, p. 366).

[28] The reason is that courts are reluctant to be *seen* as legislating. If a party comes before a court, domestically or internationally, admitting it has violated the law and agreeing to pay damages, the court will almost invariably regard the case as closed; it will virtually never reject that guilty plea and award judgment against the other party, who everyone agrees had (existing) legal right on its side.

Many cases of civil disobedience are like that. Think of the Freedom Riders. Often, they flagrantly violated Jim Crow laws of the state of Mississippi, precisely with a view to testing the constitutionality of those laws in appeals to the federal courts.[29]

Internationally, would-be law-makers might proceed similarly. Instead of forthrightly admitting that they are "breaking customary international law in order to change it," they might say that – while what they are doing might seem contrary to customary international law as presently construed – the correct interpretation of customary law is actually otherwise.

Here is one example: Customary international law has long permitted the use of force for "national self-defense." Many states over the years have used that as an excuse for armed interventions abroad, in defense of their nationals or their interests. Sometimes those claims have been generally accepted, and customary international law amended accordingly.[30] Other times they have not.

So admitting outright that they are "breaking the law to change it" is not the only way for would-be law-makers to proceed, in attempting to alter customary law. Arguing for a change in the prevailing interpretation of received precepts is another equally good strategy; and as part and parcel of that, it is essential for would-be law-makers to deny that they are "really" breaking customary law, at all.

Nonetheless, the constraints of publicity remain. Even would-be law-makers pursuing this re-interpretavist strategy still need to do so publicly, rather than surreptitiously. Furthermore, if their intervention is to result in a change in the *general pattern* of interpretation of customary law (rather than just in this particular application), they need to acknowledge openly that they are arguing against the old interpretation and in favor of some new one. So even would-be law-

---

[29] Wasserstrom, "Disobeying the Law," p. 647. Rawls, however, may be right in thinking that bringing "trial cases" lies in the penumbra of "civil disobedience" (Rawls, *Theory of Justice*, p. 367).

[30] As in the case of Israel's raid on the Entebbe Airport to rescue Israelis held hostage there, or the US interception of the Egyptian airliner carrying terrorists responsible for the death of a US citizen on the hijacked ship, the *Achille Lauro*. This is the "passive personality principle" discussed in Louis Henkin et al., *Restatement of the Law (Third): The Foreign Relations Law of the United States* (Washington, DC: American Law Institute, 1987), Section 404 (comment a) and Section 402 (comment g). See further: Malvina Halberstam, "Terrorism on the High Seas: The Achille Lauro, Piracy and the IMO Convention on Maritime Safety," *American Journal of Internatinal Law* 82 (1988), pp. 269–310; and David Rodin, *War & Self-Defense* (Oxford: Clarendon Press, 2002), p. 110.

makers pursuing this re-intepretavist strategy need to acknowledge publicly that what they have done would be a breach of customary law, under the presently prevailing interpretations that they hope their intervention will alter.

3.2. *Accepting the Consequences of Breach*

Let us turn now to the second requirement that, to show respect for the "rule of law," one must be prepared to accept the legal consequences for one's breach of the law.[31]

When protesting an iniquitous law domestically, civil disobedients accept the legal consequences of their actions in part to distinguish themselves from ordinary law-breakers who would strive assiduously to avoid detection and penalties. Civil disobedients strike a contrast by boldly accepting the legal consequences of their breach, thus emphasizing the moral seriousness of their protest at the injustice of the existing law and of their petition for its change.

But beyond that vaguely strategic consideration, there is a larger point of principle. By accepting the legal consequences for breaking the law, even one that they deem iniquitous, civil disobedients signal their respect for the law as such. Their paying the penalty is a material token of their respect for the "rule of law." That is a familiar theme of civil disobedients, from Socrates through Martin Luther King, Jr.[32]

Why is it so important that actors – individuals and states alike – be willing to "accept the consequences" and pay the legal penalty for laws they have broken, even when breaking laws which they think is deeply wrong? One obvious answer has to do with "fairness."[33]

Any complex code is a bundle of provisions, some of which benefit you and others of which benefit me. Adhering to the provisions that benefit you is the price I pay for your adherence to the provisions that

[31] Of course, if (or when) the change is accepted there will be no legal consequences to be accepted. Even customary international law can sometimes change moderately quickly. On "instant custom," see Bin Cheng, "Custom: The Future of General State Practice in a Divided World," in R. St. J. Macdonald and Douglas M. Johnston (eds.), *The Structure and Process of International Law* (The Hague: Martinus Nijhoff, 1983), pp. 513–554.

[32] Martin Luther King, Jr., "Letter from Birmingham City Jail," in Hiego Bedau (ed.), *Civil Disobedience: Theory and Practice* (New York: Pegasus, 1969), pp. 73–89.

[33] John Rawls, "Legal Obligation and the Duty of Fair Play," in Sidney Hook (ed.), *Law and Philosophy* (New York: New York University Press, 1967), pp. 3-18; and Rawls, *A Theory of Justice*, Chapter 5.

benefit me. We cannot pick apart the package, each adhering only to those provisions that benefit us and ignoring the rest, without the whole ensemble collapsing; and even if we could, it would be morally wrong to do so. Accepting the legal consequences for one's conscientious breach of the law is part and parcel of what it is to accept the package as a whole, and respect the "rule of law" in its full generality.

Paying the penalty for your breach is obviously not "just the same" as complying with the requirements of the law. Maybe it is sometimes "just as good" (as in certain civil contexts like contracts), but often it definitely is not (as in criminal contexts, clearly, and perhaps some civil contexts like irreparable torts). Sometimes international delicts might be more like the first case, sometimes the second. But even where paying the penalty fails to compensate fully for the wrong done, at least it goes some way toward righting the wrong – or anyway toward acknowledging that one has done wrong, if only in the sense of disappointing someone else's legitimate expectations.[34]

It is clear what is involved in a domestic civil disobedients presenting themselves before the bar of justice and accepting whatever penalty is lawfully imposed by the court. Occasionally there is a strict international analogue. Take the case of a tribunal that is empowered to hear the case and impose penalties under some treaty to which all parties are signatories. There, "accepting the consequences of one's breach" involves broadly the same thing internationally as it does domestically: submitting to the jurisdiction of the tribunal; presenting one's case before it; accepting its decision; complying with its orders; and so on.

Even where there is no tribunal with compulsory (treaty-based or other) jurisdiction, states can always voluntarily submit a disputed case to arbitration – as for example when France and New Zealand submitted issues arising from the Rainbow Warrior affair to the UN Secretary-General for a ruling that they agreed would be binding on both of them.[35] Here again, "accepting the consequences of one's

---

[34] This criterion is used, among other things, to distinguish "civil disobedients" from "revolutionaries." But note that even revolutionaries might "respect the rule of law," at least in the sense that what they want to institute is a law-governed order (simply one with a whole different set of laws).

[35] "Ruling Pertaining to the Differences between France and New Zealand arising from the Rainbow Warrior Affair," *American Journal of International Law* 81 (1987), pp. 325–328. How "binding" the arbitration was might be queried in light of the fact that the French subsequently secured transfer of their agents on disingenuous health grounds to French territory; reparations were paid, however [see more generally Oran R. Young, *The Intermediaries* (Princeton: Princeton University Press, 1967)].

breach" would involve consigning the case to such an adjudicator; cooperating with the adjudicator in supplying information required for the adjudication; accepting the judgment of the adjudicator, rather than repudiating it; performing such actions as are required under the terms of that judgment; and so on.

That, I submit, is precisely what would-be law-makers would do, if they were genuinely attempting to engineer a change in customary international law. If a country wants to get some new principle or interpretation ensconced in customary international law, it needs to appeal to some independent authority standing outside the controversy. It needs to get that principle endorsed by neutral, reflective agents who are conscientiously attempting to assess the proposed principle's relation to the existing canon of customary international law.

Any state that refuses to submit to impartial adjudication or that resiles from its determinations – as the US did from the ruling of the International Court of Justice in *Nicaragua v. United States*[36]—will not have been breaching customary international law in order to change it. Such a state is an international law-breaker, pure and simple, with no law-making aspiration to serve as an excuse for its delict.

4. The Rule of Soft Law

Contemporary theorists of "soft law" would grumble that that is an insistently old-fashioned, "hard law" way of looking at those things.

"Hard law" is the law of die-hard positivists. It is the law of a sovereign who makes orders and backs them with threats. It is the law of courts with compulsory jurisdiction, empowered to interpret rules authoritatively and to apply them to particular cases, bringing sanctions to bear for their breach. "Hard law," in short, is characterized by "*binding* obligations that are *precise* (or can be made precise through adjudication or the issuance of detailed regulations) and that *delegate* authority for interpreting and implementing law."[37]

---

[36] *Nicaragua v. United States* (1986): Judgment available at www.icj-cij.org/icjwww/Icases/iNus/inus_ijudgment/inus_ijudgment_19860627.pdf (accessed October 30, 2003). With due notice, of course, the US could have withdrawn from the jurisdiction of the Court altogether; but that had not been done before the ruling was handed down.

[37] Kenneth W. Abbott and Duncan Snidal, "Hard and Soft Law in International Governance," *International Organization* 54 (2000), p. 421 (emphasis mine).

International law has never been like that, to any very large extent. Customary international law in particular is certainly "soft" along all those crucial dimensions: its obligations are not very precise and not very binding; and there are rarely any authorities empowered to interpret and implement it.[38] "So much the worse for international law," positivists have traditionally supposed. But that view mistakes the very important ways in which soft law might nonetheless become institutionalized and come to guide the behavior of people and of states.[39]

4.1. *The Growth of Soft Law*

This process starts (logically if not literally) from the situation of "international lawlessness" described earlier. Suppose there are no norms of international conduct internalized by any state; suppose that each pursues its purposes and presses its advantage as far as it is able, given the power and purposes of others around it. Even in a fundamentally competitive environment, however, there will always be some scope for mutual gains from cooperation or mutual restraint. The process is probably more one of "mutual accommodation" rather than a quest for "common purposes," in the first instance. But on those islands of cooperation an increasingly dense undergrowth of norms begins to take root.[40] States begin to adhere to those norms, even where at the margin (and eventually well beyond the margin) doing so is contrary to their immediate interests and aims. International norms that start out being very "soft" indeed get progressively hardened, whether by treaty or by custom.

Now, in this world of "soft law" it is never quite so clear what it is to "break" the law, as it is in a world of "hard law." "Soft law" is by definition imprecise, and has no authoritative interpreter to make it more precise. Neither is it clear in the world of "soft law" what exactly would be involved in "accepting the legal consequences for

---

[38] Kunz, "The United Nations and the Rule of Law," p. 504.

[39] More efficiently and effectively than hard law, perhaps. See, in addition to Abbott and Snidal, "Hard and Soft Law in International Governance"; Kenneth W. Abbott, Robert O. Keohane, Andrew Moravcsik, Anne-Marie Slaughter and Duncan Snidal, "The Concept of Legalization," *International Organization* 54 (2000), pp. 457–488; and Robert O. Keohane, *After Hegemony* (Princeton: Princeton University Press, 1984).

[40] The process is effectively described by Christian Reus-Smit, "Politics and International Legal Obligation," *European Journal of International Relations* 9 (2003), pp. 591–625.

breaking the law." "Soft law" by definition lacks any agency authoritatively empowered to enforce it.

Even though there is no "enforcement by any central organ," soft international law can still be regarded as "binding" and "obligatory," however. As Hart observes,

> [T]here is general pressure for conformity to the rules; claims and admissions are based on them and their breach is held to justify not only insistent demands for compensation, but reprisals and countermeasures. When the rules are disregarded, it is not on the footing that they are not binding; instead efforts are made to conceal the facts.[41]

In short, there is serious social pressure within the community of nations to obey what are deemed to be "settled norms" according to the customs and standards of the regime governing the body of "soft law" in question. And that comes pretty close to satisfying Hart's "necessary and sufficient conditions for the existence of a legal system."

4.2. *Respecting Soft Law*

Realpolitik analysts might question what it can mean to "accept the consequences" of one's breach of customary international law, where judgment and enforcement are left purely to the interaction of offending states with other states. It would be unclear what it means to "accept" the consequences, in *realpolitik* terms, because it would be unclear what it might mean in those terms *not* to accept them. Other states simply do whatever they do in response to your breach; you do whatever you do, in response to their responses; and so on. From a *realpolitik* perspective, what they do is simply a fact about the external world – a fact that you are no more free to "accept or reject" than you are facts about gravity or electromagnetism.

But that *realpolitik* perspective overlooks the internal aspect of law, found even (indeed, perhaps especially) in "soft law." A state that is trying to alter or amend or extend some principle of "soft law" itself fundamentally accepts the corpus of existing norms which it is trying to amend. It internalizes those norms as ones with which it should generally try to comply, for their own sake in the first instance (even if perhaps for reasons of self-interest, in the final analysis). When generally accepted norms are violated, such a state accepts that others have legitimate grounds for complaint.

---

[41] Hart, *The Concept of Law*, pp. 214–215.

In consequence of that recognition, a state that is engaged in an attempt to alter, amend or extend some principle of "soft law" would refrain from resisting other countries' complaints with all the means at its disposal. Such a state would signal that it is genuinely attempting to alter, amend or extend "soft law" by paying compensation or reparations, even when power relations are such that it might be able to evade doing so.

4.3. *Enforcing Soft Law*

Realpolitik analysts see international outcomes as the vector sum of forces, where each state is playing its advantages to the hilt. States engaged in the process of building up a rule of law (even just of "soft law") would stay their hand, initially occasionally and then increasingly often, in deference to at least some of the more settled norms of that body of law.

Where the states concerned are rough co-equals, considerations of interest and principle unite in commending reciprocal compliance with the constraints of soft law. Some states may comply more fully than others. Some states may gain marginally more than others, overall, from the soft laws in question. Some states might do marginally better than others if the regime broke down into international anarchy. But as long as that variation is all within the substantial margins of uncertainty inevitably surrounding the outcomes of any *realpolitik* power plays, the "soft law" will generally be respected.[42] As it is, it will naturally be increasingly internalized and hence acquire increasing normative force.

Those conditions are missing in a world with a single superpower. True, the weaker could always gang up on the stronger; and that might give the superpower pause.[43] But the larger the coalition would need to be to counter the hegemon's power, the less likely it would be that such collective action could be organized and sustained. If the

[42] What Hart says *a propos* norms against aggression generalize to various other soft norms of international law: "To initiate a war is, even for the stronger power, to risk much for an outcome which is rarely predictable with reasonable confidence" (Hart, *The Concept of Law*, p. 214).

[43] Hart, *The Concept of Law*, p. 214. Enfeebled though Russia might now be, it retains a serious nuclear arsenal, so the US might well have second thoughts about its new doctrine of preemptive self-defense when President Vladimir Putin announced, "If the principle of preventive use of force continues to develop in international practice, then Russia reserves the right in an analogous manner to defend its national interests" (*Canberra Times*, November 5, 2003, p. 16).

hegemon needs only pick off a very few partners from the counter-coalition, then that counter-coalition is unlikely to be able to hold the hegemon to an international rule of soft law.

On the *realpolitik* account, soft law works through self-interest in the first instance, and it is increasingly internalized and normativized the more it is respected in practice.[44] But that process of internalization and normativization simply never gets going, for the single superpower with no self-interested reason to respect those laws in the first instance. *Other* states might abide by an increasingly internalized code of increasingly "harder" law. But the sole superpower can simply go its merry way, doing whatever it fancies, oblivious to any constraints from an international "rule of soft law."

5. Generalizability: Testing State Sincerity

One rule-of-thumb we can use in testing whether states (even sole superpowers) are really respecting the "rule of soft law" harks back to a central feature of the "rule of law" as such. It is key to the very idea of a "rule of law, not men" that there be "one law for all."[45] Law, to be law, must be general in form. *Ad hominem* orders (bills of attainder and such like) represent edicts, not laws.[46]

[44] Self-interest, in the first instance, in these sorts of ways: our not dumping toxic chemicals into rivers flowing into their territory is a *quid pro quo* for their not dumping chemicals into rivers flowing into our territory; our not abusing the human rights of their citizens is a *quid pro quo* for their not abusing the human rights of our citizens; and so on.

[45] Waldron, *The Law*, p. 37.

[46] This is one of the first things that any writer on "the rule of law" invariably says [see, e.g., Lon L. Fuller, *The Morality of Law*, 2nd edition (New Haven: Yale University Press, 1964), pp. 46–49; Cass R. Sunstein, *Legal Reasoning and Political Conflict* (New York: Oxford University Press, 1996), p. 104; and William N. Eskridge, Jr. and John Ferejohn, "Politics, Interpretation and the Rule of Law," in Ian Shapiro (ed.), *Nomos XXXVI: The Rule of Law* (New York: New York University Press, 1994), p. 265]. Of course, it is a familiar problem with "generalization tests" in both ethics and law that principles that appear to be general in form might be extensionally equivalent to specifying one named individual [for an example from tax law, see Russell Hardin, *Collective Action* (Baltimore: Johns Hopkins University Press, 1982), p. 78]. Thus, this requirement ought be construed as demanding generality both in form and in substance. Note that generalizability is only one among several necessary conditions for the rule of law being respected, however.

Among a group of rough co-equals developing a regime of "soft law" for themselves, ordinary reciprocity is usually sufficient to effectively impose that "generalizability" test on whatever rules get proposed. Where each can and will hold the other to the norms to which others have held them, no one state would propose the very same norm that it was not prepared to have applied to it as well.

There, reciprocal tit-for-tat ensures that any deviation by anyone will promptly be repeated by everyone. Under such circumstances, no actor would deviate from the existing norms unless it were prepared to see everyone do likewise. No actor would break the existing rules without intending (or anyway anticipating and accepting) that that become the new rule.

In a single-superpower world, that is not necessarily the case. The single superpower can expect to hold others to standards that it has the power to evade. More powerful states have long done that *vis-a-vis* less powerful ones, whenever their interests are substantially at stake.[47] A single-superpower would be in a position to do so in trumps – if it so chooses.

Of course, the sole-superpower might decide not to press its power to the hilt. It might internalize international norms, even when in *realpolitik* terms it would not have to do so. When deviating from the customary rules of international law, it *might* be genuinely proposing an amendment to the old rules in light of new circumstances, rather than just plain declaring itself exempt from the law.

In deciding which it is, we therefore need to cast the generalizability test in hypothetical form. We know that the same rules will probably not actually apply to hegemon as everyone else.[48] But *would* hegemon be prepared to be held to the same rules as it proposes applying to others?

Hypothetical questions like that are often hard to assess. But sometimes the answers seem straightforward. Take these two examples:

- In sending secret agents to assassinate Fidel Castro, or organizing the Chilean military to assassinate Salvador Allende, was the US

[47] "It is an ancient observation that powerful states, when they are belligerents, impose upon the neutrals the breaking off of trade relations with their enemy, whereas the same powerful states, when they are neutrals in a war between minor Powers, insist in the strictest way on the rule of international law, according to which neutrals have ... a right to trade with all the belligerents" (Kunz, "The United Nations and the Rule of Law," p. 504).

[48] Or the effect of applying the same rules will be very different, given differential resources with which to take advantage of those rules.

simply breaking international law, or was it proposing an amendment to international law according to which assassination of heads of state ought be deemed permissible?[49] Well, the test would be whether the US would accept as equally legitimate the assassination of John F. Kennedy by Cuban agents (if that is how it happened).

- In launching the invasion of Iraq, the US said it was entitled to do so in order to forestall "terrible threats before they're fully formed."[50] Was the U.S. genuinely proposing a new principle of international law, according to which any state that is under any distant threat from any other ought be allowed to attack in preemptive self-defense? Well, the test would be whether the U.S. would accept as equally legitimate an Iraqi attack on Texas, when Texans were clearly intent on attacking it.[51]

Presumably not. Presumably in those cases the US was in effect claiming exemption from the ordinary standards of conduct, rather than genuinely proposing changes along those lines to customary international law.[52]

---

[49] At least in "relevantly similar circumstances" – which someone wanting to differentiate these cases might claim were present in these cases but absent in the Kennedy case.

[50] George W. Bush, "Remarks at Fort Drum, NY, July 19, 2002"; quoted in Michael Byers, "Preemptive Self-defense: Hegemony, Equality and Strategies of Legal Change," *Journal of Political Philosophy* 11 (2003), p. 181.

[51] Subsequent defenses of the Iraq invasion might invoke other rationales – humanitarian intervention in defense of an oppressed people, for example – which the US might more plausibly be prepared to see generalized. But those are different from the Bush doctrine of preemptive self-defense as announced at Fort Drum. Note that one problem with notions of preemptive self-defense in general is that the remoteness of the threat elides the distinction between aggressor and defender: insofar as the hostile intentions in view are not "fully formed," your preemptive self-defense against my merely-inchoate hostile intentions appear from my perspective as a much firmer intention on your part to attack me, against which I have a correspondingly more robust right to defend myself against by preemptively attacking you.

[52] Or perhaps claiming special exemption from the general rules, on the grounds that special powers must come with its special responsibilities as the *de facto* world policeman. Remember, however, the police are bound by the law just like everyone else, and any special powers they have must be incorporated into the law in the ordinary way – which, in customary international law, must be via the consent and customary practice of the community of nations overall.

In other cases, though, I think we can find examples of strong states breaking the existing norms of customary international law, precisely in hopes that others will do likewise and some new norm will thereby emerge. Here are four cases in point:

- "Britain used its position as the leading naval power of the nineteenth century to suppress piracy on the high seas, which eventually led to agreements and concerted action among the major states to protect ocean shipping."[53]
- A country's territorial waters were traditionally defined in terms of some fixed distance from the shore (traditionally, three miles: as far as a cannonball could be projected from an on-shore battery), and that alone.[54] In 1945, US President Harry S. Truman unilaterally declared the US extended instead all the way to the edge of the continental shelf. In so doing, he anticipated and accepted that all other nations would follow suit, and eventually they did in the Convention on the Law of the Sea.[55]
- "President Nixon unilaterally 'closed the gold window' of the Bretton Woods monetary regime in the early 1970s, which upset Japan and European countries but eventually led to the creation of the International Monetary Fund and the G-8 summit process."[56]
- Just as in the 19th century Britain sought to establish piracy on the high seas a crime of universal jurisdiction, ideally (eventually) in virtually all countries, the much less powerful state of Belgium would presumably be equally happy to see others

[53] G. John Ikenberry, "Is American Multilateralism in Decline?" *Perspectives on Politics* 1 (2003), p. 540. See further Oded Lowenheim, "'Do Ourselves Credit and Render a Lasting Service to Mankind:' British Moral Prestige, Humanitarian Intervention and the Barbary Pirates," *International Studies Quarterly* 47 (2003), pp. 23–48.

[54] Goldsmith and Posner, "A Theory of Customary International Law," p. 1158.

[55] Harry S Truman, "Presidental Proclamation No. 2667: Policy of the United States with Respect to the Natural Resources of the Subsoil and Sea Bed of the Continental Shelf," 28 September 1945, available at www.oceanlaw.net/texts/truman1.htm (accessed April 8, 2004). The Convention on the Law of the Sea, concluded in 1982, came into effect in 1994.

[56] Ikenberry, "Is American Multilateralism in Decline?," p. 540.

> following its lead in allowing prosecutions in their courts for violation of universal human rights anywhere in the world.[57]

So there are, I believe, some real cases of would-be law-makers breaking customary international law genuinely with a view to remaking it.[58] Alas, that seems not to be the way today's sole superpower chooses to play the great game of international politics.[59]

Social & Political Theory and Philosophy Programs
Research School of Social Sciences
Australian National University
Canberra ACT 0200
Australia
E-mail: goodinb@coombs.anu.edu.au

[57] As in a limited way the US Alien Tort Claim Act of 1789 does, in giving US federal courts "jurisdiction of any civil action by an alien for a tort only, committed in violation of the law of nations or a treaty of the United States." The interpretation and scope of that statute is judicially disputed, most recently in the US Supreme Court in *Sosa v. Alvarez-Machain*, No. 03-339, consolidated with *U.S. v Alvarez-Machain*, No. 03-485 (oral argument July 2004).

[58] In their own interests, to be sure – certainly in the first three cases, anyway, although the worst that even the most cynical arch-realist can say against Belgium is that it is easy for it to adopt that policy because it does not have many troops stationed overseas who might get caught up in any generalization of this policy (which is the official US worry about the International Criminal Court).

[59] Earlier versions were presented at the University of Stockholm and the American Philosophical Association, Pacific Division, Mini-Conference on "Global Justice." I am grateful for comments, then and later, from Gustaf Arrhenius, Lars Bergstrom, Jim Bohman, John Gardner, Lena Halldenius, Dora Kostakopoulou, Larry May, Eric Posner, John Tasioulas and Janna Thompson.

JOHN W. LANGO

PREVENTIVE WARS, JUST WAR PRINCIPLES, AND THE UNITED NATIONS*

(Received 14 May 2004; accepted in revised form 7 June 2004)

ABSTRACT. This paper explores the question of whether the United Nations should engage in preventive military actions. Correlatively, it asks whether UN preventive military actions could satisfy just war principles. Rather than from the standpoint of the individual nation state, the ethics of preventive war is discussed from the standpoint of the UN. For the sake of brevity, only the legitimate authority, just cause, last resort, and proportionality principles are considered. Since there has been disagreement about the specific content of these principles, a third question also is explored: How should they be formulated? Moreover, these questions are addressed in the context of a particular issue: the goals of the non-proliferation and the abolition of weapons of mass destruction.

KEY WORDS: ethics of war, just war principles, pre-emptive wars, preventive military actions, preventive wars, Security Council, United Nations, war and morality, weapons of mass destruction

At the beginning of *Prevention of Armed Conflict: Report of the Secretary-General*, Kofi Annan relates that, "Since assuming office, I have pledged to move the United Nations from a culture of reaction to a culture of prevention."[1] In broad agreement with his report, I want to explore a question that he does not consider sufficiently: Should a UN culture of prevention include an option of preventive war? Note that "war" is used broadly. What Annan terms an "armed conflict" is a war, and the actual use of military force – a military action – is an act of war.[2] Hence the question can be restated as

* I would like to thank an anonymous referee, Carol C. Gould, George R. Lucas, Jr., Darrel Moellendorf, Andrew Oldenquist, Andrew Valls, Harry van der Linden, and Virginia Warren for their helpful comments on various drafts of this paper. This work was supported in part by a grant from the City University of New York Research Award Program.

[1] Kofi A. Annan, *Prevention of Armed Conflict: Report of the Secretary-General* (New York: United Nations, 2002), p. vii.

[2] For a discussion of the terms "war" and "armed conflict," see Ingrid Detter de Lupis, *The Laws of War* (Cambridge: Cambridge University Press, 1987), pp. 16–18.

follows. Should a UN culture of prevention include an option of preventive military actions?

Correlatively, I shall explore the question of whether UN preventive military actions could satisfy just war principles. Instead of discussing the ethics of preventive war abstractly, I shall discuss it concretely by orienting it from the standpoint of the UN. For the sake of brevity, I shall consider only the legitimate authority, just cause, last resort, and proportionality principles. Since there has been disagreement within the just war tradition about the specific content of these principles, I shall also have to ask how they should be formulated.[3] (Those who hold that preventive wars violate current just war principles might understand my question thus: how should they be revised?) Again for the sake of brevity, my answer to this question has to be incomplete.

Usually, however, discussions of the ethics of war are oriented from the standpoint of the individual nation state. On 20 September 2002, the George W. Bush administration released a document containing a new national security strategy for the US. In this document, it is declared that the US maintains "the option of pre-emptive actions to counter a sufficient threat to our national security," that "we will not hesitate to act alone, if necessary," but that this option will be exercised only when "the cause [is] just."[4] Evidently, this appeal to (something like) the just cause principle is oriented from the standpoint of the US. But could preventive military actions that are waged alone – unilaterally – satisfy just war principles?[5] Because I am skeptical that this question should

[3] The topic of preventive war is discussed from a "cosmopolitan normative perspective" in Allen Buchanan and Robert O. Keohane, "The Preventive Use of Force: A Cosmopolitan Institutional Proposal," *Ethics & International Affairs* 18 (2004), p. 1. Although what they propose – namely, a new cosmopolitan "institutional framework" governing the preventive use of force – includes "traditional just war principles," they do not consider the question of how such principles should be formulated. In contrast, a main goal of my paper is to answer this question.

[4] "The National Security Strategy of the United States of America," 2002, http://www.whitehouse.gov/nsc/nss.html (accessed 16 March 2004). The first quotation (p. 15) and the second quotation (p. 16) are from a chapter about weapons of mass destruction, whereas the middle quotation (p. 6) is from a chapter about terrorism (page references are to the PDF version). Although this unilateralist declaration is not repeated explicitly in the former chapter, it is implicit there.

[5] I use the term "preventive," since (for a reason to be stated shortly) the term "pre-emptive" is misleading.

be answered affirmatively, I am concentrating instead on the question of whether multilateral preventive military actions that are authorized by the UN Security Council could satisfy them.

According to Chapter VII (Article 39) of the UN Charter, it is the duty of the Security Council to ascertain not only whether there is a "breach of the peace" or an "act of aggression" but also whether there is a "threat to the peace."[6] The mere possession of weapons of mass destruction (WMD), or even the attempt to possess them – not just by Iraq and North Korea,[7] but by any state, including Russia and the US – constitutes, I shall argue, a threat to the peace. Accordingly, in discussing the ethics of preventive war, I shall advocate both the goal of the non-proliferation of weapons of mass destruction and the goal of their abolition.[8] Let us term a state that possesses or is striving to possess WMD a "WMD state," and preventive military actions with the limited aim of causing a WMD state not to possess WMD a "WMD preventive war." Of course, a WMD state might be persuaded or coerced not to possess WMD by the use of measures other than military force – such as various political, diplomatic, or economic measures. However, my view is that, if a WMD state is sufficiently threatening, a WMD preventive war against it could be a just cause. Nonetheless, even if such a preventive war would satisfy the just cause principle, it would not be a just war if it did not also satisfy the other just war principles. With the aim of illustrating the above questions with a challenging issue, I shall be especially concerned with the more specific question:

---

[6] "Charter of the United Nations," http://www.un.org/aboutun/charter (accessed 16 March 2004). Henceforth references for quotations from the UN Charter are omitted.

[7] Admittedly, my writing of this paper is motivated considerably by current events, but I want to discuss the ethics of preventive war largely in abstraction from them. Instead of focusing on particular wars or international crises, I am focusing on principles and policies. Therefore, with the exception of a few scattered remarks, I shall ignore the cases of Iraq and North Korea.

[8] It is often forgotten that the Nuclear Non-Proliferation Treaty incorporates the goal of the abolition of nuclear weapons. More specifically, Article VI commits signatories to engage in "negotiations in good faith" about "effective measures" for bringing about "nuclear disarmament" [see "The Treaty on the Non-Proliferation of Nuclear Weapons (NPT)," http://disarmament.un.org:8080/wmd/npt (accessed 16 March 2004)].

Could a WMD preventive war authorized by the Security Council satisfy just war principles?[9]

I. The United Nations and Threats to the Peace

Motivated particularly by the case of genocide in Rwanda, Annan proposes that the UN "has a moral responsibility to ensure that vulnerable peoples are protected and that genocides never occur again."[10] My view is that this moral responsibility should include ensuring that vulnerable peoples are protected from weapons of mass destruction and that nuclear or biological or chemical genocides never occur. Moreover, Annan thinks that the prevention of armed conflict is "best undertaken" in accordance with Chapter VI of the UN Charter.[11] Entitled "Pacific Settlement of Disputes," Chapter VI (Article 33) names such measures as negotiation, mediation, and judicial settlement. Throughout his report, Annan advocates a "comprehensive approach" to armed conflict prevention, one that includes political, diplomatic, and economic measures.[12] Among the measures in his comprehensive approach are peacekeeping operations, but UN peacekeeping operations require the "consent of the States concerned."[13] In general, all of the measures named above presuppose such consent.[14]

Although mainly concerned with peaceful measures under Chapter VI, Annan does admit, albeit briefly, "that certain measures under

[9] The topics of the international community, just war principles, and pre-emptive war (and also humanitarian military intervention) are discussed by George R. Lucas, Jr., "The Role of the 'International Community' in Just War Tradition – Confronting the Challenges of Humanitarian Intervention and Preemptive War," *Journal of Military Ethics* 2 (2003), pp. 122–144. Although our two papers overlap somewhat – in particular, we are both concerned with the question of how just war principles should be formulated or revised – there are significant differences. Let me provide a few examples. He is primarily concerned with decisions by individual states to engage in military interventions, whereas I am primarily concerned with decisions by the Security Council to authorize preventive military actions. He restricts the use of military force to threats that are "imminent," whereas I challenge such a restriction. He considers the issue of weapons of mass destruction peripherally, whereas I consider it centrally.

[10] Annan, *Prevention of Armed Conflict: Report of the Secretary-General,* p. 86.

[11] Annan, *Prevention of Armed Conflict: Report of the Secretary-General,* pp. viii, 90.

[12] Annan, *Prevention of Armed Conflict: Report of the Secretary-General,* pp. ix, 90.

[13] Annan, *Prevention of Armed Conflict: Report of the Secretary-General,* p. 45.

[14] Annan, *Prevention of Armed Conflict: Report of the Secretary-General,* p. 87.

Chapter VII of the Charter such as sanctions, can have an important deterrent effect."[15] Entitled "Action with Respect to Threats to the Peace, Breaches of the Peace, and Acts of Aggression," Chapter VII includes both non-military measures such as sanctions (Article 41) and "such action by air, sea, or land forces as may be necessary to maintain or restore international peace and security" (Article 42). Obviously, such coercive measures do not presuppose the consent of the states concerned. Should Chapter VII be understood as encompassing actions by air, sea, or land forces that are preventive of armed conflict?

When there is a breach of the peace, Chapter VII (Article 39) authorizes the Security Council to decide which such measures should be taken to "restore" peace. And, when there is a threat to the peace, Chapter VII (Article 39) authorizes the Security Council to decide which such measures should be taken to "maintain" peace. A plain reading of the words "threat" and "maintain" implies, I submit, that Chapter VII authorizes the Security Council to exercise an option of preventive military actions – military actions that are designed to prevent a threat to the peace from eventuating in a breach of the peace.

Chapter VII (Article 40) also authorizes the Security Council to pass resolutions that require a state that is threatening the peace to cease doing so. And, if the state fails to comply with the resolutions, the Security Council may then call for military actions to compel compliance.[16] Although occasioned by the state's failure to comply, the Security Council's aim in calling for military actions is to prevent the state from breaching the peace. For example, in Resolution 687 (1991), the Security Council decided (as a Gulf War cease fire measure) that Iraq must not possess WMD, and recently the Security Council deliberated whether Iraq should be compelled to comply with this resolution by means of military actions. Plainly, the motive for the decision that Iraq must not possess WMD was preventive – the aim was to prevent Iraq from using (or threatening to use) WMD in the future.

A UN option of multilateral preventive military actions is compatible with the UN Charter, but is the US option of unilateral preventive military actions compatible with it? Chapter VII (Article

[15] Annan, *Prevention of Armed Conflict: Report of the Secretary-General,* p. 90.

[16] See Rosalyn Higgins, *Problems and Process: International Law and How We Use It* (Oxford: Clarendon Press, 1994), pp. 257–259.

51) does recognize that, prior to action by the Security Council, states have a "right of individual or collective self-defence if an armed attack occurs." Nevertheless, it is not recognized in Chapter VII that, prior to action by the Security Council, states have a right of individual or collective preventive war. It might be objected that, in accordance with international law, a pre-emptive first strike could be legitimate in the face of an imminent attack.[17] However, in the document in which this US option is declared, it is asserted that "We must adapt the concept of imminent threat" – for "pre-emptive" military actions could still be legitimate "even if uncertainty remains as to the time and place of the enemy's attack."[18] So that this adaptation is not confused with the usual meaning of the term "pre-emptive," I have been using the term "preventive" in discussing the US option. Even if unilateral pre-emptive military actions are compatible with the UN Charter, unilateral preventive military actions are not.

Roughly speaking, to satisfy the legitimate authority principle, a war must be declared and controlled by persons who are legally authorized to do this.[19] My view is that the principle should involve a concept of legal authorization that transcends the individual nation state. In particular, since 191 states are members of the UN, the principle should encompass the procedure of legal authorization that is formulated in the UN Charter.[20] Therefore, a preventive war could satisfy the principle only if it is authorized by the Security Council. Indeed, a US preventive war could satisfy the principle only if it is authorized by the US Congress. But, additionally, since the US is a signatory of the UN Charter, and thus must be in compliance with it (cf. Article VI of the US Constitution), a US preventive war could satisfy the principle only if it also is authorized by the UN Security Council.

In endorsing Annan's report by Resolution 1366 (2001), the Security Council emphasized that, in order for the prevention of armed conflict to be successful, "the United Nations needs the consent and support of the Government concerned."[21] I want to

[17] See Higgins, *Problems and Process*, pp. 242–243.

[18] "The National Security Strategy of the United States of America," p. 15.

[19] See Richard J. Regan, *Just War: Principles and Cases* (Washington, DC: Catholic University of America Press, 1996), p. 20.

[20] Cf. Regan, *Just War: Principles and Cases*, pp. 24–27.

[21] This resolution is reprinted in Annan, *Prevention of Armed Conflict: Report of the Secretary-General,* p. 96.

emphasize that there is no explicit endorsement in this resolution of coercive measures under Chapter VII. Even though the Security Council is authorized by the UN Charter to decide whether coercive measures should be taken, and even though Annan's report alludes to them, this resolution does not. Concerning the concept of consent, let me make a quasi Hobbesian point. Each member of the UN, in signing the UN Charter, has committed itself to comply with Chapter VII, and, therefore, it has consented to being coerced, should it become a threat to the peace.

In light of the irresolution in Resolution 1366 about coercive measures – and also because any permanent member of the Security Council may veto any resolution that authorizes coercive measures – it might be argued that the US option of unilateral preventive military actions is necessary because the UN is ineffective. Admittedly, to have a sufficiently effective UN option of preventive military actions, UN culture has to be transformed. But the Bush administration, by its policy of unilateral preventive military actions, would also transform international culture. Given that there are threats to the peace that warrant preventive military actions, we need to ask which transformation is best. My suggestion is that the US should, instead of acting alone, act together with other states to realize a sufficiently effective UN option of preventive military actions.

Alternatively, it might be argued that, in order to have a truly legitimate transnational authority, the ineffective UN ought to be superseded by a different global institution. For instance, such a global institution might be founded by a treaty among all those states that are sufficiently democratic (i.e., in addition to the obvious European states, such states as Brazil, Israel, Japan, Mexico, Russia, South Africa, and Turkey). To envisage it, we might imagine NATO expanded into a Pacific and Atlantic Treaty Organization (PATO). By reading the terms "United Nations (UN)" and "Security Council" as standing for such a global institution, those who agree with this sort of argument might find much of the remainder of this paper acceptable.[22]

[22] For a detailed proposal of an institutional model involving a "democratic coalition" that would supplement the Security Council, see Buchanan and Keohane, "The Preventive Use of Force," pp. 18–20. My view is that this proposal is in conflict with the UN Charter, for it permits the democratic coalition to engage in a preventive war that is not authorized by a Security Council resolution.

II. The Mere Possession of Weapons of Mass Destruction

Even though a UN option of preventive military actions is compatible with the UN Charter, we still may ask whether such an option could satisfy just war principles. Since the legitimate authority principle has already been considered, it remains to consider the just cause, last resort, and proportionality principles. With the aim of answering this question in the context of a particular issue, I shall first discuss the topic of weapons of mass destruction.[23]

The controversy today concerning the Bush administration's preventive war policy is reminiscent of the controversy two decades ago concerning the Ronald Reagan administration's nuclear war fighting policy. In the midst of the earlier controversy, McGeorge Bundy advocated the efficacy of "existential deterrence": Instead of relying on credible threats about nuclear retaliation – such as threats about escalation dominance in a limited nuclear war – existential deterrence does not need "provocative threats."[24] For the mere possession of nuclear weapons – their mere existence – creates "terrible and unavoidable uncertainties" about how (or even whether) they would be used in retaliation, uncertainties that are sufficient for deterrence.[25] Analogously, my claim is that the mere possession of WMD by states – even ones that do not (apparently) have aggressive intentions – creates terrible and unavoidable uncertainties about what could happen, uncertainties that constitute a threat to the peace.

For an illustration of this claim, let us consider the problem of the proliferation of biological weapons (BW). More than 100 states are

---

[23] There is no space here to discuss topics such as armed humanitarian intervention. However, as what might prove to be an acceptable counterexample to a negative answer to the question, let me mention a case. UN peacekeepers were in Rwanda for several months before the outbreak of genocide in April 1994, but their Rules of Engagement only allowed them to use military force in self-defense. Had preventive military actions been allowed, they might have been able to prevent some of the future slaughter – e.g., by seizing some of the machetes that were being imported in unusually large numbers. Concerning the role of machetes in the genocide, see Alison Des Forges, *Leave None to Tell the Story: Genocide in Rwanda* (New York: Human Rights Watch and International Federation of Human Rights, 1999), pp. 5, 8, 127–128.

[24] McGeorge Bundy, "Existential Deterrence and Its Consequences," in Douglas MacLean, (ed.), *The Security Gamble: Deterrence Dilemmas in the Nuclear Age* (Totowa: Rowman and Allanheld, 1984), p. 10.

[25] Bundy, "Existential Deterrence and Its Consequences," p. 8.

presently capable of manufacturing BW,[26] and so very many states might in future possess BW, if BW proliferation is not stemmed. However, during the Cold War the bipolar nuclear deterrence regimen (presumably) proved stable, and so we might expect that in future a multi-polar WMD deterrence regimen will be stable. Nevertheless, there still was considerable worry during the Cold War about the possibility of the accidental or inadvertent or unauthorized use of nuclear weapons.[27] Similarly, we still should be quite worried about the possibility of an accidental or inadvertent or unauthorized use (or release) of a BW agent (i.e., a microorganism or toxin), especially one that would result in a catastrophic plague (briefly, a "BW plague").

Granted, it is uncertain at present whether there will be in future a BW plague, but this is a terrible and unavoidable uncertainty. Indeed, because each state possessing BW (i.e., each "BW state") can be expected to have safeguards against accidental or inadvertent or unauthorized uses of its BW agents, the probability that its possession of BW will unintentionally result in a BW plague is perhaps very low. For simplicity, let us suppose that this probability is .01. Nonetheless, if there were 10 BW states, the probability that the possession of BW by one of these ten will unintentionally result in a BW plague is about .1. (To obtain this result, it is assumed that the probability that the possession of BW by the 10 states will not unintentionally result in a BW plague is $.99^{10}$.) And, if there were 30 BW states, the probability that the possession of BW by one of these 30 will unintentionally result in a BW plague is about .26 (i.e., $1 - .99^{30}$.) These probabilities, although conjectural, symbolize a generalization about BW proliferation that is not conjectural: the larger the number of BW states, the greater the probability of a BW plague. Just as there were terrible and unavoidable uncertainties during the Cold War about nuclear intentions, so there are terrible and unavoidable uncertainties today about what could happen with BW agents unintentionally.

There also are terrible and unavoidable uncertainties about what could happen with BW agents intentionally. In particular, we should

[26] US Congress, Office of Technology Assessment, *Technologies Underlying Weapons of Mass Destruction, OTA-BP-ISC-115* (Washington, DC: US Government Printing Office, 1993), p. 85.

[27] See Paul Bracken, "Accidental Nuclear War," in G. T. Allison, A. Carnesale, and J. S. Nye, Jr. (eds.), *Hawks, Doves, and Owls: An Agenda for Avoiding Nuclear War* (New York: Norton, 1985).

admit that we actually are uncertain about whether a multi-polar WMD deterrence regimen would remain stable. For the larger the number of BW states, the greater the probability that one of them will use BW in warfare. Note that such a use of BW could result in a BW plague, because of technical difficulties in limiting BW agents to the battlefield.[28]

Having considered the problem of BW proliferation, I want now to ask whether we can reasonably demand that states not possess chemical and biological weapons (CBW), when some states continue to possess nuclear weapons. First, we still should be very worried about the accidental or inadvertent or unauthorized use of nuclear weapons. Second, in light of the nuclear arms race during the Cold War, we also should be very worried that the possession of nuclear weapons by some states could stimulate other states to arm themselves with CBW. Third, if the US were to respond to a CBW attack with the "overwhelming force" of a nuclear weapon, there could be catastrophic radioactive fallout on non-belligerents (consider Chernobyl).[29] Fourth, a conventional war between two states with nuclear weapons (e.g., India and Pakistan) could escalate to an inadvertent nuclear war. Fifth, in general, the larger the number of WMD states, the greater the probability that a weapon of mass destruction will be used. And so forth.

Additionally, there are terrible and unavoidable uncertainties about WMD possession by non-governmental agents – e.g., revolutionaries, mercenaries, arms dealers, and, of course, terrorists.

Because of such terrible and unavoidable uncertainties about what could happen with WMD, my conclusion is that the mere possession of them – or even the attempt to possess them – constitutes a threat to the peace. Note that one of the reasons stated in Resolution 687 (1991) for the decision at the end of the Gulf War that Iraq must not possess WMD was that the Security Council was "Conscious of the threat that all weapons of mass destruction pose to peace and security

[28] US Congress, Office of Technology Assessment, *Technologies Underlying Weapons of Mass Destruction,* p. 73.

[29] In a supplementary national security document released by the Bush administration in December 2002, it is declared that, to deter the use of WMD by an enemy state, the US "reserves the right to respond with overwhelming force – including through resort to all of our options." And among these options is a "nuclear response" [see "National Strategy to Combat Weapons of Mass Destruction," 2002, p. 3, http://www.whitehouse.gov/nsc (accessed 16 March 2004)].

(in the Middle East)."[30] Therefore, my proposal is that, in accordance with Chapter VII of the UN Charter, the Security Council ought to maintain the peace by taking actions with the aim of realizing the goals of WMD non-proliferation and WMD abolition. In particular, in accordance with Article 42, the Security Council ought to have the option of preventive military actions.

Obviously, in order to carry out this proposal, UN culture would have to be transformed. To appreciate the difficulty of the requisite transformation, consider that the Security Council would have to take actions with the aim of abolishing the nuclear weapons possessed by its own permanent members. Let me suggest again that the US should, instead of acting alone, act together with other states to bring about such a transformation of UN culture.

III. UN Preventive Military Actions and the Just Cause Principle

I want now to return to the question of whether a UN option of preventive military actions could satisfy just war principles. To begin with, let us recall a widely held thesis in the recent literature on just war theory: whereas there are circumstances under which a preemptive attack could satisfy just war principles (The Six Day War is a paradigm case), a preventive war cannot be a just war. For instance, William V. O'Brien claims that "the right of defense" includes a right of "anticipatory self-defense," a right that can be exercised only when three criteria are satisfied.[31] First, there is a criterion of intent: "There must be a clear indication of an intent on the part of the alleged aggressor to attack."[32] Second, there is a criterion of imminence: "There must be adequate evidence that preparations for the attack have advanced to the point where it is imminent."[33] Third, there is a criterion of proportionality: "The advantages of a preemptive attack must be proportionate to the risks of precipitating a

[30] "United Nations Security Council Resolution 687," 1991, http://www1.umn.edu/humanrts/peace/docs/scres687.html (accessed 11 April 2004).

[31] William V. O'Brien, *The Conduct of Just and Limited War* (New York: Praeger, 1981), p. 132.

[32] O'Brien, *The Conduct of Just and Limited War*, p. 133.

[33] O'Brien, *The Conduct of Just and Limited War*, p. 133.

war that might be avoided."[34] Presumably, his imminence criterion serves to demarcate pre-emptive attacks from preventive wars. For he also claimed parenthetically that "Defense does not go so far as to justify preventive war," a claim that he did not elaborate.[35]

But why should imminence matter? In *Just and Unjust Wars*, Michael Walzer stated three conditions for a morally legitimate first strike. First, there is a condition of intent: "a manifest intent to injure."[36] Second, there is a condition of degree: "a degree of active preparation that makes that intent a positive danger."[37] Third, there is a condition of urgency: "a general situation in which waiting, or doing anything other than fighting, greatly magnifies the risk."[38] It is notable that, in contrast to O'Brien, Walzer does not require imminence. "The line between legitimate and illegitimate first strikes," Walzer wrote, "is not going to be drawn at the point of imminent attack but at the point of sufficient threat."[39] On the other hand, Walzer also supported "the moral necessity of rejecting any attack that is merely preventive in character."[40] But notice the use of "merely." Presumably, it is not merely preventive to launch a first strike against a sufficient threat (i.e., one that satisfies the stated three conditions) that happens not to be imminent. Accordingly, my conclusion is that he has in effect stated three conditions for morally legitimate preventive military actions.

By revising his intent and degree conditions, I shall propose an answer to the question of whether an option of UN preventive military actions could satisfy the just cause principle.[41] (His urgency condition has relevance mainly to the last resort principle, and so it is discussed in the next section.) Concerning his intent condition, which is remarkably similar to O'Brien's criterion of intent, my main question is why it is limited to manifest threats of injury that are

[34] O'Brien, *The Conduct of Just and Limited War*, p. 133.

[35] O'Brien, *The Conduct of Just and Limited War*, p. 132.

[36] Michael Walzer, *Just and Unjust Wars: A Moral Argument with Historical Illustrations* (New York: Basic Books, 1977), p. 81.

[37] Walzer, *Just and Unjust Wars*, p. 81.

[38] Walzer, *Just and Unjust Wars*, p. 81.

[39] Walzer, *Just and Unjust Wars*, p. 81.

[40] Walzer, *Just and Unjust Wars*, p. 80.

[41] See the "slight re-wording and generalizing" of Walzer's three conditions by Lucas, "The Role of the 'International Community' in Just War Tradition," pp. 131–133.

intentional. The *Model Penal Code* of the American Law Institute distinguishes four kinds of culpability, which are based on whether a person acts purposely (i.e., intentionally) or knowingly or recklessly or negligently.[42] Of course, during a trial the members of the jury are deciding retrospectively about culpability, whereas I am concerned here with prospective decisions about sufficiency of threat. Nonetheless, similar to these four kinds of culpability, there are four kinds of threat. Accordingly, I would revise Walzer's intent condition as follows: a manifest threat of injury made (or done) either intentionally or knowingly or recklessly or negligently. Because of the greater generality of the revised condition, I shall rename it the *threat condition*.

Let me sketch some disputable illustrations. If fundamentalists were to seize power in Pakistan, the increased likelihood of accidental or inadvertent or unauthorized use of Pakistan's nuclear weapons would constitute a manifest threat of injury through negligence. Even if North Korea's nuclear weapons program does not involve a manifest intent to injure, it still involves a manifest threat of injury through recklessness. Implicit in the US threat to respond to a WMD attack with the overwhelming force of a nuclear weapon is a manifest threat of knowingly (even if not intentionally) injuring civilians.

Correspondingly, I would revise Walzer's degree condition as follows: The magnitude of the threat is sufficiently large to make the threat an extreme danger. And I shall rename it the *magnitude condition*. But what are the thresholds of sufficiency for the magnitudes of various threats? This question and comparable threshold questions are considered in the final section of this paper.

What, then, is the relevance of these two revised conditions for the just cause principle? There is widespread agreement that there is a just cause for war when a state's territorial integrity is violated. But this sort of just cause should be understood to encompass not only intentional violations of territorial integrity but also knowing, reckless, and negligent violations of territorial integrity. Indeed, the intentional invasion of a state by the armed forces of an aggressor is a violation of territorial integrity, but then so is the invasion of a BW plague due to an accidental or inadvertent or unauthorized use of a BW agent. And so is the invasion of radioactive fallout due to the use of a nuclear weapon elsewhere. Additionally, this sort of just cause should be understood to encompass both actual violations of

---

[42] *Model Penal Code* (Philadelphia: American Law Institute, 1962), Section 2.02.

territorial integrity and sufficient threats of such violations. Accordingly, my view is that there is a just cause for UN preventive military actions when a threat of a violation of territorial integrity satisfies both the threat and magnitude conditions.

To generalize, there is a just cause for UN preventive military actions when there is a threat to the peace that satisfies both the threat and magnitude conditions. Of course, when there is a threat to the peace that satisfies the threat condition but not the magnitude condition, there still could be enough justification for UN non-military measures. In the preceding section, I argued that the mere possession of WMD, or even the attempt to possess WMD, constitutes a threat to the peace. Such a threat is, I now want to add, a manifest threat of injury (whether intentional or knowing or reckless or negligent). Nevertheless, there is a just cause for UN preventive military actions only if the magnitude of such a threat is sufficiently large to make the threat an extreme danger.

IV. UN Preventive Military Actions and the Last Resort Principle

Even if a preventive war authorized by the Security Council would satisfy the just cause principle, it would not be a just war if it did not also satisfy the last resort principle. Measures other than military force must be tried first. It is especially because of the last resort principle that there is considerable skepticism about whether a preventive war could be a just war. For, since the peace is only threatened – and the threat is not imminent – it would seem that there is ample time to try non-military measures first – until the threat becomes imminent or the peace is breached. In the present section, I shall challenge such skepticism. In particular, I shall contend that an option of UN preventive military actions could satisfy the last resort principle.[43]

Roughly speaking, the last resort principle requires that measures other than war must be tried sufficiently first. Hence a key question concerns the standards for determining whether non-military measures have been tried first sufficiently. In brief, what are the sufficiency standards?

[43] Although Buchanan and Keohane state that their cosmopolitan institutional proposal includes "traditional just war principles," they do not mention the last resort principle (see Buchanan and Keohane, "The Preventive Use of Force," p. 4).

In his study of just war principles, James Childress claimed that the last resort principle does not require "that all possible [non-military] measures have to be attempted and exhausted if there is no reasonable expectation that they will be successful."[44] Note that, when we reasonably expect that a measure will succeed, we also have to recognize that there is a significant risk that it will fail. Thus his standard of sufficiency is that there is no reasonable expectation that additional non-military measures will be successful. While agreeing that this *unsuccessfulness standard* is correct, I want to investigate whether there should be other sufficiency standards, ones that pertain specifically to preventive wars.

To begin with, let us recall Walzer's urgency condition: "A general situation in which waiting, or doing anything other than fighting, greatly magnifies the risk."[45] Let me revise his condition in terms of the language of my threat and magnitude conditions. Suppose that there is a manifest threat of injury, and the magnitude of the threat is sufficiently large to make the threat an extreme danger. Moreover, if we were to delay taking preventive military actions in order to attempt non-military measures first, the magnitude of the threat would be greatly increased. In brief, the revised condition is that delaying taking preventive military actions greatly increases the magnitude of the threat. The main point is that this condition amounts to a second sufficiency standard, one that pertains specifically to preventive wars. Let us term it the "*magnitude standard*." Even if we could reasonably expect that a non-military measure will succeed, we also have to recognize that there is a significant risk that it will fail. And so the last resort principle does not require that it has to be attempted if the magnitude of the threat would thereby be greatly increased. But, to satisfy the magnitude standard, how great does the increase in magnitude have to be? This threshold question too is considered later.

The last resort principle requires that non-military measures must be attempted first unless a sufficiency standard is satisfied. However, it does not require that, once a sufficiency standard is satisfied, non-military measures must no longer be attempted. For in some circumstances it could be most effective to use both preventive military actions and non-military measures concurrently. For instance, to

---

[44] James F. Childress, "Just-War Theories: The Bases, Interrelations, Priorities, and Functions of Their Criteria," *Theological Studies* 39 (1978), p. 75. See the term "reasonable" in Regan, *Just War: Principles and Cases,* p. 64.

[45] Walzer, *Just and Unjust Wars*, p. 81.

coerce a WMD state not to possess WMD, limited military strikes could help to bring about a diplomatic solution. Indeed, war must be a last resort, but it also may be a concurrent resort.

In light of this qualification, let me propose a third sufficiency standard, termed the "*minimization standard*." (There might be other sufficiency standards, but I cannot pursue this possibility here.) In summarizing his strategy of the indirect approach in a set of maxims, Basil Liddell Hart included the maxim: "Exploit the line of least resistance."[46] For the purpose of strategy is "to diminish the possibility of resistance."[47] By exploiting the line of least resistance, one aims both to increase the likelihood of securing one's military objective and to decrease one's costs in doing so. His military maxim has a moral analogue: Exploit the line of least harm. For the purpose of just war theory is to diminish the destructiveness of war, but the purpose of morality also includes diminishing the harm of unjust threats. I want to stress that the line of least harm is sometimes best exploited by using non-military measures concurrently with military actions. Most importantly, it is sometimes best to use as many non-military measures as possible concurrently with as little military force as possible. Therefore, the last resort principle should permit using minimal preventive military actions and maximal non-military measures concurrently if the magnitude of an extremely dangerous threat to the peace would thereby be greatly decreased. In short, the minimization standard is that using minimal preventive military actions and maximal non-military measures concurrently decreases greatly the magnitude of the threat. But, to satisfy the minimization standard, how great does the decrease in magnitude have to be? Again there is a threshold question to be considered later.

Let us imagine an arguable example set in the future. North Korea has sold a nuclear weapon to Syria, and the nuclear weapon is on a ship at sea. The possession by Syria of this nuclear weapon would constitute a manifest threat of injury to other states, and the magnitude of the threat would be sufficiently large to make the threat an extreme danger. However, there is a reasonable expectation that Syria would be persuaded to relinquish the nuclear weapon by means of diplomacy, and so the unsuccessfulness standard is not satisfied. Although there is a significant risk that diplomacy would fail, the

---

[46] Basil Liddell Hart, *Strategy*, second revised edition (New York: Praeger, 1967), p. 348. Italics removed.

[47] Hart, *Strategy*, p. 337. Italics removed.

magnitude of the threat would not be greatly increased by attempting it, and so the magnitude standard is not satisfied. Nevertheless, the line of least harm would be to immediately use limited military force, to board the ship and seize the nuclear weapon, while using a variety of non-military measures to prevent further escalation of the ensuing crisis. Even though the other sufficiency standards are not satisfied, the minimization standard is satisfied.

V. UN Preventive Military Actions and the Proportionality Principle

Even if a preventive war authorized by the Security Council would satisfy the just cause and last resort principles, it would not be a just war if it did not also satisfy the proportionality principle. It might be thought that the just cause and last resort principles, as I have interpreted them in the preceding two sections, are too permissive, that they allow recourse to preventive war too readily. I want to emphasize that the proportionality principle, as I shall interpret it in the present section, is highly restrictive. A common aim of just war theories is to constrain war, and my particular aim in this paper is to show how UN preventive military actions should be constrained.

Roughly speaking, the proportionality principle requires that the probable good consequences achieved by war should outweigh the probable harmful consequences caused by it.[48] In short, benefits should outweigh harms. But what are benefits and harms, and how should they be weighed? In particular, how should we weigh immediate (and often relatively certain) benefits and harms against remote (and often relatively uncertain) benefits and harms? Evidently, as Nick Fotion asserts, the principle "suffers from a severe measurement problem."[49] This problem is very severe for preventive wars, especially when the threat to the peace is far from imminent.

Whatever our measurement procedures, we will ordinarily distinguish three sorts of cases: cases where we are reasonably certain that benefits outweigh harms, cases where we are reasonably certain that harms outweigh benefits, and intermediate cases. Therefore, as

[48] See O'Brien, *The Conduct of Just and Limited War*, p. 27.

[49] Nick Fotion, "Proportionality," in Bruno Coppieters and Nick Fotion (eds.), *Moral Constraints on War: Principles and Cases* (Lanham: Lexington Books, 2002), p. 93.

Fotion remarks, the proportionality principle is "best applied at the extremes."[50] Note also that, concerning intermediate cases, he claims that the principle is "permissive": even when we are not reasonably certain whether benefits outweigh harms, the principle is satisfied.[51] By contrast, concerning intermediate cases, my claim is that the principle is prohibitive: when we are not reasonably certain that benefits outweigh harms, the principle is not satisfied. For with the aim of constraining war, just war theories are (usually) based on a strong moral presumption against war. To override this moral presumption, we have the burden of proving that the just war principles are satisfied.[52] In particular, we have the burden of proving that the proportionality principle is satisfied. When we are not reasonably certain that benefits outweigh harms, we have not fulfilled this burden of proof (because we also have the burden of proving that the just cause and last resort principles are satisfied, they also are quite restrictive, even as I have interpreted them in the preceding two sections).

Consequently, to ensure that we can fulfill the burden of proving that projected UN preventive military actions satisfy the proportionality principle, we ought to follow this roughly stated rule: Use minimal military force. Let us term it the "*minimization rule*." Similarly, O'Brien claimed that, to satisfy the proportionality principle, "a military action must conform to the principle of economy of force."[53] But the economy of force principle is limited to military actions, for it requires that no more military force should be employed "than is necessary to achieve the [military] objective."[54] By contrast, the minimization rule is not limited to military actions. As has already been noted, the line of least harm is sometimes best exploited by using as many non-military measures as possible concurrently with as little military force as possible. Accordingly, the minimization rule can be elaborated as follows. To

---

[50] Fotion, "Proportionality," p. 93.

[51] Fotion, "Proportionality," p. 93.

[52] I discuss these ideas of moral presumption and burden of proof more fully in John W. Lango, "Is Armed Humanitarian Intervention to Stop Mass Killing Morally Obligatory?," *Public Affairs Quarterly* 15 (2001), pp. 173–191. For an interpretation of just war principles in terms of W. D. Ross's conception of *prima facie* duties, see Childress, "Just-War Theories."

[53] O'Brien, *The Conduct of Just and Limited War*, p. 228.

[54] O'Brien, *The Conduct of Just and Limited War*, p. 227. The quoted words are from a US Army Manual.

ensure that we can fulfill the burden of proving that UN preventive military actions satisfy the proportionality principle, we ought to follow the rule: use minimal military actions and maximal non-military measures concurrently.

In striving to satisfy the proportionality principle, we should always keep in mind that the smallest quantity of military force is 0. For coercive threats of military action (whether deterrent or compellent) are themselves (in a broad sense of the term) military actions. When a coercive threat is successful – when military force does not actually have to be exerted – the quantity of military force is 0. "In peacekeeping, we have a doctrine that you sometimes have to show force in order not to use force," Annan remarked, "that you arrive in such a robust, credible manner that the other side may do what you wish to see done, without having to fight."[55] Ideally, non-military measures should be buttressed merely by robust, credible threats of preventive military actions. Therefore, in accordance with the minimization rule, let me propose a rule of coercion: Use maximal non-military measures and coercive threats of minimal military actions concurrently.

VI. Thresholds and Treaties

Of course, sometimes non-zero military force has to be used, and so there still is a threshold question about the minimization rule: how minimal do preventive military actions have to be? Now recall that comparable threshold questions were asked about the just cause principle's magnitude condition and the last resort principle's magnitude and minimization standards. Concerning his conception of supreme emergencies, Walzer stated: "We need to make a map of human crises and to mark off the regions of desperation and disaster."[56] Analogously, to answer these questions, we need to make a map of threats to the peace and to mark off the regions that warrant U.N. preventive military actions.

---

[55] Annan is quoted in "UN Secretary General Faces His 'Most Difficult' Moment," *New York Times* (30 March 2003), p. B1.

[56] Walzer, *Just and Unjust Wars*, p. 253. I have no room to consider the question: "In a supreme emergency, may one or more of the just war principles be set aside?" Even if the question is answered affirmatively, it still is important to understand how the principles hold of preventive wars. For before we can decide whether a principle may be set aside, we first have to understand how it holds.

To articulate the map, a tool of threat cartography is conceptual analysis, but I have no space here to continue using this tool. Additionally, there are more pragmatic tools, ones that are political or diplomatic. More specifically, let me suggest that a principal goal of the Security Council ought to be to formulate procedures for answering the questions that are politically acceptable. And let me also suggest that no state should answer them unilaterally. Again I have to admit that, to realize this goal, UN culture would have to be transformed. Let me sketch one course that this transformation might follow. In accordance with Chapter VII (Article 43) of the UN Charter, and with the aim of contributing "to the maintenance of international peace and security," the Security Council might negotiate "special agreements" with UN members that would establish and govern "armed forces."[57] In so doing, the Security Council might negotiate procedures for answering the questions that are politically acceptable.

But what might be the purposes of such UN armed forces? Without attempting to answer this question completely, let me suggest one purpose. The Biological Weapons Convention (BWC) is not sufficiently effective, and so attempts have been made to negotiate a protocol designed to enhance its effectiveness. However, the BWC does provide minimally for compliance in terms of the Security Council. According to Article VI of the BWC, "Any State Party to the Convention which finds that any other State Party is acting in breach of obligations deriving from the provisions of the Convention may lodge a complaint with the Security Council of the United Nations."[58] Note also that Article VII of the BWC can be interpreted as providing for collective military action authorized by the Security Council. What the history of WMD inspections by the UN in Iraq indicates is, I think, that sometimes compliance with the BWC might be secured by means of UN preventive military actions, or by means of coercive threats of such actions. To generalize, in negotiating or renegotiating treaties to limit or abolish WMD, provisions for non-military measures might be buttressed by provisions for an option of UN preventive military actions. To generalize further, an option of UN preventive military

[57] See Alton Frye (ed.), *Humanitarian Intervention: Crafting a Workable Doctrine* (New York: Council on Foreign Relations, 2000), pp. 31–32.

[58] "Convention on the Prohibition of the Development, Production and Stockpiling of Bacteriological (Biological) and Toxin Weapons and on their Destruction," http://disarmament.un.org:8080/wmd/bwc (accessed 16 March 2004).

actions might be embodied in an appropriate framework of Security Council resolutions, international treaties, and international laws.[59]

In conclusion, let us imagine a future Security Council resolution:

The Security Council,

Emphasizing its responsibility under Article 39 of the United Nations Charter to determine the existence of threats to the peace and to take actions to maintain the peace,

Expressing its determination that both the continued possession and the further proliferation of weapons of mass destruction constitute threats to the peace,

Recognizing that it is an erroneous double standard to require some states to abolish such weapons while allowing other states to possess them,

Finding that existing arms control treaties do not provide for compliance measures that are sufficiently effective,

Stressing the importance of the option of military actions as a compliance measure,

Emphasizing its responsibility under Article 42 to take military actions, if necessary,

Affirming its responsibility under Article 43 to negotiate a special agreement with Members of the UN whereby armed forces will be made available to it,

Recognizing the unique standing of the US as a military power,

1. *Requires* that the states possessing nuclear weapons take prompt and verifiable steps to destroy them,
2. *Requires* that the states possessing chemical or biological weapons take prompt and verifiable steps to destroy them,
3. *Requires* that all states sign the Nuclear Non-Proliferation Treaty, the Chemical Weapons Convention, and the Biological Weapons Convention,
4. *Requires* the negotiation of protocols for these three treaties that provide for effective compliance measures, including measures about taking military actions,
5. *Convenes* Members of the UN to negotiate a special agreement for making armed forces available to it,
6. *Declares* that it will, if necessary, use these armed forces to compel compliance with the three treaties,

---

[59] Additionally, such a framework might incorporate the conception of "accountability" that is central to the cosmopolitan institutional proposal of Buchanan and Keohane, "The Preventive Use of Force."

7. *Calls upon* the US, which led in the founding of the UN at the close of the Second World War, and was a leader of an alliance of nations in that war, to once again lead the world in taking "effective *collective* measures for the prevention and removal of threats to the peace."[60]

Hunter College
City University of New York
695 Park Avenue
New York, NY 10021
USA
E-mail: john.lango@hunter.cuny.edu

[60] Article 1 of the UN Charter, emphasis provided.

GOPAL SREENIVASAN

DOES THE GATS UNDERMINE DEMOCRATIC CONTROL OVER HEALTH?

(Received 14 May 2004; accepted in revised form 7 June 2004)

ABSTRACT. This paper examines the General Agreement on Trade in Services (GATS), which is one of the World Trade Organisation's free trade agreements. In particular, I examine the extent to which the GATS unduly restricts the scope for national democratic choice. For purposes of illustration, I focus on the domestic health system as the subject of policy choice. I argue that signatories to the GATS effectively acquire a *constitutional obligation* to maintain a domestic health sector with a certain minimum degree of privatisation. Like constitutional obligations, the restrictions the GATS imposes on the freedom of future generations to structure their domestic health sector are (i) very difficult, though not strictly impossible, to alter; and (ii) not chosen in any ordinary sense by the subject generation. To gain democratic legitimacy, therefore, the relevant provisions of the GATS must pass some higher standard of democratic scrutiny, such as ratification by a super-majority. Ordinary legislative ratification does not suffice.

KEY WORDS: democracy, free trade, GATS, health, health care system, legitimacy, services, WTO

At least since the famous demonstrations in Seattle, Washington, the World Trade Organisation (WTO) has been in the forefront of attention and concern about the widespread changes grouped under the rubric of "globalisation." Where this concern has focused more specifically on health and health care, the lion's share of attention paid to the WTO has concentrated on the agreement on Trade Related aspects of Intellectual Property (TRIPS). This attention is often driven by concern with HIV/AIDS and the question of access to antiretroviral drugs, particularly in developing countries. However, TRIPS is not the only WTO agreement with important implications for health.[1] In this paper, I shall consider another of the core WTO agreements, the General Agreement on Trade in Services (GATS). The GATS is to trade in services what the older, and perhaps more familiar, GATT is to trade in goods.

[1] D. Lipson, "The World Trade Organization's Health Agenda," *British Medical Journal* 323 (2001), pp. 1139–1140.

I shall be interested, in particular, in the extent to which the GATS unduly restricts the scope for *national choice* concerning the structure of the domestic health system. Critics of the GATS have argued, among other things, that the agreement forcibly increases the degree of privatisation within domestic health systems; and they charge that this is undemocratic.[2] While their criticisms reflect a concern with both the political and the empirical impact of the GATS, my own focus will simply be on its political impact. As yet, there is little evidence concerning how far the GATS has actually affected trade in health services.[3]

I proceed on the background assumption that the question of how to structure the domestic health system is properly a matter for national decision – national *democratic* decision, to be precise. Although I shall not defend this assumption here, we shall see that a proper grasp of its upshot requires one to distinguish between national sovereignty and democratic legitimacy. My question, then, is whether the GATS unduly restricts the scope for democratic control over the degree of privatisation within the domestic health system.

I

Let me begin with a brief description of the GATS.[4] The agreement came into force on 1 January, 1995 and aims to create a favourable climate for trade in services. It does so by allowing nations to make binding commitments to reduce various barriers to trade in services. Over 120 nations are signatories.

---

[2] See, e.g., S. Sinclair, *GATS: How the WTO's New "Services" Negotiations Threaten Democracy* (Ottawa: Canadian Centre for Policy Alternatives, 2000); A. M. Pollock and D. Price, "The Public Health Implications of World Trade Negotiations on the General Agreement on Trade in Services and Public Services," *Lancet* 362 (2003), pp. 1072–1075; A. M. Pollock and D. Price, "Rewriting the Regulations: How the World Trade Organisation Could Accelerate Privatisation in Health-Care Systems," *Lancet* 356 (2000), pp. 1995–2000; D. Price, A. M. Pollock, and J. Shaoul, "How the World Trade Organisation is Shaping Domestic Policies in Health Care," *Lancet* 354 (1999), pp. 1889–1892; and D. Bolwell, *The WTO and the GATS: What Is at Stake for Public Health?* (Ferney-Voltaire: Public Services International, 1999).

[3] World Health Organisation and WTO, *WTO Agreements and Public Health* (Geneva: WTO, 2002), Section 228, http://www.wto.org/english/res_e/booksp_e/who_wto_e.pdf (accessed 12 March 2004).

[4] For the text of the GATS, see http://www.wto.org/english/docs_e/legal_e/26-gats_01_e.htm (accessed 12 March 2004).

There are two kinds of rules in the GATS: conditional rules and unconditional rules. The conditional rules apply to a given service sector only if a nation has formally and explicitly committed to maintain a certain degree of openness to trade in that sector. It does so by listing the sector in its official schedule of GATS commitments – in GATS parlance, by "scheduling" it. The unconditional rules apply to all of a nation's service sectors, simply in virtue of its having signed the GATS. Neither kind of rule applies to a service supplied "in the exercise of governmental authority," which Article I Section 3(c) defines as a service supplied *neither* on "a commercial basis" *nor* "in competition with one or more service suppliers."[5]

We can therefore divide the restrictions the GATS may impose on national choice into two groups, corresponding to its two kinds of rule. Some restrictions are unconditional, while others are conditional. *Unconditional* restrictions apply to a nation's service sectors whether they have been scheduled under the GATS or not. These restrictions are grounded in the general obligations defined in Part II of the GATS. For example, members must not discriminate between suppliers of different nations. Under Article II, the so-called "Most-Favoured-Nation Treatment" (MFN) provision, a member must treat services and service suppliers from one nation no less favourably than those from another.

Conditional restrictions arise, by contrast, only once a nation has scheduled a service sector under the GATS. They would apply to a nation's health insurance sector, for example, *only if* that nation had specifically listed "health insurance" in its schedule of sectors committed under the GATS.[6] The most obvious of these restrictions are defined by the provisions on market access (Article

[5] It is rather controversial how much protection from the GATS this exemption affords public services, since it is quite unclear how these categories are to be interpreted. Indeed, one legal scholar has argued that they have "no clear meaning" according to generally accepted methods of legal interpretation [see M. Krajewski, *Public Services and the Scope of the GATS* (Geneva: Center for International Environmental Law, 2001, http://www.ciel.org/Publications/PublicServicesScope.pdf (accessed 12 March 2004)].

[6] Or, more usually, had listed "life insurance," which includes health insurance, without specifically excluding the health insurance sub-sector [see WTO Council for Trade in Services, *Financial Services: Background Note by the Secretariat* S/C/W/72 (1998), Section 9, www.wto.org/english/tratop_e/serv_e/w72.doc (accessed 12 March 2004)].

XVI) and national treatment (Article XVII).[7] These Articles constitute the central means by which the GATS's aim of liberalising trade in services is to be achieved. To this end, they offer to impose a battery of restrictions on how scheduled sectors may be structured.[8]

A full commitment to provide "market access" to other nations entails refraining, for example, from establishing such barriers to trade as quotas that limit the number of providers of a given service or the volume of service supplied by each. Under the "national treatment" provision, a member is also committed to treating foreign service suppliers no less favourably than it treats *domestic* ones. This means that it could not, for example, exclude foreign-owned hospitals from subsidies given to domestic hospitals.

II

To focus our discussion, let us concentrate on a specific example. Article VIII of the GATS governs monopolies. Since the general obligation it defines is only triggered in relation to scheduled sectors, the restriction it entails is best understood as a conditional restriction. Article VIII countenances the pre-existence of monopoly suppliers (Section 1). However, when the introduction of a new service monopoly – or the extension of an existing one – encroaches upon another member's trade in services in a scheduled sector, Article VIII Section 4 makes the member introducing the monopoly liable to pay compensation. The force of this restriction depends on the prospective cost of the compensation due.

It is instructive to consider the application of Article VIII to the health insurance sector in particular. Not only is the financing of health care a fundamental component of any health system, but at least 76 members of the WTO (i.e., a majority) have already

[7] For a more detailed presentation, see R. Adlung and A. Carzaniga, "Health Services Under the GATS," *Bulletin of the World Health Organization* 79 (2001), pp. 352–364.

[8] I say they "offer to impose" these restrictions, since the Articles also allow a member to re-write the standard battery at its discretion.

scheduled health insurance under the GATS.[9] The 76 includes, for example, the European Union member states, as well as Canada, Mexico, and the United States. Thus, the GATS's conditional restrictions already apply to all of their health insurance sectors.

Now, as long as their health insurance sector contains *some element* of competitive (i.e., non-monopolistic) provision,[10] Article VIII appears to restrict the freedom of these nations to structure even public provision of health insurance. For even if public services supplied by an existing monopoly are exempt from restriction under Article I, Section 3 (see note 5), these nations are still not free to *extend the (public) monopoly* (if there is one) to services previously supplied on a competitive basis.

In Canada, for example, there is a public insurance monopoly on health services falling within the scope of the medicare system. But services not covered by medicare are insured privately – at present, these services include prescription drugs and home care. Recent reform proposals have recommended bringing prescription drugs and home care within the ambit of the medicare system.[11] This would involve extending the public insurance monopoly to services previously supplied on a competitive basis. Since Canada has already scheduled health insurance under the GATS, implementing these reforms may well make it liable under Article VIII to compensate members whose insurance trade is adversely affected.[12]

Is this restriction on Canada's freedom to structure its domestic health system *undue*?

---

[9] See WTO Council for Trade in Services, *Health and Social Services: Background Note by the Secretariat* S/C/W/50 (1998), Table 3, www.wto.org/english/tratop_e/serv_e/w50.doc (accessed 12 March 2004).

[10] To be precise, the non-monopolistic suppliers of health insurance must also include *foreign* firms. Otherwise the resultant encroachment on trade in services will not harm *another WTO member's* trade, and so not violate Article VIII. The Canadian example described in the text below satisfies this more precise condition (see note 12).

[11] A. S. Detsky and C. D. Naylor, "Canada's Health Care System – Reform Delayed," *New England Journal of Medicine* 349 (2003), pp. 804–810.

[12] M. Sanger, *Reckless Abandon: Canada, the GATS and the Future of Health Care* (Ottawa: Canadian Centre for Policy Alternatives, 2001), Chapter 4; and Canadian Centre for Policy Alternatives, *Putting Health First: Canadian Health Care Reform, Trade Treaties, and Foreign Policy, Summary Report on Globalization and Health* (Ottawa: Commission on the Future of Health Care in Canada, 2002), Chapter 5, www.hc-sc.gc.ca/english/pdf/romanow/pdfs/Summary_Globalization_E.pdf (accessed 12 March 2004).

III

In one sense, the answer is obviously "no." Canada not only signed the GATS, but it specifically decided – presumably, freely – to schedule health insurance. More generally, since the GATS's conditional restrictions are only triggered by a national government's own decision to schedule the sector in question, they hardly count as *undue* restrictions on its choice.[13] Not surprisingly, this is exactly the line the WTO has taken in rebutting the criticism that the GATS is undemocratic.[14]

From the standpoint of national *sovereignty*, this rebuttal is perfectly correct. By and large, it is fair to say that the conditional restrictions entailed by the GATS do not derogate from a nation's sovereignty.[15] Volunteering for treaty obligations is an *exercise of* sovereign authority, and so does not limit it in any objectionable way. However, it does not follow that the restrictions are equally consistent with *democratic* control, for sovereignty and democratic legitimacy are not the same thing. Not all sovereign decisions are democratically legitimate.

As a first approximation, a nation's sovereign decision will be democratically legitimate only if it conforms to the *vox populi* in some suitable sense.[16] To illustrate the distinction, consider various cases of

---

[13] A similar retort could be made in relation to the GATS's *un*conditional restrictions, since even these require that a nation has *signed* the agreement.

[14] See, e.g., WTO, *GATS: Fact and Fiction* (2001), pp. 15–16, www.wto.org/english/tratop_e/serv_e/gatsfacts1004_e.pdf (accessed 12 March 2004). Compare OECD Working Party of the Trade Committee, *Open Service Markets Matter* TD/TC/WP(2001)24/PART1/REV1 (Geneva: Organisation for Economic Cooperation and Development, 2001), p. 38; R. Adlung, "Effects of World Trade on Public Health," *Lancet* 357 (2001), p. 1626; and R. Adlung, "Health Care Systems and the WTO: No Grounds for Panic" (2001), www.wto.org/english/tratop_e/serv_e/comments_lancet_e.doc (accessed 12 March 2004).

[15] It is fair by and large. Nevertheless, there are circumstances under which even this point could be questioned. If the consequence of a sovereign decision was impossible to anticipate, it may plausibly be argued that it does not inherit the stamp even of sovereign approval. In fact, various consequences of the decision to schedule a sector under the GATS *are* arguably impossible to anticipate, since their significance depends upon the correct interpretation of Article I Section 3's governmental authority exemption, which is extremely unclear (see note 5).

[16] It is controversial what precise sense is the most suitable to require here. For simplicity, I shall frame the discussion in the familiar language of "popular mandates." But this is not meant to prejudge the underlying issue of how best to understand democratic legitimacy. The problem I go on to introduce arises independently of the simplified terms in which I frame it. See note 23, below.

manifest non-conformity. Most clearly, if a nation's government is not democratic – for example, if it is a dictatorship – then its decisions may be perfectly sovereign, but they still will not be democratically legitimate. The same holds of a nation whose government claims to be democratic, but is not in fact meaningfully representative. Even if a nation's government is uncontroversially democratic, some of its particular decisions may lack democratic legitimacy – despite being fully sovereign – if they were taken in the absence of a suitable popular mandate.

It would therefore be worth asking, for different WTO members, what kind of popular mandate existed for various decisions taken in relation to the GATS – the decision to sign it, to schedule health insurance, and so on.[17] In Switzerland, for example, the decision to sign the GATS was subject to the possibility of a popular referendum, although in the event an insufficient number of signatures was collected to trigger a referendum.[18] By contrast, in the United States, the GATS was not actually formally ratified as a treaty. Rather, the decision to sign it was approved, along with all the other Uruguay Round agreements, by an ordinary legislative action of Congress – or, perhaps, "quasi"-ordinary, since Congress was subject to the rigours of a "fast-track" approval process, according to which the results of the entire Uruguay Round had to be accepted or rejected as a package deal.[19]

Despite its interest, however, the question of whether the operative governmental decisions actually enjoyed a popular mandate is not, in fact, the critical issue. For one thing, it might well be argued that the ordinary decisions – especially, the legislative ones – of a duly

[17] For an account of the ratification (and implementation) procedures followed in eleven different jurisdictions, see J. Jackson and A. Sykes (eds.), *Implementing the Uruguay Round* (Oxford: Clarendon Press, 1997).

[18] T. Cottier and F. Schefer, "Switzerland: The Challenge of Direct Democracy," in J. Jackson and A. Sykes (eds.), *Implementing the Uruguay Round* (Oxford: Clarendon Press, 1997), Chapter 9.

[19] D. Leebron, "Implementation of the Uruguay Round Results in the United States," in J. Jackson and A. Sykes (eds.), *Implementing the Uruguay Round* (Oxford: Clarendon Press, 1997), Chapter 6. While this approach was heavily criticised at the time – on the ground, *inter alia*, of being undemocratic – it should also be noted that, as it happened, the measure did gain the Senate's approval by more than the two-thirds majority that treaties require under the Constitution. For some discussion, see J. Jackson, "The Great 1994 Sovereignty Debate: United States Acceptance and Implementation of the Uruguay Round Results," in his *The Jurisprudence of the GATT and the WTO* (New York: Cambridge University Press, 2000), Chapter 19.

constituted democratic government are, eo ipso, *presumed* to enjoy a popular mandate. But the more important point is that even if the relevant sovereign decision did enjoy a popular mandate – for example, because the presumption that it enjoyed one was not defeated in the case at hand – this fact would still not suffice to establish that the decision was democratically legitimate.

IV

To see why not, we need to recall why it is that voluntarily incurred obligations do not restrict choice unduly in the first place. Why, for example, do voluntarily incurred obligations not constitute objectionable limitations on *individual* freedom? Fundamentally, it is because the person imposing the obligation and the person subject to it are one and the same. A structurally similar answer can be given in the case of sovereign nations, to the extent that it is plausible to rely on the legal fiction of "national personality." While this fiction is often plausible, it breaks down – at least for some purposes – when the obligation in question spans *different generations* within the "same nation." In that case, the imposer of the obligation (generation N) and its subject (generation $N + M$) are manifestly not the same. As far as democratic legitimacy is concerned, this is sufficient to void the fiction,[20] and so to re-instate the presumption that the resultant restrictions on national choice are objectionable. While a popular mandate is required to confer democratic legitimacy on an obligation, the only popular mandates that count are ones issued by the generation *subject to* the obligation.

In a sense, therefore, it does not matter whether Canada's decision, for example, to schedule health insurance under the GATS enjoyed a popular mandate, either actually or presumptively. It does not matter because, even if the decision enjoyed a popular mandate when it was taken, the democratic legitimacy thereby conferred on Canada's resultant obligations under the GATS is only temporary. Canada will eventually come, quite obviously, to be populated by a generation that did not even exist when the GATS was signed or health insurance scheduled. Yet when this future generation does

[20] For sovereign legal purposes, the fiction may be stipulative – it may hold for any group of people, however temporally or otherwise disconnected, as long as they are (were) all inhabitants of the same constitutional order. This merely reinforces the distinction between sovereignty and democratic legitimacy.

come into existence, it will also find its freedom to structure its (i.e., "the Canadian") health insurance sector restricted by the GATS – for example, by the provisions on monopolies in Article VIII. From the standpoint of this future generation, the fact that its freedom to extend the public monopoly on health insurance to new services is restricted *on account of some past national decision* will not shield the GATS from the charge of being undemocratic. The origin of this restriction in a choice by a government of today does not suffice to legitimate it for the people of tomorrow.

Of course, it is in the nature of legal obligations generally to persist into the (indefinite) future. One might therefore wonder whether there is anything special about GATS obligations that makes them particularly vulnerable to the temporary character of popular mandates, and hence of democratic legitimacy. There is and it lies in a feature of the GATS that I have not yet explained, namely, the effective permanency of scheduling decisions. Once a commitment to schedule a sector has been "bound," the commitment cannot be withdrawn – that is, the sector cannot be un-scheduled – except at great cost. A nation can quit the GATS altogether or, after a lapse of three years, it can rescind its decision and be liable to pay compensation to other nations whose trade the change damages (Article XXI).[21] The rescinding option is presumably the easier of the two. But it is not clear how "easy," if at all, this option really is. It depends on the cost of the compensation due. For present purposes, I shall simply assume that it is very difficult, though not strictly impossible, for a nation to withdraw one of its bound scheduling commitments. The plausibility of this assumption is confirmed by the following description from the WTO's own website:

> These clearly defined commitments are "bound": like bound tariffs for trade in goods, they can only be modified after negotiations with affected countries. Because "unbinding" is difficult, the commitments are virtually guaranteed conditions for foreign exporters and importers of services and investors in the sector to do business.[22]

---

[21] Compensation may take various forms. The nation rescinding its decision could liberalise equivalent service sectors in exchange or, as a last resort, the nation whose service providers are affected by the change could withdraw equivalent market access from the rescinding nation (i.e., from its service providers).

[22] The quotation is from an introductory description of the GATS. See http://www.wto.org/english/thewto_e/whatis_e/tif_e/agrm6_e.htm (accessed 12 March 2004).

We should thus distinguish two different kinds of legal obligation, the ordinary and the effectively compulsory. *Ordinary* obligations can be modified or dissolved at the pleasure of the legislature (or other relevant national decision-maker). By contrast, *effectively compulsory* obligations either cannot be so modified or can be only with great difficulty. Ordinary legal obligations are not especially vulnerable to the temporary character of popular mandates because it is plausible to suppose that the presumption of a popular mandate is *self-renewing* in the specific context where a duly constituted democratic government retains a *standing option to modify or dissolve* the obligation in question.

But where the legislature has no power (or effectively none) to modify or dissolve an obligation, it makes no sense to credit the obligation with a new popular mandate, not even if the legislature's decisions are presumed to enjoy one. It makes no sense because the obligation – that is, any effectively compulsory obligation – binds quite independently of anything the legislature decides. Hence, any mandate its decisions enjoy is irrelevant to the existence of the obligation. Likewise, it makes no sense to say that the popular mandate an effectively compulsory obligation may once have enjoyed can be presumed to *renew* itself, not even if the legislature in question remains democratic and duly constituted. As a result, effectively compulsory obligations, unlike ordinary ones, are notably vulnerable to the temporary character of popular mandates.[23]

V

As we have seen, the fact that obligations entailed by bound scheduling commitments under the GATS are effectively compulsory

[23] Notice that this argument begins from the legislature's *disability* (lack of a power) to modify or dissolve an effectively compulsory obligation. This disability certainly raises a problem for future generations if the democratic legitimacy of an obligation requires that it enjoy a popular mandate. But a problem for effectively compulsory obligations will arise on *any* account on which democratic legitimacy seems to require that the people (or its representatives) retain the power to modify the obligations to which it is subject, whether or not the account sanctions the specific requirement of a popular mandate. (That is why I said my analysis would not depend on the simplified language of popular mandates. See note 16 above.) For an account of democratic legitimacy that requires the people to have the power to modify the obligations to which it is subject, but does *not* require these obligations to enjoy a popular mandate, see, e.g., P. Pettit, *Republicanism* (Oxford: Clarendon Press, 1997), Chapter 6.

for future generations raises a special problem of democratic legitimacy. Still, it would be a mistake to conclude that the problem cannot be solved – to conclude that nothing can confer democratic legitimacy on effectively compulsory obligations that span the generations. If that were true, then no *constitutional* obligations – no Bills of Rights, for example – could be democratically legitimate. That would certainly be going too far.

What is of great significance in the present context, however, is that constitutional obligations are standardly held to require *special* measures of democratic scrutiny in order to gain legitimacy. Constitutional conventions, for example, often require that measures be passed by a super-majority. Constitutional amendments, which perhaps offer a better analogy, often require both a super-majority and a dedicated referendum. That is, not only is a higher standard of agreement demanded, but the people themselves must be more directly involved in the decision.

Moreover, it is plausible to see the rationale for requiring constitutional obligations to pass a higher standard of democratic scrutiny as being precisely that they possess the very features of effectively compulsory obligations that we have singled out: Once a nation moves beyond its founding generation, its constitutional obligations are both (i) very difficult, though not strictly impossible, to alter; and (ii) not chosen in any ordinary sense by the subject generation.

In the constitutional case, the effect (and also the point) of making the relevant obligations effectively compulsory is to lock a certain set of arrangements – recognition of certain fundamental rights and liberties – into place. These arrangements are locked into place by making it impossible for certain decision-makers (e.g., the legislature acting alone) and very difficult for others (the co-ordinated set of those entitled to amend the constitution) to alter them. With the GATS, the effect of making its obligations effectively compulsory is similar: It locks a set of arrangements into place – only here, it is the existing degree of privatisation in scheduled service sectors that is locked into place. For example, as we saw, Article VIII treats changes in a scheduled sector's degree of privatisation *asymmetrically*. Reductions are inhibited, while increases are permitted. In 76 jurisdictions that belong to the WTO, then, the freedom of future generations to have a health insurance sector with a *lesser* degree of privatisation than exists in their respective jurisdictions today is severely restricted.

We might capture this by saying that the various GATS obligations we have discussed are *tantamount to a constitutional obligation* to maintain a health insurance sector with a certain minimum degree of privatisation.[24] The main conclusion I wish to draw from this analogy is that ordinary legislative decisions are not sufficient to legitimate the restrictions the GATS imposes on the freedom of future generations to structure their domestic health sector. Like decisions to amend the constitution, decisions to bind a scheduling commitment under the GATS must be held to a higher standard of democratic scrutiny.[25] It does not matter here exactly which procedures are deemed to satisfy this higher standard. For concreteness, we may assume that ratification by a super-majority is required to confer democratic legitimacy on a constitutional obligation.[26] But the significant point is simply that sovereign commitments under the GATS should be treated on a par with constitutional amendments.

If the restrictions the GATS imposes on national choice are not, therefore, to undermine democratic control of the health sector by future generations, bound scheduling commitments under the GATS should at least be ratified by a national super-majority (or some such equivalent). In principle, of course, there is also another alternative. To wit, the effective permanency of the obligations that scheduling

[24] This is rhetorically correct, though technically imprecise. To be precise, the GATS obligations are tantamount to a constitutional disability to have a health insurance sector with anything other than a certain minimum degree of privatisation.

[25] Just *how* higher standards of democratic scrutiny contribute to the legitimacy of effectively compulsory obligations for future generations remains an open question. In my view, the answer turns on the effect higher standards (are likely to) have on the *content* of the obligations that can be made effectively compulsory. But nothing in the present discussion requires one answer to this question rather than another, as long as one agrees that constitutional amendments must be held to a higher standard of democratic scrutiny. For an instructive discussion of the largely salutory effects that liability to the prospect of a popular referendum had on Switzerland's position(s) in the GATS negotiations, see Cottier and Schefer, "Switzerland: The Challenge of Direct Democracy," pp. 340–342 and 354–363.

[26] This is not, of course, to say that such procedures *suffice* to legitimise constitutional obligations democratically. It seems to me that the problem of how constitutional obligations gain their legitimacy is actually one to which insufficient attention has been paid. For some discussion of related issues, see Gopal Sreenivasan "Judicial Review and Individual Self-rule," *Revista Argentina de Teoría Jurídica* 2 (2001), pp. 1–13, www.utdt.edu/departamentos/derecho/publicaciones/rtj1/primeraspaginas/2nro2.htm (accessed 12 March 2004).

decisions trigger could be significantly relaxed. But this alternative would likely come at the cost of the predictability of the GATS framework, which the WTO has emphasised as one of its signal advantages.[27] So ratification in accordance with some higher standard of democratic scrutiny may be preferable. If neither of these options is exercised, however, the restrictions entailed by bound scheduling commitments under the GATS may plausibly be regarded as undemocratic.[28]

Canada Research Chair
Department of Philosophy
University of Toronto
215 Huron Street
Toronto, Ontario
Canada M5S 1A1
E-mail: gopal.sreenivasan@utoronto.ca

---

[27] WTO, *GATS: Fact and Fiction* (2001), pp. 5, 13–14.

[28] Earlier versions of this paper were presented to a conference on "Globalisation, Justice, and Health," organised by the Department of Clinical Bioethics at the National Institutes of Health and held in Washington, DC; and to the Mini-Conference on Global Justice held in conjunction with the Pacific Division meeting of the American Philosophical Association in Pasadena, California. For helpful comments, I am grateful to Richard Arneson, Avi Astor, Margaret Battin, Leah Belsky, Ezekiel Emanuel, David Estlund, Henry Richardson, and the audiences on both occasions.

JAMES P. STERBA

GLOBAL JUSTICE FOR HUMANS OR FOR ALL LIVING BEINGS AND WHAT DIFFERENCE IT MAKES

(Received 14 May 2004; accepted in revised form 7 June 2004)

ABSTRACT. I begin with an account of what is deserved in human ethics, an ethics that assumes without argument that only humans, or rational agents, count morally. I then take up the question of whether nonhuman living beings are also deserving and answer it in the affirmative. Having established that all individual living beings, as well as ecosystems, are deserving, I go on to establish what it is that they deserve and then compare the requirements of global justice when only humans are taken into account with the requirements of global justice when all living beings are taken into account.

KEY WORDS: anthropocentric, distant peoples, future generations, liberty, libertarianism, nonanthropocentric, population policy

1. Introduction

Justice requires giving what is deserved. That in turn requires figuring out both what is deserved and who it is that deserves it. Here priority should be given to *who* it is that is deserving rather than *what* it is that is deserved. This is because the more there are who are deserving, other things being equal, the less good things each of them can deserve. Political philosophers have long recognized this priority when they are trying to determine what the human members of a particular society or state deserve; they have acknowledged that this question cannot be conclusively resolved without taking into account distant peoples and future generations as also deserving. Unfortunately, most political philosophers tend to stop there; they do not take the next logical step of asking whether nonhuman living beings are also deserving. In this paper, I will begin with an account of what is deserved in human ethics, an ethics that assumes without argument that only humans, or rational agents, count morally. I will then take up the question of whether nonhuman living beings are also deserving and answer it in the affirmative. Having established that all individual living beings, as well as ecosystems, are deserving, I will go on to establish what it is that they deserve and then compare the requirements of global justice when only humans are taken into account with the requirements of global justice when all living beings are taken into account.

Needless to say, in human ethics, there is considerable disagreement over what it is that people deserve. For libertarian justice, what people deserve is determined by an ideal of liberty. For welfare liberal justice, it is determined by an ideal of fairness. For socialist justice, it is determined by an ideal of equality. For communitarian justice, it is determined by an ideal of the common good. And for feminist justice, it is determined by an ideal of a gender-free society. Now I have argued elsewhere that when these five conceptions of justice are correctly interpreted, they all can be seen to support the same basic practical requirements.[1] Since I cannot in this paper lay out my entire practical reconciliation argument, what I propose to do is to focus on the most contentious part of that argument where I attempt to show that libertarians should endorse a right to a basic needs minimum that extends to both the distant peoples and future generations before arguing that all living beings are deserving as well.

2. Liberty and Welfare

Let us begin by interpreting the ideal of liberty as a negative ideal in the manner favored by libertarians.[2] So understood, liberty is the absence of interference by other people from doing what one wants or is able to do. Libertarians go on to characterize their political ideal as requiring that each person should have the greatest amount of liberty commensurate with the same liberty for all.[3] Interpreting their ideal in this way, libertarians claim to derive a number of more specific requirements, in particular, a right to life, a right to freedom of speech, press and assembly, and a right to property.

Here it is important to observe that the libertarian's right to life is not a right to receive from others the goods and resources necessary for preserving one's life; it is simply a right not to be killed unjustly. Correspondingly, the libertarian's right to property is not a right to

[1] See James P. Sterba, *How to Make People Just* (Totowa: Rowman and Littlefield, 1988); and also James P. Sterba, *Justice for Here and Now* (New York: Cambridge University Press, 1998).

[2] Sterba, *How to Make People Just;* Sterba *Justice for Here and Now.*

[3] See John Hospers, "The Libertarian Maniesto," in James P. Sterba (ed.), *Morality in Pratice,* 7th edition (Belmont: Wadsworth Publishing Company, 2003).

receive from others the goods and resources necessary for one's welfare, but rather a right to acquire goods and resources either by initial acquisition or by voluntary agreement.

Of course, libertarians would allow that it would be nice of the rich to share their surplus resources with the poor. Nevertheless, they deny that government has a duty to provide for such needs. Some good things, such as providing of welfare to the poor, are requirements of charity rather than justice, libertarians claim. Accordingly, failure to make such provisions is neither blameworthy nor punishable. As a consequence, such acts of charity should not be coercively required. For this reason, libertarians are opposed to coercively supported welfare programs.

Moreover, it does little good to argue here, as Henry Shue does, that the libertarian ideal, like the welfare liberal ideal or the socialist ideal, entails both negative and positive duties.[4] This is because libertarians can grant this point and still argue that what is crucial for them is not this entailment but which rights are basic, and what is basic for them are negative rights, that is, rights of noninterference, and these rights, they claim, do not entail a right to welfare, even if they do entail some positive duties.

Now in order to see why libertarians are mistaken about what their ideal requires, consider a typical conflict situation between the rich and the poor. In this conflict situation, the rich, of course, have more than enough resources to satisfy their basic needs.[5] By contrast, the poor lack the resources to meet their most basic needs even though they have tried all the means available to them that libertarians regard as legitimate for acquiring such resources. Under circumstances like these, libertarians usually maintain that the rich should have the liberty to use their resources to satisfy their luxury needs if they so wish. Libertarians recognize that this liberty might well be enjoyed at the expense of the satisfaction of the most basic needs of the poor; they just think that liberty always has priority over other political ideals, and since they assume that the liberty of the poor is not at stake in such conflict situations, it is easy for them to

---

[4] See Henry Shue, *Basic Rights*, 2nd edition (Princeton: Princeton University Press, 1996), p. 155.

[5] Basic needs, if not satisfied, lead to significant lacks or deficiencies with respect to a standard of mental and physical well-being, Thus, a person's needs for food, shelter, medical care, protection, companionship and self-development are, at least in part, needs of this sort. For a discussion of basic needs, see Sterba, *How To Make People Just*, pp. 45–48.

conclude that the rich should not be required to sacrifice their liberty so that the basic needs of the poor may be met.

Of course, libertarians would allow that it would be nice of the rich to share their surplus resources with the poor. Nevertheless, according to libertarians, such acts of charity are not required because the liberty of the poor is not thought to be at stake in such conflict situations.

In fact, however, the liberty of the poor is at stake in such conflict situations. What is at stake is the liberty of the poor not to be to interfered with in taking from the surplus possessions of the rich what is necessary to satisfy their basic needs.

Now when the conflict between the rich and the poor is viewed as a conflict of liberties, we can either say that the rich should have the liberty not to be interfered with in using their surplus resources for luxury purposes, or we can say that the poor should have the liberty not to be interfered with in taking from the rich what they require to meet their basic needs. If we choose one liberty, we must reject the other. What needs to be determined, therefore, is which liberty is morally preferable: the liberty of the rich or the liberty of the poor.

2.1. *The "Ought" Implies "Can" Principle*

I submit that the liberty of the poor, which is the liberty not to be interfered with in taking from the surplus resources of others what is required to meet one's basic needs, is morally preferable to the liberty of the rich, which is the liberty not to be interfered with in using one's surplus resources for luxury purposes. To see that this is the case, we need only appeal to the "ought" implies "can" principle, a principle common to all moral and political perspectives. According to this principle, people are not morally required to do what they lack the power to do or what would involve so great a sacrifice that it would be unreasonable to ask, and/or in cases of severe conflict of interest, unreasonable to require them to abide by.

Now applying the principle to the case at hand, it seems clear that the poor have it within their power willingly to relinquish such an important liberty as the liberty to take from the rich what they require to meet their basic needs. Nevertheless, it would be unreasonable in this context to ask or require them to make so great a sacrifice. In the extreme case, it would involve asking or requiring the poor to sit back and starve to death. Of course, the poor may have no real alternative to relinquishing this liberty. To do anything else may involve worse consequences for themselves and their loved ones and may invite a painful death. Accordingly, we may expect that the poor would acquiesce, albeit unwillingly, to a political system that denied them the right to welfare supported by such a liberty, at the same time that we recognize that such a system imposed an unreasonable sacrifice upon the poor – a sacrifice that we could not morally blame the poor for trying to evade.[6] Analogously, we might expect that a woman whose life was threatened would submit to a rapist's demands, at the same time that we recognize the utter unreasonableness of those demands.

By contrast, it would not be unreasonable to ask and require the rich in this context to sacrifice the liberty to meet some of their luxury needs so that the poor can have the liberty to meet their basic needs.[7] Naturally, we might expect that the rich, for reasons of self-interest and past contribution, might be disinclined to make such a sacrifice. We might even suppose that the past contribution of the rich provides a good reason for not sacrificing their liberty to use their surplus for luxury purposes. Yet, unlike the poor, the rich could not claim that relinquishing such a liberty involved so great a sacrifice that it would be unreasonable to require it of them; unlike the poor, the rich could be morally blameworthy for failing to make such a sacrifice.

Consequently, if we assume that however else we specify the requirements of morality, they cannot violate the "ought" implies "can" principle, it follows that, despite what libertarians claim, the right to liberty endorsed by them actually favors the liberty of the poor over the liberty of the rich, and thus provides the basis for a right to welfare on libertarian premises.

3. Distant Peoples and Future Generations

Now for libertarians, fundamental rights are universal rights, that is, rights possessed by all people, not just those who live in certain places or at certain times. Given then the universal character of the

---

[6] See James P. Sterba, "Is There a Rationale for Punishment?," *Philosophical Topics* 18 (1990), pp. 105–125.

[7] By the liberty of the rich to meet their luxury needs I continue to mean the liberty of the rich not to be interfered with when using their surplus possessions for luxury purposes. Similarly, by the liberty of the poor to meet their basic needs I continue to mean the liberty of the poor not to be interfered with when taking what they require to meet their basic needs from the surplus possessions of the rich.

libertarian right to welfare that we have just established, we need to determine its implications for distant peoples and future generations.

Consider that at present there is probably a sufficient worldwide supply of goods and resources to meet the normal costs of satisfying the basic nutritional needs of all existing persons. According to the former United States Secretary of Agriculture, Bob Bergland, "For the past 20 years, if the available world food supply had been evenly divided and distributed, each person would have received more than the minimum number of calories."[8] Other authorities have made similar assessments of the available world food supply.[9]

Needless to say, the adoption of a policy of supporting a right to welfare for all existing persons would necessitate significant changes, especially in developed societies. For example, the large percentage of the U.S. population whose food consumption clearly exceeds even an adequately adjusted poverty index would have to substantially alter their eating habits. In particular, they would have to reduce their consumption of beef and pork so as to make more grain available for direct human consumption (currently, 37% of worldwide production of grain and 70% of US production is fed to animals).[10] Thus, at least the satisfaction of some of the nonbasic needs of the more advantaged in developed societies would have to be forgone, leading to greater equality, so that the basic nutritional needs of all existing persons in developing and underdeveloped societies could be met. Furthermore, to raise the standard of living in the Second and Third World will require substantial increases in the consumption of energy and other resources. But such an increase would have to be matched by a substantial decrease in the consumption of these same goods in the First World, otherwise global ecological disaster would result

[8] Bob Bergland, "Attacking the Problem of World Hunger," *The NationalForum* 69 (1979), p. 4.

[9] For example, see World Watch Institute, *Vital Signs 2003* (New York: W.W. Norton & Co., 2003), pp. 28–31 (http://www.bread.org/hungerbasics/international.html).

[10] For example, see World Watch Institute, Vital Sigus 2003, pp. 28–31. Stuart Pimm, *The World According to Pimm* (New York: McGraw-Hill, 2001), Chapter 2; World Watch Institute, *Vital Signs 1996* (New York: W.W. Norton & Co., 1996), pp. 34–35; Jeremy Rifkin, *Beyond Beef* (New York: Penguin, 1992), p. 1.

from increased global warming, ozone depletion and acid rain, lowering virtually everyone's standard of living.[11]

In addition, once the basic nutritional needs of future generations are also taken into account, then the satisfaction of the nonbasic needs of the more advantaged in developed societies would have to be further restricted in order to preserve the fertility of cropland and other food-related natural resources for the use of future generations. And once basic needs other than nutritional needs are taken into account as well, still further restrictions would be required. For example, it has been estimated that presently a US citizen uses 75 times more resources than an Indian. This means that in terms of resource consumption the US population is the equivalent of roughly 22.5 billion Indians.[12] So unless we assume that basic resources such as arable land, iron, coal, oil, etc. are in unlimited supply, this unequal consumption would have to be radically altered if the basic needs of distant peoples and future generations are to be met.[13] In effect, recognizing a universal right to welfare applicable both to distant peoples and future generations would lead to an equal sharing of resources over place and time.[14] It would lead us to provide each individual with the goods and resources that are required for a decent life – but no more.

In brief, I have argued that in human ethics when a libertarian ideal of liberty is correctly interpreted, it leads to a universal right to welfare and further that the recognition of this universal right to

---

[11] For a discussion of these causal connections, see Linda Starke, (ed.), *State of the World 2003* (New York: W.W. Norton & Co., 2003), Chapter 1; Cheryl Silver, *One Earth One Future* (Washington, DC: National Academy Press, 1990); Bill McKibben, *The End of Nature* (New York: Random, 1989); Jeremy Leggett (ed.), *Global Warming* (New York: Oxford University Press, 1990); Lester Brown (ed.), *The World Watch Reader* (New York: W. W. Norton & Co., 1991).

[12] Linda Starke, *State of the World 2004* (New York: W. W. Norton & Co., 2004), p. 8.

[13] See Starke, *State of the World 2004*. There is no way that the resource consumption of the US can be matched by developing and underdeveloped countries, and even if it could be matched, doing so would clearly lead to ecological disaster. See, Constance Mungall and Digby McLaren (eds.), *Planet under Stress* (Oxford: Oxford University Press, 1990); and Frances Lappe and Joseph Collins, *World Hunger: Twelve Myths* (New York: Grove Press, 1986).

[14] Once basic needs are met among existing generations, however, it may be that renewable resources can used to for meeting nonbasic needs in ways that do not jeopardize the meeting the basic needs of future generations.

welfare leads to considerable equality in the shares of goods and resources over place and time.

4. The Moral Deservingness of All Living Beings

Most political philosophers, as I have indicated, are committed to anthropocentrism; they just assume without argument that all or only human beings, or all or only rational agents, are deserving or count morally. In order to show that this view is mistaken, I will need a non-question-begging argument that nonhuman living beings are deserving or count morally. Is there such an argument?

Consider that we clearly have the capacity of entertaining and acting upon both anthropocentric reasons that take only the interests of humans into account and nonanthropocentric reasons that also take the interests of nonhuman living beings into account. Given that capacity, the question we are seeking to answer is what sort of reasons it would be rational for us to accept.

Now right off, we might think that we have nonquestion-begging grounds for only taking the interests of humans into account, namely, the possession by human beings of the distinctive traits of rationality and moral agency. But while human beings clearly do have such distinctive traits, the members of nonhuman species also have distinctive traits that humans lack, like the homing ability of pigeons, the speed of the cheetah, and the ruminative ability of sheep and cattle. Nor will it do to claim that the distinctive traits that humans possess are more valuable than the distinctive traits that members of other species possess because there is no nonquestionbegging standpoint from which to justify that claim. From a human standpoint, rationality and moral agency are more valuable than any of the distinctive traits found in nonhuman species, since, as humans, we would not be better off if we were to trade in those traits for the distinctive traits found in nonhuman species. Yet the same holds true of nonhuman species. Generally, pigeons, cheetahs, sheep and cattle would not be better off if they were to trade in their distinctive traits for the distinctive traits of other species.[15] So there would appear to be no nonquestion-begging perspective from which to judge that

[15] See Paul Taylor, *Respect for Nature* (Princeton: Princeton University Press, 1987), pp. 129–135; and R. and V. Routley, "Against the Inevitability of Human Chauvinism," in K. E. Goodpaster and K. M. Sayre (eds.), *Ethics and Problems of the 21st Century* (Notre Dame: University of Notre Dame Press, 1979).

distinctively human traits are more valuable than the distinctive traits possessed by other species, and so no nonquestion-begging justification for only taking anthropocentric reasons into account. Judged from a nonquestion-begging perspective, we would seemingly have to grant the *prima facie* relevance of both anthropocentric and non-anthropocentric reasons for action and then try to determine which reasons we would be rationally required to act upon, all things considered.

In this regard, there are two kinds of cases that must be considered. First, there are cases in which there is a conflict between the relevant anthropocentric and nonanthropocentric reasons for action. Second, there are cases in which there is no such conflict.

It seems obvious that where there is no conflict and both reasons are conclusive reasons of their kind, both reasons should be acted upon. In such contexts, we should do what is favored both by anthropocentrism and by nonanthropocentrism.

Now when we turn to assess rationally the relevant reasons in conflict cases, three solutions are possible. First, we could say that anthropocentric reasons always have priority over conflicting non-anthropocentric reasons. Second, we could say, just the opposite, that nonanthropocentric reasons always have priority over conflicting anthropocentric reasons. Third, we could say that some kind of compromise is rationally required. In this compromise, sometimes anthropocentric reasons would have priority over non-anthropocentric reasons, and sometimes nonanthropocentric reasons would have priority over anthropocentric reasons.

Once the conflict is described in this manner, the third solution can be seen to be the one that is rationally required. This is because the first and second solutions give exclusive priority to one class of relevant reasons over the other, and only a question-begging justification can be given for such an exclusive priority. Only by employing the third solution, and sometimes giving priority to anthropocentric reasons, and sometimes giving priority to nonanthropocentric reasons, can we avoid a question-begging resolution. What we need, therefore, are conflict resolution principles that specify these priorities.

5. Conflict Resolution Principles

But how are these priorities to be specified? Now surely, even if we hold that all living beings should count morally, we can justify a preference for humans on grounds of preservation. Accordingly, we have

> A Principle of Human Preservation: Actions that are necessary for meeting one's basic needs or the basic needs of other human beings are permissible even when they require aggressing against the basic needs of individual animals and plants, or even of whole species or ecosystems.[16]

In human ethics, there is no principle that is strictly analogous to this Principle of Human Preservation. There is a principle that permits actions that are necessary for meeting one's own basic needs or the basic needs of other people, even if this requires *failing to meet* (through an act of omission) the basic needs of still other people. For example, we can use our resources to feed ourselves and our families, even if this necessitates failing to meet the basic needs of people in underdeveloped countries. But, in general, we do not have a principle that allows us to *aggress against* (through an act of commission) the basic needs of some people in order to meet our own basic needs or the basic needs of other people to whom we are committed or happen to care about. One place where we do permit aggressing against the basic needs of other people in order to meet our own basic needs or the basic needs of people to whom we are committed or happen to care about is our acceptance of the outcome of life and death struggles in lifeboat cases, where no one has an antecedent right to the available resources. For example, if you had to fight off others in order to secure the last place in a lifeboat for yourself or for a member of your family, we might say that you justifiably aggressed against the basic needs of those whom you fought to meet your own basic needs or the basic needs of the members of your family.

Now the Principle of Human Preservation does not permit aggressing against the basic needs of humans even if it is the only way to meet our own basic needs or the basic needs of other human beings. Rather this principle is directed at a different range of cases with respect to which we can meet our own basic needs and the basic needs of other humans simply by aggressing against the basic needs of nonhuman living beings. With respect to those cases, the Principle of Human Preservation permits actions that are necessary for meeting one's own basic needs or the basic needs of other human

[16] For the purposes of this paper, I will follow the convention of excluding humans from the denotation of "animals."

beings, even when they require aggressing against the basic needs of individual animals and plants, or even of whole species or ecosystems.

Of course, we could envision an even more permissive principle of human preservation, one that would permit us to aggress against the basic needs of both humans and nonhumans to meet our own basic needs or the basic needs of other human beings. But while adopting such a principle by permitting cannibalism would clearly reduce the degree of predation of humans on other species and so would be of some benefit to other species, it would clearly be counterproductive with respect to meeting basic human needs. This is because implicit nonaggression pacts based on a reasonable expectation of a comparable degree of altruistic forbearance from fellow humans have been enormously beneficial and probably were necessary for the survival of the human species. So it is difficult to see how humans could justifiably be required to forgo such benefits.

Moreover, beyond the prudential value of such implicit nonaggression pacts against fellow humans, there appears to be no morally defensible way to exclude some humans from their protection. This is because any exclusion would fail to satisfy that most basic principle of morality, the "ought" implies "can" principle, given that it would impose a sacrifice on at least some humans that would be unreasonable to ask and/or require them to accept.

But are there no exceptions to the Principle of Human Preservation? Consider, for example, the following real-life case.[17] Thousands of Nepalese have cleared forests, cultivated crops, and raised cattle and buffalo on land surrounding the Royal Chitwan National Park in Nepal, but they have also made incursions into the park to meet their own basic needs. In so doing, they have threatened the rhino, the Bengal tiger, and other endangered species in the park. Assume that the basic needs of no other humans are at stake.[18] For this case, then, would would-be human guardians of these nonhuman endangered species be justified in preventing the Nepalese from meeting their basic needs in order to preserve these endangered species? It seems to me that before the basic needs of disadvantaged Nepalese could be

---

[17] See Holmes Rolston III, "Enforcing Environmental Ethics: Civil Law and Natural Value," in James P. Sterba (ed.), *Social and Political Philosophy: Contemporary Perspectives* (New York: Routledge, 2001) where Rolston uses this example to object to my Principle of Human Preservation and I respond.

[18] This did not hold in the real-life case that Rolston actually presented. See my response in Sterba (ed.), *Social and Political Philosophy: Contemporary Perspectives*.

sacrificed, the would-be human guardians of these endangered species first would be required to use whatever surplus was available to them and to other humans to meet the basic needs of the Nepalese whom they propose to restrict. Yet clearly it would be very difficult to have first used up all the surplus available to the whole human population for meeting basic human needs. Under present conditions, this requirement has certainly not been met. Moreover, insofar as rich people are unwilling to make the necessary transfers of resources so that poor people would not be led to prey on endangered species in order to survive, then, the appropriate means of preserving endangered species should be to use force against such rich people rather than against poor people, like the Nepalese near Royal Chitwan National Park.[19] So for all present purposes, the moral permissibility in the Principle of Human Preservation remains that of strong permissibility, which means that other humans are prohibited from interfering with the aggression against nonhumans that is permitted by the principle.

Nevertheless, preference for humans can still go beyond bounds, and the bounds that are required are captured by the following:

A Principle of Disproportionality: Actions that meet nonbasic or luxury needs of humans are prohibited when they aggress against the basic needs of individual animals and plants or even of whole species or ecosystems.

This principle is strictly analogous to the principle in human ethics that similarly prohibits meeting some people's nonbasic or luxury needs by aggressing against the basic needs of other people. Without a doubt, the adoption of such a principle with respect to nonhumans would significantly change the way we live our lives. Such a principle is required, however, if there is to be any substance to the claim that the members of all species count morally. We can no more consistently claim that the members of all species count morally and yet aggress against the basic needs of some animals or plants whenever this serves our own nonbasic or luxury needs than we can consistently claim that all humans count morally and then aggress against the basic needs of other human beings whenever this serves our nonbasic

[19] In a nonideal world, the Nepalese and their human allies should press against rich people to acquire the available surplus to meet the basic needs of the Nepalese until their own lives are threatened and then regrettably the Nepalese would be justified in preying on endangered species as the only way for them to survive.

or luxury needs. Consequently, if saying that species count morally is to mean anything, it must be the case that the basic needs of the members of nonhuman species are protected against aggressive actions that only serve to meet the nonbasic needs of humans, as required by the Principle of Disproportionality. Another way to put the central claim here is to hold that counting morally rules out domination, where domination means aggressing against the basic needs of some for the sake of satisfying the nonbasic needs of others.

Nevertheless, in order to avoid imposing an unacceptable sacrifice on the members of our own species, we can also justify a preference for humans on grounds of defense. Thus, we have

> *A Principle of Human Defense:* Actions that defend oneself and other human beings against harmful aggression are permissible even when they necessitate killing or harming individual animals or plants, or even destroying whole species or ecosystems.

This Principle of Human Defense allows us to defend ourselves and other human beings from harmful aggression first against our persons and the persons of other human beings that we are committed to or happen to care about and second against our justifiably held property and the justifiably held property of other human beings that we are committed to or happen to care about.

Here there are two sorts of cases. First, there are cases where humans are defending their own basic needs against harmful aggression from nonhumans. In cases of this sort, not only would the human defenders be perfectly justified in defending themselves against aggression but also no would-be human guardians of nonhuman interests would be justified on grounds of what we could reasonably require of humans in opposing that defense.

Second, there are cases where humans are defending their own nonbasic needs against harmful aggression from nonhumans which, let's assume, are trying to meet their basic needs. In cases of this sort, would it be justified for would-be human guardians of the interests of nonhuman living beings to assist them in their aggression against humans? In analogous cases in human ethics, we can see how just this type of aggression can be justified when the poor, who have exhausted all the other means that are legitimately available to them, take from the surplus possessions of the rich just what they require to meet their basic needs. Expressed in terms of an ideal of negative liberty endorsed by libertarians, the justification for this aggression is the priority of the liberty of the poor not to be interfered with when taking from the surplus possessions of the rich what they require to meet their basic needs over the liberty of the rich not to be interfered with when using their surplus for luxury purposes.[20] Under this libertarian justification, would-be guardians of the poor (e.g., real or idealized Robin Hoods) would certainly be justified in assisting the poor in their aggression against the rich. Would then would-be human guardians of nonhuman living beings (e.g., real or idealized Earth Firsters) be similarly justified in assisting plants and animals in their aggression against the nonbasic needs of humans to meet the basic needs of nonhumans?

There are two reasons why this is unlikely to be the case. First, as the above justification from human ethics suggest, achieving libertarian justice for humans will require a considerable redistribution of resources in order to meet the basic needs of humans in both existing and future generations.[21] So if justice is done in this regard, it will significantly constrain the availability of resources for legitimately meeting nonbasic human needs, and thereby limit the possibilities where humans could be justifiably defending their nonbasic needs against aggression from nonhumans. Second, the Principle of Disproportionality further constrains those possibilities where humans could be justifiably defending their nonbasic needs against aggression from nonhumans. This is because the principle prohibits humans from aggressing against the basic needs of nonhumans in order to meet their own non-basic needs, and thereby significantly constrains the ways that humans could legitimately acquire resources that are used simply for meeting nonbasic human needs. For these two reasons, therefore, the possibilities for legitimately exercising the Principle of Human Defense for the sake of nonbasic needs would be drastically limited, thus providing few occasions where would-be human guardians of the interests of nonhumans could have any role with regard to its exercise. Of course, some nonbasic human needs can still be legitimately met indirectly through meeting basic human needs. But any attempt by would-be human guardians of the interests of nonhumans to help nonhumans aggress against the non-basic needs of other humans in such contexts would most likely result in

[20] For a detailed discussion of this argument, see James Sterba, "From Liberty to Welfare," *Ethics* 104 (1994), pp. 64–98; and Sterba, *Justice for Here and Now*, Chapter 3.

[21] For further argument for this conclusion, see Sterba, *Justice for Here and Now*, Chapter 3; and Sterba, *How To Make People Just*, Chapters 2–10.

aggressing against the basic needs of those humans as well, and thus would not be justified. Of course, in the nonideal societies in which we live, many humans still have access to a surplus for meeting nonbasic needs. But in these circumstances, other humans would surely have a claim to significant part of that surplus, and much of what remains would have been illegitimately acquired in violation of the Principle of Disproportionality. In any case, the Principle of Defense would rarely apply because it presupposes for its application that the means for meeting the nonbasic needs of humans have been legitimately acquired.

Lastly, we need one more principle to deal with violations of the above three principles. Accordingly, we have

> *A Principle of Rectification:* Compensation and reparation are required when the other principles have been violated.

Obviously, this principle is somewhat vague, but for those who are willing to abide by the other three principles, it should be possible to remedy that vagueness in practice. Here too would-be human guardians of the interests of nonhumans could have a useful role figuring out what is appropriate compensation or reparation for violations of the Principle of Disproportionality, and, even more importantly, designing ways to get that compensation or reparation enacted.

Taken altogether, these four principles, I claim, constitute a defensible set of principles for resolving conflicts between human and nonhuman living beings.

6. Comparing the Requirements of Global Justice

We are now in a position to compare the requirements of global justice when only humans are taken into account with the requirements of global justice when all living beings are taken into account. When only humans are taken into account, I argued on libertarian grounds that we are only entitled to the goods and resources required to meet our basic needs for a decent life – no more. Otherwise, we would be violating the rights of distant peoples and future generations. Somewhat surprisingly, that is almost the *same conclusion* I arrived at after also taking nonhuman living beings into account. Specifically, the Principle of Human Preservation only permits aggression against nonhuman nature for the sake of what we need for a decent life and the Principle of Disproportionality prohibits aggression against nonhuman nature for the sake of nonbasic or luxury needs.

Still, the more inclusive account of global justice does impose some additional obligations. First, in order to avoid unnecessary harm to nonhuman nature, we will have an obligation to meet our basic needs in some ways rather than others. For example, if there were no negative effects on our fellow human beings, it would be permissible for us to meet our basic needs through the consumption of meat and dairy products provided by factory farming, but we cannot do this once the interests of particularly farm animals are appropriately taken into account. Second, we will have additional obligations to help nonhuman living beings based on restitution. For example, where we humans have endangered nonhuman species by aggressing against them for the sake of our luxury needs, we would have an obligation to try to restore those species to a flourishing condition. Third, we have an obligation to control our population to a greater extent under a more inclusive global justice than we would under a human-centered global justice. Of course, even in a human-centered global justice, we would need restrictions on population growth. While existing people are not required to sacrifice their basic needs for the sake of future generations, they are required to do what they can to restrict the membership of future generations so that those generations will be able to meet their basic needs.[22]

But what does this entail? We could limit human reproduction to the legitimate exercise of the basic human need to procreate, which I think would be roughly one child per family. It is unclear whether such a restrictive population policy would be necessary for respecting the rights of future generations. Suppose it was. At some point, it would be possible to abandon such a policy because the welfare rights of future generations were no longer threatened. Even at that point, however, nonhuman species could still be threatened by the size of the human population. So a global justice that took all living beings into account would still want to continue this restrictive population

[22] James P. Sterba, "The Welfare Rights of Distant Peoples and Future Generations: Moral Side-Constraints on Social Policy," *Social Theory and Practice* 7 (1981), pp. 99–124.

policy. Nevertheless, at some point even a global justice that took all living beings into account would favor relaxing such a population policy in favor of one that served basic human needs and the long-term survivability of the human species, consistent with maintaining humans within their environmental niche, where, unlike today, they would be in balance with the rest of the biotic community. Thus, if there were two or more ways that served basic human needs and the long-term survivability of the human species, a global justice that took all living beings into account would favor the alternative that was most consistent with maintaining humans within their environmental niche, where they would be in balance with the rest of the biotic community. Of course, more would have to be said to specify more precisely this requirement of a more inclusive global justice.

Summing up, I have argued that in a human-centered global justice, even the libertarian ideal of liberty supports a right to welfare that extends to both distant people and future generations, and that this right would lead us to provide each individual with the goods and resources necessary for a decent life, but no more. I also argued that in a more inclusive global justice that took all living beings into account, the Principle of Human Preservation, Disproportionality, Human Defense, and Restitution would provide a nonquestion-begging resolution of the conflicts between human and nonhuman living beings, and, in so doing, this more inclusive global justice would also restrict us to acquiring the goods and resources we need for a decent life, but no more. Yet I further argued that this more inclusive, and hence more adequate global justice, imposes some additional obligations on us that are absent from a less defensible human-centered global justice. These additional obligations require that we meet our basic needs in a way that avoids unnecessary harm to nonhuman living beings, that we attempt to restore species which we have endangered, and that we accept a restrictive population policy that protects endangered species consistent with serving basic human needs and long-term survivability of the human species. As far as theories of justice go, this is about as demanding as it gets.

7. EPILOGUE

Different versions of this paper have been presented to a variety of audiences. Invariably, at some point in the question period, someone asks the question of how do I distinguish basic from nonbasic needs. Usually, the questioner does not realize how widespread the use of this distinction is. While the distinction is surely important for global ethics, as its use in this paper attests, it is also used widely in moral and political philosophy generally; it would really be impossible to do much moral, political, or environmental philosophy without a distinction between basic and nonbasic needs.

Typically, I respond to the question by pointing out that the fact that not every need can be clearly classified as either basic or non-basic, as similarly holds for a whole range of dichotomous concepts like moral/immoral, legal/illegal, living/nonliving, human/nonhuman, should not immobilize us from acting at least with respect to clear cases. This puts our use of the distinction in a still broader context suggesting that if we cannot use the basic/nonbasic distinction in moral, political, and environmental philosophy, the widespread use of other dichotomous concepts is likewise threatened. It also suggests how our inability to clearly classify every conceivable need as basic or non-basic should not keep us from using such a distinction at least with respect to clear cases.

There is also a further point to be made here. If we begin to respond to clear cases, for example, stop aggressing against the clear basic needs of nonhuman nature for the sake of clear luxury needs of humans, we will be in an even better position to know what to do in the less clear cases. This is because sincerely attempting to live out one's practical moral commitments helps one to interpret them better, just as failing to live them out makes interpreting them all the more difficult. Consequently, we have every reason to act on the moral requirements that I have defended in this paper, at least with respect to clear cases.

Department of Philosophy
University of Notre Dame
Notre Dame, IN 46556
USA
E-mail: Sterba.1@nd.edu

INDEX

Studies in Global Justice

---

1. A. Føllesdal and T.W. Pogge (eds.): *Real World Justice*. Grounds, Principles, Human Rights, and Social Institutions. 2005 ISBN 1-4020-3141-6

2. G. Brock and D. Moellendorf (eds.): *Current Debates in Global Justice*. 2005 ISBN 1-4020-3347-8

---

springeronline.com